Renewing the Vision

Rabbis Spe[illegible]
Modern Je[illegible] Issues

Essays marking the Fortieth Anniversary
of the Leo Baeck College

Edited by Jonathan A. Romain

SCM PRESS LTD

0 334 02657 1

First published 1996
by SCM Press Ltd,
9–17 St Albans Place, London N1 0NX

Typeset at The Spartan Press Ltd,
Lymington, Hants
and printed in Great Britain by
Biddles Ltd, Guildford and King's Lynn

Contents

Foreword by Rabbi Professor Jonathan Magonet vii

Preface ix

Leo Baeck and the College xi
Jonathan Romain

CURRENT CROSSROADS 1

Principles of Our Faith 3
Tony Bayfield

Confrontation or Co-operation? The Relationship between Orthodox and Progressive Judaism 15
David Soetendorp

Anti-Judaism in Christian Feminist Theology 26
Rachel Montagu

German Jewry Fifty Years after the Holocaust 38
Henry Brandt

From USSR to FSU – From Oppression to Opportunity 48
Robert Shafritz

THE NEEDS OF THE PEOPLE 57

Radio Religion 59
Lionel Blue

Towards a New Jewish Sexual Ethic 64
Elizabeth Sarah

Judaism in School Classrooms 74
Douglas Charing

A Jewish Response to Mental Illness 82
Jeffrey Cohen

Ageing and the Role of the Synagogue 90
Chaim Wender

Attitudes to Life and Death in Judaism 98
Julia Neuberger

Working with the Dying 106
Sylvia Rothschild

THE PAST IS STILL PRESENT 115

The Book of Many Voices 117
Jonathan Magonet

The Last Temptation of Noah 126
Howard Cooper

John's Gospel through Jewish Eyes 135
Sybil Sheridan

Christian Influences on the Reading of the Prophets 146
Michael Hilton

Spinoza – A Jewish Heretic for Our Time? 156
Reuven Silverman

1956 and All That 165
Michael Leigh

PREPARING FOR THE FUTURE 171

The Future of the Jews 173
Dow Marmur

British Jewry, The Eleventh Tribe, Lost or Saved? 182
Jonathan Romain

Repairing the World – A Task for Jews? 192
Barbara Borts

The Challenge for Reform Judaism in a Jewish State 203
Michael Boyden

Jews and Arabs: Can We Make Our Enemies Our Friends? 212
Jeffrey Newman

Collective Survival: Judaism and the Environment 221
Hillel Avidan

Glossary 230

Contributors 234

Rabbinic Graduates of the Leo Baeck College 239

In memory of Leo Baeck
and all other refugee rabbis
whose learning and dedication
helped to transform
Progressive Judaism in Britain

Foreword

Jonathan Romain has admirably charted the history of Leo Baeck College in his introduction which gives me the opportunity to express the gratitude of the College to him for his work in editing this volume. But how do you measure the achievements of such an institution? Clearly the number of graduates and students, their worldwide impact, the renewal of our teaching staff out of the ranks of our own graduates, the innovations we have brought to rabbinic training with our emphasis on pastoral care and community skills and inter-faith dialogue, particularly between Jews and Muslims – all of these point to an institution driven by the need to re-establish a Jewish civilization that was almost destroyed and a visionary sense of the future role of Judaism on the European and wider scene.

The essays in this volume give testimony to the quality of leadership offered to the Jewish community and beyond by graduates of the College. In their diversity and unity they truly represent a new post-war generation of rabbis and teachers who have made and continue to make an impact at the level of the individual and the community as much as within the wider society. Through its openness to a wide variety of students, the calibre of its lecturing staff and the quality of its courses, the Leo Baeck College has truly earned the mantle bequeathed to it by the Berlin *Hochschule für die Wissenschaft des Judentums*.

It is a privilege as Principal of the College to be able to introduce this important book, which is also a tribute to a young but already significant Jewish institution of learning.

Rabbi Professor Jonathan Magonet

Preface

Renewing the Vision celebrates the fortieth anniversary of the Leo Baeck College through the talents of its graduates. They include its earliest students and recent ones, men and women, those serving British congregations and those abroad, those in Reform synagogues and those in Liberal ones. The essays reveal both the remarkable range of skills they have developed in their careers and the key issues that occupy British Jewry today. They include questions such as: What do we believe? Where is God in a post-Holocaust world? How do we tackle practical matters, such as mental illness or bereavement? How do we communicate with the non-Jewish community around us? Can we establish better relations with Orthodox Jews? Should Judaism be repackaged for a media world of God-slots and religious sound-bites? What effect do the new realities in Israel have upon us? How can we best come to terms with new trends within British Jewry, be they sexual mores, marriage patterns, social action or ecological concerns? Can we relate Jewish wisdom of the past to current developments? Will we be able to ensure a Jewish future? They are questions that all Jews ask at some stage of their lives. They also parallel the curriculum of the Leo Baeck College as it seeks to prepare rabbis who will be both scholars and pastors, who will both guide fellow Jews and speak to society at large, and who will both transmit faithfully the Judaism of the past and re-interpret it daringly for new situations.

My thanks are due to the twenty-three other contributors to *Renewing the Vision*, both for their pieces and for the way in which they allowed me to make additional suggestions, to omit their favourite phrases, and subject them to severe word-capping. Their good-natured approach has eased my task as editor considerably, and has also given me the pleasure of debating some fascinating points with them in the process. My one regret is that so many other highly talented graduates of the College were unable to be included because of limitations of space. They, too, have brought honour to the good name of the College through their work, and it is hoped that they can be represented in a further volume. Particular mention must go to the principal of the College, Rabbi Professor Jonathan Magonet, for his enthusiasm and encouragement when I first mooted the idea of the book, while Ruth Cohen assisted with many of the practical arrangements. Revd Dr John Bowden was most gracious with his time, and Catherine Marshall provided invaluable support. I am grateful also to David Liebling, Sylvia Morris, Barbara Rosenberg, Joyce Rose, Rabbi Elizabeth Sarah and Rabbi Sybil Sheridan for the help they gave at various stages.

Jonathan A. Romain
Maidenhead 1996

Abbreviations

BCE	Before the Common Era, the Jewish equivalent of BC
CE	Common Era, the Jewish equivalent of AD
RSGB	Reform Synagogues of Great Britain
ULPS	Union of Liberal and Progressive Synagogues

Leo Baeck and the College

Jonathan Romain

It is no exaggeration to say that the Leo Baeck College has provided the same outstanding leadership to post-war British Jewry that Leo Baeck himself gave to German Jewry before and during the war. Moreover, just as Leo Baeck's enormous personal influence extended to a wide range of other Jewish communities, so the College named after him is making an increasingly deep impact on world Jewry through the work of its graduates.

Leo Baeck was born in Lissa (now Leszno, Poland) in 1873, and trained for the rabbinate at the Conservative Jewish Theological Seminary of Breslau and then at the Liberal Hochschule für die Wissenschaft des Judentums in Berlin. After serving congregations in Oppeln and Düsseldorf, he moved to Berlin in 1912 and in 1933 became the president of the Reichsvertretung, the representative body of German Jewry. Renowned both as a preacher and teacher, he also found time for numerous articles and books, including *The Essence of Judaism*, *Judaism and Christianity*, and *This People Israel*. Many of his works presented a robust yet dignified defence of Judaism from the criticism of contemporary Christian polemics, both exposing false assumptions about the Jewish faith and giving voice to the high ideals it espoused. This literary battle was to be transformed into the most severe of practical struggles when the rise of Nazism led to increasingly oppressive measures against German Jewry, culminating in its destruction.

Leo Baeck saw his primary role as that of pastor – which is why he accompanied a group of German Jewish schoolchildren to safety in England in August 1939; and it is also why, despite the chance of staying in England and ensuring his own survival, he then returned to Germany to be with the remnant of his diminishing flock. If the story of his inspirational role had ended there, it would have marked him out as a notable rabbi – like the song *dayenu* ('It would have been enough') at the Passover meal. However, he refused subsequent offers to escape from Germany and instead was among the thousands of other German Jews taken to Theresienstadt concentration camp. Moreover, once there he acted as a source of spiritual illumination amid the dark cruelty that pervaded the camp. Through his lectures at night in the barracks on Jewish philosophy and moral teachings he not only provided a welcome distraction from the terrible surroundings, but encouraged his listeners to retain their human dignity and sense of moral purpose. Equally important was the personal example he set whilst working at the degrading and exhausting chores during the day – never losing either his own self-respect or his concern for others around him.

After the war, Leo Baeck settled in England, where – despite already being in his seventies – he maintained an active communal role. Living in North London, he was a member of the North Western Reform Synagogue, and served as its President. He also worshipped regularly at the West London Synagogue, and would often be called upon to pronounce the final blessing at the end of the service. He was a leading participant in the series of Monday lectures held at West London at which several other German Reform refugee rabbis who had survived the war – many of whom were his former pupils – regrouped and presented papers, continuing the transmission of Jewish learning and research that had been so badly disrupted, but not ended, by the Nazis. He was also the President of the Society for Jewish Study, which was established in 1945 partly as a vehicle to open his teachings to the wider public. He became the President of the Association of Synagogues in Great Britain (later known as the Reform Synagogues of Great Britain) in 1951, taking an active interest in affairs, albeit in a non-executive role. He was also made President of the World Union for Progressive Judaism, in which capacity he visited both new communities and those struggling to re-establish themselves after the Holocaust.

The following year Baeck – along with Rabbi Dr Arthur Loewenstamm and Rabbi Dr Max Katten – examined a rabbinic student, Charles Berg, whose studies in Germany had been interrupted by the war and which were completed privately in England afterwards. It was the first rabbinic ordination in England by a non-Orthodox authority. He fully supported moves to establish a rabbinic training seminary in England, which was designed both to provide ministers for the growing Reform movement here and to rekindle the light of Jewish learning in Europe which had been extinguished with the destruction of the Berlin Hochschule and the Breslau Theological College during the war. It was to be called the Jewish Theological College and was inaugurated in September 1956. Addressing the assembled dignitaries, the philosopher Leon Roth hailed the move as 'a signal act of faith and affirmation' – in both British Jewry and Judaism in general – and remarked that, given the recent devastation and the demoralization that ensued in so many quarters, 'it is to my mind not only a great, but an astonishing act'. Two months later Leo Baeck died (2 November, 28 Cheshvan) and the college was renamed after him. By then he had become a legend in his own lifetime – for his immense scholarship, his pastoral care, the influence he had on a whole generation of rabbis, the spiritual resistance he had displayed against the Nazis, and his unflagging energy and sage advice after the war in restoring a shattered Jewry. He had become a living symbol of Jewish survival, and he used his stature to promote the cause of Reform Judaism in whatever way he could. In a unique tribute to his greatness, Baeck's body lay on a high bier in the Stern Hall at West London for two days. At the funeral service the coffin was brought into the synagogue and set before the Ark before being taken to Hoop Lane cemetery. It was attended by a wide cross-section of Jewish leaders, including members of the Chief Rabbi's Court and other Orthodox ministers.

The establishment of a rabbinic college had been one of the original Aims and Objects drawn up by the Reform congregations in 1946 shortly after they had banded together to form an association. Until then there was no institution for training Reform rabbis in England, and all ministers had either received their training in the United States or had been graduates of the Orthodox Jews' College who later switched allegiance and served Reform synagogues. There were lengthy discussions over how to implement the proposal – including the foundation of a theological college together with the Union of Liberal and Progressive Synagogues (ULPS) at Oxford or Cambridge – but disagreements on joint policy and concern over financial implications prevented any progress. The breakthrough came in 1956 thanks to the persistent drive of Rabbi Dr Werner van der Zyl – then minister of the North Western Reform Synagogue, but a graduate of the Hochschule who had served the Berlin Jewish community before seeking refuge in England. He persuaded the movement to provide the resources to establish a college for the training of rabbis and teachers, and was appointed its first Director of Studies.[1]

The college was housed at West London Synagogue and opened its doors with two students – Lionel Blue and Michael Leigh, both of whom were to carve out distinguished careers. They were joined later by Henry Brandt, Michael Goulston and Dow Marmur. There was an impressive list of lecturers – all of whom had been refugees.[2] Van der Zyl was not only the prime mover of the college, but went on to guide its progress for the next ten years as director and be responsible for much of its success. He also helped to secure the support of the ULPS, and from 1964 onwards the College was jointly sponsored by both movements, with its graduates serving both Reform and Liberal congregations. Van der Zyl's work was furthered by many others, including Rabbis Hugo Gryn and John Rayner, who had supervised the College's affairs after his retirement. In 1972 Rabbi Dr Albert Friedlander became Director, and during his tenure both the student body and library grew in size. As German members of the teaching staff gradually retired, they were replaced with a new generation of English-born lecturers, including scholars outside the Progressive movements such as Rabbi Dr Louis Jacobs and Professor Raphael Loewe. Female students had been admitted from the College's inception, although none had graduated as rabbis until Jacqueline Tabick in 1973.[3] The need for larger premises became increasingly apparent and eventually resulted in the College's move in 1981 to the Manor House in North Finchley (later known as the Sternberg Centre), along with other institutions within the Progressive movement. This in turn led to a major growth in the College's activities. Its Extra-Mural Department provided a wide range of day-time and evening activities for the wider public, its Teachers Training Department expanded, while courses for Christian theological students began to have an important influence on a whole new generation of Christian religious leaders. These and other developments were assisted by the great contribution made by Professor Ben Segal, who was appointed principal of the College in 1982, having recently retired as Professor of Semitic Languages at the School of Oriental and African Studies, London University. He significantly tightened the College's academic discipline and revamped its organizational structure. In 1985, he was succeeded by Rabbi Dr Jonathan Magonet, himself a graduate of the College and head of its Bible Department. His prolific lectures and writings in other theatres helped give the College a high profile in both Jewish and non-Jewish circles, as well as in the religious and scholarly worlds. Another milestone came in 1989 when the College gained the right to confer degrees, initially from the CNAA and then from the Open University, including BAs, MAs and PhDs. It was the smallest academic establishment in the country to be entrusted with this right, which was a tribute to its scholastic standards.

By 1996 the College had 120 rabbinic graduates, including 22 women rabbis. It provided the vast majority of all Reform and Liberal ministers in Britain and supplied the rabbinic needs of most European Progressive communities, as well as those in Australia and South Africa. It had also begun training rabbinic students from Eastern Europe following the collapse of the Soviet Union. A month-long intensive seminar in Jewish studies that took place in 1989 for ten students from Hungary, and the arrival in 1991 of the first of several students from Russia and the former Soviet Union to train for the rabbinate, symbolized both the massive changes in the Jewish life of Eastern Europe and the pioneering role the College was playing. Its world-wide influence was second only to that of the rabbinic seminaries in the United

States. The 79 students enrolled at the College in 1996 for rabbinic and academic courses included students from the Czech Republic, France, Germany, the Netherlands, India, Israel, Russia, South Africa, Ukraine and the United States, providing a rich mix of cultures and Jewish expressions. When books that had been saved from the former Hochschule Library were donated to the College library, it was recognition of the College's role in continuing its tradition of liberal scholarship and effectively being its direct descendant. Leo Baeck would have been very proud.

Notes

1. For a fuller picture of the Reform movement and its relationship with the College see Anne J. Kershen and Jonathan A. Romain, *Tradition and Change: A History of Reform Judaism in Britain*, Vallentine Mitchell 1995.
2. For further details of this period see Michael Leigh's essay below, and Ellen Littmann, 'The First Ten Years of the Leo Baeck College', in *Reform Judaism*, ed. Dow Marmur, RSGB 1973.
3. Jacqueline Tabick, 'I Never Really Wanted To Be First', in *Hear Our Voice*, ed. Sybil Sheridan, SCM Press 1994.

CURRENT CROSSROADS

Critical issues that confront Jewish life today

In this section Tony Bayfield tells how he and others tried to define the central tenets of Reform Judaism in the Manna Platform. He tackles the traditional theological structure of God, Torah and Israel in a refreshingly honest and modern way, sharing both his doubts and certainties, and warning of the gulf between Jews and Jewish theology that has arisen and needs addressing urgently. David Soetendorp focuses on an equally acute problem, the relationship between the different religious groupings within Jewry. On the basis of his own experiences, he suggests that the hostility that has so often been the dominant theme until now need not always be the case, and he urges moves towards conciliation and tolerance for the greater good of all concerned. Rachel Montagu's concern is that the very welcome development of Christian feminist theology has certain aspects to it that are unwelcome. This is the tendency towards a strong anti-Jewish bias in the works of many such writers. She both exposes their misconceptions and points to a way forward in which all the prejudices of the past can be jettisoned in a mutual pursuit of feminist creativity. The way in which the past impinges on the present has occupied much of the ministry of Henry Brandt, who has served several Jewish communities in post-war Europe. He looks at German Jewry fifty years after the Holocaust and presents his conclusions. Another example of the Jewish spirit rising from the ashes is explored by Robert Shafritz through his involvement with the Jewish life in the former Soviet Union. He describes movingly the struggles such Jews are facing, but also cautions Jews elsewhere to let Russian Jews be Russian Jews and develop in their own way, giving help, but not stifling their new-found freedom.

Principles of Our Faith

Tony Bayfield

Unlike its American counterpart, British Reform Judaism, characteristically pragmatic and suspicious of theory, has never produced a platform or statement of guiding principles. With one recent exception. The spring 1990 issue of *Manna*, the quarterly journal of the Sternberg Centre for Judaism, contained 'Progressive Judaism, a Collective Theological Essay and Discussion Paper'.[1] The title drips with tact. But what lies behind it is a platform of a slightly idiosyncratic kind.

Why was it written, this disingenuously titled Manna Platform? The motivation, I must confess, was essentially a private one. It is true that British Reform is consistently and justly criticized for not presenting a clear and unequivocal message. A broad brush statement of Reform Jewish beliefs which could be read within half an hour would remedy a real lack. But my own fundamental motivation as its editor was more personal. We are frequently told that Judaism lacks systematic theology. It is true that a host of factors have led to a different degree of emphasis in Judaism from Christianity but, as Rabbi Dr Louis Jacobs points out, Jews have always thought profoundly about God and written about theological matters – and Jacobs' own *A Jewish Theology*, following a medieval schema, is as thorough and systematic as they come.[2] I was accustomed to addressing individual topics – afterlife or theodicy – as needs required. Moreover, I had found, from time to time, that my rational, intellectual scepticism ran counter to my intuitive, existential perceptions of God at moments of stress or challenge. I wondered whether it would be possible to give a clear overall picture of what it is I believe and what I think Reform Judaism believes, a picture where the parts cohere and in which the reasoning is reflective of feeling and experience.

The Platform was sent to a significant number of theologians around the world, who took it with great seriousness and responded to what they clearly saw as a coherent, overall picture and set of principles.[3] Of course, in a broad, liberal 'church', one cannot speak for everyone, and I suspect that the 50,000 members of the two British Progressive Movements could offer at least 50,000 sets of emendations and qualifications. But what the Manna Platform may just contain are the characteristic hallmarks of Progressive Jewish theology in Britain in the last decade of the twentieth century.

Milieu

An obvious preliminary decision that needed to be made was what shape to give the Platform, what structure, what organizing principle to adopt. We toyed with Maimonides' 'Thirteen Principles of Faith', formulated in the twelfth century, both because it is hallowed by time and because scholars like Louis Jacobs have used it as their organizing principle. But it felt constricting, a potential strait-jacket, reflective of medieval questions and concerns which are not necessarily ours. In the end, we utilized the older and broader format of God, Torah and Israel, into which most of our concerns seemed naturally to fall. However, we began with an introduction headed 'Preliminary Principles and Observations' – though 'Milieu' might have been a more illuminating term.

What the section brings out is a degree of self-consciousness and awareness of our place in history and in wider society. The setting allows us to acknowledge the profound nature of our own subjectivity, the dynamism of history and the dialogue with modernity.

The self-consciousness is one of a number of hallmarks. It is an acknowledgment of the extent to which who we are – in terms of education, class, gender, experience – affects how we think and what we believe. It adds a distinctive degree of provisionality to our theology, a fundamental acknowledgment of humanity's endlessly changing perceptions of the nature and actions of God. Reform theology consciously eschews the authority of claiming permanence and absolute truth. It accepts the limitations, the relativity, the partiality of human thought.

Much the same is true of the acceptance of the full significance of the historical process. Judaism is the Jewish response to God, a divinely inspired human construct. Judaism has been shaped by history, both when responding and resisting. Once again, Reform theology is a stage on a journey, not journey's end.

Perhaps most characteristic of all as a hallmark is the dialogue with modernity. The milieu, the setting, is the modern world of which Reform Jews are wholly (as well as holy) a part even if they aspire to a life of what the American rabbi Professor Eugene Borowitz describes as 'creative maladjustment'. That world contains much that we challenge and reject but, a defining characteristic, much that is positive and to be embraced. Characteristic values such as egalitarianism, personal autonomy and democracy are allowed to inform and develop theology. Thus, as we shall see, egalitarianism shapes the language in which we speak of God, personal autonomy influences our responses to the commands of Torah, and democracy informs our understanding of the role of Israel as people and the way that people develops its tradition.

This positive dialogue with modernity stands in sharp contrast to the stance taken by so many of the leading exponents of contemporary Orthodox Judaism. Rabbi Dr Jonathan Sacks uses the Talmudic case of the *tinok shenishbah*, the child brought up by idolaters, as his strategy to avoid writing Reform Jews out of the Jewish people as heretics.[4] Just as children brought up by idolaters cannot help themselves and are therefore not fully culpable in respect of their errors, so Reform Jews, blinded by modernity, are similarly not fully culpable. What that says about modernity is clear and stands in sharp contrast to the view taken by the Manna Platform of its milieu.

The milieu, then, becomes part of the theology itself – provisional and partial, historically shaped and dialogical. The milieu is also a world that is, without doubt, a very narrow bridge, a tightrope as far as Jewish faith and survival is concerned. It is a world in which Reform Jews seek distinctiveness rather than separation and a world in which secularism, questioning, doubts and alternative religious perspectives are endemic. The final hallmark of this section is a theology of outreach. Many Jews live outside the synagogue, on the margins, with more doubts and uncertainties than any platform could contain. The theology beckons to them, acknowledging the doubts as themselves containing truths; accepting that, today, the question may be more important than the answer; finding teachers in unexpected places and far beyond the confines of schools of traditional Jewish learning. The outreach not only starts from where people are and welcomes them in but accepts that what they bring with them may introduce new insights and further change, which is where walking before God leads.

God

There are almost as many different portraits of God as there are people who have tried to explain what they mean by God with the limited vocabulary and conceptual apparatus of human beings. But it might be convenient to suggest that, in contemporary Jewish writing, the portraits can often be grouped under four headings.

We can perhaps best term the first category the traditional portrait – the supernatural, interventionist God of the Bible and of much of post-biblical Jewish literature, particularly the liturgy. In the second category, God is still supernatural – it may well be that the most appropriate word is 'external'. This latter – liberal-traditional – portrait grapples with a number of pressing issues thrown up by contemporary experience as a challenge to the older characteristics of intervening, rewarding and punishing. In the third category, or portrait, God is still external but fundamentally limited: God is 'becoming'. God will only become fully God when the partnership between God and humanity reaches its fulfilment. And in the fourth and final category, God ceases to be supernatural, external, but is, rather, the sum total of immanent values and, in some sense, a human construct.

The God of the Manna Platform clearly falls within the second category. One should, however, add that one of the theologians who commented upon the Platform, Louis Jacobs, was less than clear about this and questioned whether the concept of a metaphysical or supernatural God was being rejected. But it is difficult to understand his comments as anything other than a simple misreading, and it was certainly not a conclusion that any other commentator reached.

During 1993–94, a very interesting debate took place within the Church of England in which a Christian priest, Anthony Freeman, attempted to recast the Christian God in 'category four', or Christian humanist terms.[5] His book was almost immediately the subject of a firm and reasoned rebuttal by the Bishop of Oxford, Richard Harries, who restated the 'category two' or liberal-traditional position.[6] In an intriguing comment on the debate, Rabbi Howard Cooper defined the Freeman position as follows: 'Instead of the word "God" referring to a Someone/something existing independently of human beings, the term God is now applied "to the sum of all my values and ideals in life". This involves a subtle but fundamental shift in perspective.'[7]

Cooper goes on to argue that Jewish mystics 'have known and taught of God as Nothing . . . as a subjective experience to be approached through and created by the imagination'. His sympathies appear to lie with Freeman rather than with Harries, for whom 'the real God exists beyond us'. The debate is a fascinating one and, without doubt, one of the key theological issues of the late twentieth century. The indications are, both from the Manna Platform and from the three Reform prayer books published between 1977 and 1995, that the liberal-traditional position is the one that contemporary British Reform as a collectivity maintains.

If the 'post-theistic' position is rejected, so too are radical notions of a 'becoming' God. But there is, nevertheless, a sense of deep divine involvement in the *enterprise* of Creation, of a purpose which can only be fulfilled through and in partnership with humanity.

This takes us naturally and inevitably to a theological issue of almost equal importance, namely that which is technically termed theodicy. Theodicy is, broadly speaking, the attempt to make sense of three propositions, namely that God is good; God is all-powerful; and evil is real. How is the apparent paradox of a good and all-powerful God and human suffering to be resolved?

The Manna Platform expressly rejects the equation of suffering with punishment which has been a dominant feature of Jewish theology through the centuries, even though Jewish theologians have frequently also rejected the equation. The most notable and earliest rejection was that of Job, and his response – which contains a profound mistrust of all who try to explain human suffering – is embodied in the Platform. The Manna Platform also reasserts both that God is *Ein Sof*, The One Without End, about Whom we can say nothing or almost nothing, and also that God, as it were, has human attributes, amongst which is the propensity to weep at suffering. A withdrawal in order to make space for the world, a voluntary self-limitation, the granting of free will, a daring acknowledgment of the role of chance, all feature in the theodicy of the Manna Platform.

This brings us to the third and final hallmark of the God portrayed in the Platform. One of the great challenges to Jewish theology presented by the events of the twentieth century is to the traditional understanding of the place of God in history. Judaism is the faith *par excellence* which sees the hand of God as human history unfolds. Three major Jewish festivals, Pesach, Shavuot and Sukkot, celebrate God's involvement in historical events. Surprisingly few post-Shoah Jewish theologians tackle the many questions that this belief throws up, and much contemporary liturgy is even more evasive. The Manna Platform seizes upon an extremely interesting and challenging passage in Arthur A. Cohen's book, *The Tremendum*, and uses his image of God as 'a glowing filament illuminating the domain of human freedom'.[8] The Platform goes on to say: 'We recognize our own terrible capacity to obscure, eclipse or burn out that filament rather than enable it to be the source of light and redemption.' The difficulty with the image lies in its impersonality and lifelessness, so far removed from a God who weeps at human suffering. But it does convey an idea of God who is perpetually available – 'only he who sees takes off his shoes' – but not interventionist, not acting independently of human beings by subverting the laws of nature, working no miracles in a literal sense.

The language in which the theology is expressed is in itself most significant. God is spoken of in gender-free language, reflective of the egalitarian values referred to earlier. Not only is God not a man but neither should our attempts to speak of God be obscured by the use of exclusively male metaphors.

Torah

Once again, three hallmarks are clearly discernible. The first is an uncompromising assertion of the role of human beings in the writing of Torah. Both the Pentateuch and the sea of literature which flowed from it are written by human beings, limited by human limitations, the product of history and environment. The fundamentalist doctrine of Torah as 'other', 'extra-historical', 'inerrant' or 'unmediated reality' is replaced by an understanding of Torah which accepts historical criticism. Torah is not 'God's word', but the profoundest Jewish attempt to discern and express God's word.

The myth implicit in the fundamentalist understanding of the phrase '*Torah min hashamayim*' (Torah from Heaven) and the political statement expressed in the opening lines of *Pirke Avot* – which begins by identifying rabbinic writing with what was spoken at Sinai – give an absolute authority to halachah (Jewish law) which historical criticism and a non-fundamentalist understanding of Torah undermine. The Manna Platform is implicitly post-halachic, acknowledging the central importance of the Jewish legal tradition but recognizing the fact of personal autonomy and the inadequacy of law to enable all Jews to express their relationship with God and with other human beings.

This particular section of the Platform prompted me to coin the phrase 'responsible autonomy', to take up Eugene Borowitz's stress upon the covenantal obligation that every Jew assumes when he or she chooses to opt in to the Jewish people and to seek a post-halachic balancing of individual rights with covenantal duties to God, to tradition and to people. Such a balancing leads to a flexibility and variety of responses, particularly in the personal, ritual area, within a framework of broad values and principles.[9]

The Torah section lays great emphasis on ethics, reasserting the classical Reform commitment to 'prophetic Judaism'. The holiness of God is essentially ethical, and human beings imitate God and worship God at least as much in their ethical conduct as in their prayers and rituals. God, in the Manna Platform, is still and unequivocally the source of ethical imperatives, the *Metzaveh*, and those ethical imperatives extend equally and unequivocally to all humanity and not just to the Jewish people. The ancient awareness of ethical responsibility for the environment strikes a contemporary chord, even as the reassertion of the centrality of social justice is familiar.

Interestingly, the section on Torah deals with two areas that play a noticeably small part in the whole – two, as it were, negative hallmarks. The muted passage on messianism is reflective of a sense that passionate Jewish messianism has all too often led to false dawns. Perhaps, less expectedly – and often remarked upon not just by Christian theologians but by Jewish scholars such as Dan Cohn-Sherbok – afterlife is scarcely a dominant theme. This is not to say that the Manna Platform rejects a belief in an afterlife; far from it. Only it impinges very little on and figures almost not at all in discussions of theodicy, in my view because the hope of an afterlife offers little existential consolation or explanation for the barbarity and cruelty of the world.

Israel

For almost nineteen centuries the term 'Israel' meant the Jewish people. The Platform acknowledges fully the change that the re-establishment of the State has wrought and gives it not merely a practical but a theological dimension. It is as if the three pillars have metamorphosed into four, with Israel as land taking its place once more alongside Israel as people, Torah and God.

In a happy phrase, the Platform declares that 'Judaism has a geography as well as a history'. The return to the land does not represent the beginning of messianic times, but it has a sacred place in the working out of the destiny of the Jewish people and

Judaism. It supplies a renewed centre and it lays down a special challenge. For much of the last nineteen centuries, Jews have lived in a state of disempowerment. The land and the State embody both the hope and challenge of empowerment, the opportunity and obligation to exercise control and responsibility to an extent denied to those Jews who live as a minority in other lands.

Yet the Platform also recognizes the continuing role and value of Diaspora, seeing a continuing partnership and in no sense asserting a hierarchy of values with an implicit obligation to seek the dismantling of one for the sake of the other.

The section begins with a paragraph headed 'Israel as People', and clearly intends to lay stress upon peoplehood, characterizing Jews as a family with all the overtones both of obligation and positive value implicit in using 'family', so significant in Jewish life, as the metaphor. A number of writers have suggested that the various contemporary streams of Judaism lay differential stress on the three pillars of God, Torah and Israel. The Manna Platform seeks to return to a balance. One sympathetic critic, Rabbi Richard Hirsch, suggested that insufficient stress had been placed on peoplehood. Nevertheless, the biblical description of the people Israel as a 'nation of priests' is taken sufficiently seriously to espouse the democratization of Judaism, allowing all Jews to play a part in its development and emphasizing the role of the rabbi as teacher and guide, rather than as exclusive decision-maker.

If two hallmarks of this section are the reincorporation into Jewish theology of Israel as land and the stress on Israel as people, family (but not as race), a third is its emphasis on pluralism.

Great stress is laid upon the value and significance of other faith traditions. With the Book of Jonah, the Platform acknowledges that God is the God of all humanity and that no one has a monopoly on truth. The importance of dialogue and co-operation stems from this theology. So, too, does the attitude to conversion. The Jewish task is not one of active mission prompted by a belief that all who remain outside the Jewish faith are beyond redemption; but there is an openness and a welcome to all who would seek to share our particular fragments of truth and insight.

The pluralism is not restricted to attitudes to and relations with other faiths. Unlike contemporary Orthodox Judaism, British Progressive Judaism is internally pluralistic as well, recognizing the continuing value of Orthodox thought and practice for many and declaring explicitly that no one expression of Judaism is likely to meet the needs of all Jews. The relationship is, of course, an asymmetrical one, and there are limits, both theoretical and practical, to internal dialogue with an Orthodox establishment which rules out internal pluralism completely and resorts to what are experienced as patronizing intellectual devices to justify to itself a so-called inclusivist stance.[10]

Finally, we can see the pluralism, the recognition that no one has a monopoly on truth, in a section on changing life-styles and social patterns, which seeks to uphold the value of monogamous marriage and family whilst recognizing that underlying values such as fidelity and mutual concern can be expressed in other forms of relationship. A section devoted to women underlines a shift which is still only in train and which expresses both the pluralism of this section and the egalitarianism described earlier.

Conclusion

At this point, I am conscious of the dangers of the exercise which I have undertaken. What about all the areas that have gone unmentioned in this essay – Shabbat, spirituality, Jewish survival, continuing revelation, for example? Are they not important? Of course they are, and in trying to single out some characteristics, some hallmarks, I must stress that there is no intention of downgrading by omission. Let me close this essay with an observation about the exercise itself. Did writing and publishing the Manna Platform fulfil the intentions of the authors and, in particular, of the editor? The answer, how very Jewish, is both yes and no!

Whilst others must decide whether the Manna Platform has a coherence and offers headings indicating a respectable, systematic theology, I am reasonably content that what emerged is both consonant with my experience of God, Torah and Israel and gives me a sense of something that can be put forward with confidence.

On the other hand, it would be vain not to acknowledge that, if I had any desires to provide Reform Jews at large with something they would find helpful and with which they could both resonate and debate, then such hopes were not fulfilled. It is somehow symbolic that the Jewish Chronicle published a short article about the Platform when it first appeared. The article concentrated exclusively on what the Reform Movement had to say about *Shabbat, kashrut* ('We're pleased to know it's in favour') and conversion. Nothing said about God was taken up.

There is a curious dichotomy both within the Reform Jewish world and, I am sure, within much of the wider Jewish world and society beyond. On the one hand, people appear to retain, if I may put it this way, an interest in the subject of God, worrying from time to time about faith and wishing that they could find a belief, even if such belief is not actual. Many of the doubts and uncertainties stem from older theologies and from beliefs and expectations not to be found in the Manna Platform. And yet theology is not the best subject for a sermon – unless the preacher wishes to speak only to him – or herself! The gulf between the mass of people and a meaningful and tenable theology that really touches them represents one of the great challenges that graduates of the Leo Baeck College and leaders of British Progressive Judaism face in the coming years.

Notes

1. Many people contributed to it, but its principal authors were Rabbi Colin Eimer, Rabbi Hugo Gryn, Rabbi Professor Jonathan Magonet, and me. Indeed, I must confess to being the initiator as well as the editor.
2. Louis Jacobs, *A Jewish Theology*, Behrman House, New York 1973.
3. *Manna* 29 (Autumn 1990), 30 (Winter 1991), 31 (Spring 1991), and 32 (Summer 1991).
4. Jonathan Sacks, *One People?*, Littman Library of Jewish Civilization 1993, 34.
5. Anthony Freeman, *God in Us*, SCM Press 1993. His work has been associated with the 'Sea of Faith' group around Don Cupitt.
6. Richard Harries, *The Real God*, Mowbray 1994.

7. Howard Cooper, 'God – Someone, Something or Nothing', *Manna* 48, Summer 1995.
8. Arthur A. Cohen, *The Tremendum*, Crossroad Publishing Co, New York 1981, 97f.
9. See my *Sinai, Law and Responsible Autonomy*, RSGB, London 1993. This owes much to the closing chapter of Eugene B. Borowitz, *Renewing the Covenant*, JPS, Philadelphia 1991.
10. See the *tinok shenishbah* device referred to in n.4.

Confrontation or Co-operation? The Relationship between Orthodox and Progressive Judaism

David Soetendorp

A few years ago I was presented by a congregant with a photograph of my father Rabbi Jacob Soetendorp shaking hands with Rabbi A. Schuster, the Chief Rabbi of Amsterdam during the 1950s and 1960s. It is an amazing photograph. On the face of it the two men shake hands enthusiastically. Closer inspection proves that this encounter is altogether less spontaneous. My father has taken hold of Schuster's hand before he can refuse to shake hands with him; and Schuster is clearly deeply embarrassed by the situation.

A photograph can bring back memories. This one certainly did. Memories of the many times father would come home ashen-faced from public meetings where Orthodox rabbis would refuse to acknowledge or speak with him, the Progressive Rabbi of Holland. Such hostility by Orthodox religious leadership to the fast-growing progressive community in Holland was indicative of the atmosphere in which I grew up. A deep divide existed between the Orthodox and Progressive communities. At that time it never struck me how deeply tragic it was that Dutch Jewry, emerging from the Shoah with its numbers reduced from 140,000 to 30,000, was so deeply divided. It was a sin that this badly wounded community was served by leadership preoccupied with in-fighting rather than co-operation.

Arriving in England in 1965 meant encountering a Jewish community which on the face of it was not affected by the Shoah and its aftershocks. The confrontation between Orthodox and Progressive in Anglo-Jewry had been brought into focus by the 'Jacobs affair'. Rabbi Dr Louis Jacobs had been the Rabbi of the New West End synagogue until 1959, when he left to take up the post of Moral Tutor at Jew's College, with the promise of appointment as its Principal when the position became vacant.

Chief Rabbi Israel Brodie of the United Synagogue first vetoed his appointment as Moral Tutor, and then blocked Jacob's return to the New West End synagogue.

What was the reason for effectively banishing Jacobs from the United Synagogue? He had written extensively, notably his book *We Have Reason to Believe*, in which he suggested that the Torah might not have been revealed in its entirety on Mount Sinai. His views were deemed controversial by the United Synagogue religious leadership. The New West End Synagogue decided to part company with the United Synagogue rather than with Louis Jacobs.

Stephen Brook in *The Club* claims that the Jacobs affair 'marked the end of the cosy accommodation of mainstream Orthodox within Anglo-Jewry . . . From the time of his (Jacobs') resignation until the present day, the United Synagogue has moved steadily to the religious right.'[1] It certainly had an effect on the relationship between Orthodox and Progressive in Anglo-Jewry. The divide marking their position became less one of institutional affiliation, more one of principle: whether to accept unquestioningly the divine authorship of the Torah or a more pragmatic approach to Torah study.

Up to the turn of the nineteenth century, European Jewry had been restricted to the Ghetto. Until the shock-waves of the French revolution hit Europe, followed by the Napoleonic Wars, European Jews perceived themselves as living in a state of isolation. They had no real identity outside the Jewish world. The conflict between the approaches of Orthodox and Progressive Judaism to Jewish continuity has its roots in the challenge of emancipation.

Jonathan Romain comments in *Faith and Practice* that the impact of ghettos being abolished in the wake of the French Revolution resulted in:

> a mass defection of Jews from Jewish life, whilst many of those who remained, found that the traditional pattern of worship compared unfavourably to the aesthetic and decorous nature of Christian services. In order to halt the flight from Judaism . . . various reforms were introduced.
>
> That, and the impact of modern biblical research which had undermined many Jewish tenets, created a fertile ground for the emergence of a Progressive Jewish Movement. This Movement saw its task as preserving Jews and Judaism from wholesale defection to assimilation. After almost 1900 years of powerless humiliation and rootlessness within European society, Jews had a choice: to exist within or outside the Jewish world. Offering the Jews being faced with this choice a Jewish movement which combined a healthy regard for what the non-Jewish world had to offer with the rich treasury of Judaism would not only stop the defection, but allow the coming into being of a vigorous Judaism capable of preparing the generations of Jews born into emancipated European society for a Jewish future.[2]

The opposition to this development was presented by the nineteenth-century German rabbi Samson Raphael Hirsch, who contested that 'Jews, not Judaism, were in need of reform'.[3] Hirsch preached and wrote of the subject of Orthodox Judaism as an ideology. He hoped for an invigorating traditional Judaism, liberated from the ghetto, to hold its own in the secular world. His philosophy of *Torah im Derech Eretz* [Torah with the way of the World] confronted the challenge of emancipation from the opposite perspective of the Reform Movement.

In the nineteenth-century developments in the Jewish world which gave birth to a revolutionary reformist movement, and a counter-reaction by the Orthodox establishment within emancipated Western European Jewry, we see a pattern emerging which foreshadows the conflict between Orthodox and Progressive Judaism a century and a half later.

In a perverse way history repeated itself. Hit by shock waves which shook European society to the core, Jews, having lived through Nazism and the Second World War, emerged from its ruins faced with a desperate struggle for Jewish survival. With eighty per cent of European Jewry massacred and the European Jewish world devastated, Jewish survivors were forced to find a response to the catastrophe which had overtaken them.

How was Judaism to go on? Progressive and Orthodox Judaism found themselves responding to this challenge in different ways. The Orthodox approach can be classified as based on the rabbinic slogan: *af al pi chen*. We must carry on regardless. The Jewish world which survived the Shoah had a responsibility to preserve Judaism.

The Progressive perception was that the Shoah had presented the Jewish world with an urgent need to keep the surviving remnant of Jewry within the fold, in a dislocated world. That required dynamic and innovative religious responses.

This becomes clear when we consider how Rabbi Jonathan Sacks in his book *Traditional Alternatives* comments on the teaching of the leading Progressive rabbi, Emil Fackenheim. Fackenheim, on the concept of an additional 614th Commandment to the Torah's 613, wrote:

> The authentic Jew . . . is now bound by a 614th Command. He is forbidden to hand Hitler yet another, posthumous victory. Jews have a heavy duty to preserve fellow Jews and to this end should all future energy be directed after the Shoah.[4]

Rabbi Sacks' response, 'Judaism survives *despite* Auschwitz, not because of it',[5] indicated his belief that the ability to keep Jewish life going as before, despite the Holocaust, will prove its capacity to survive.

In the aftermath of the Shoah, the areas in which division between the Orthodox and Progressive approaches were most marked were specifically involved with Jewish physical survival. One third of World Jewry perished as a result of Nazi domination. Progressive Judaism recognized the vulnerability of the surviving remnant, and saw it as a sacred obligation to resist the potential threat of numerical decline.

This led to the emphasis which in the Progressive Jewish world was placed on halachic issues: of Jewish status; the resolution of marital impediments; and a more humane approach to conversion to Judaism.

Writing in *Reform Judaism*, Rabbi Michael Curtis, an early convener of the RSGB Beit Din [rabbinic court], stated,

> We are primarily concerned with the rights of people, and we try to guide them in the light and spirit of the Halachah. It is a valid paraphrase, that the Halachah is for man and not man for the Halachah.[6]

This is a sentiment with which most Progressive Jews would agree. They may not be aware, however, that the Reform Beit Din was constituted in 1948 by one of the principal leaders of British Progressive Judaism, Rabbi Harold F. Reinhart, to whom a particular debt of gratitude is owed for the renaissance of Reform Judaism after the Shoah.

In 1995, Rabbi Hugo Gryn, himself a refugee from the Shoah, at a rabbinic meeting, reflected on the energy Reinhart deployed in looking for British pulpits and employment opportunities for rabbis who arrived here from the Continent after the Second World War.

His support of these rabbis was the foundation on which Reform Judaism's rapid post-war growth, both numerically and institutionally, is based. In addition to enabling a highly talented rabbinic workforce to breathe life into Reform Judaism, Reinhart surrounded himself with a rabbinate of colleagues with which to turn Reform Judaism into an institution capable of making a contribution to the preservation of Jewish life.

The establishment of a Reform Beit Din was a significant development of this process. Now Reform Judaism had a means of *systematically* dealing with issues of halachah, which, effectively, had been seen by the Orthodox establishment as their exclusive concern.

The commitment of Progressive Jewish communities to create an institutional framework to deal with conversion, Jewish status and matrimonial issues continued to be a source of greatest conflict between the post-war Orthodox and Reform Jewish establishments. The reasons for this are two-fold.

First, the Orthodox establishment was and is eager to be the only agency in control of issues relating to 'who is a Jew', and what constitutes valid Jewish marriage. Secondly, the arrival of Jews converted by other than strictly Orthodox standards and the blessing of Jewish marriages by other than Orthodox guidelines and standards created risks for the make-up of future Jewish social mix from amongst whom Orthodox Jews would be able to choose marital partners, acceptable according to Orthodox interpretation of halachah.

The Progressives' refusal to relinquish control to the Orthodox establishment over Jewish status and marital issues emerged as the most fundamental conflict between the Orthodox and Progressive rabbinates.

The other conflicts were founded on theological disagreements. Orthodox teaching accepts as binding that the Torah, its laws and teachings, were revealed, through Moses, to the People of Israel in the course of the forty days and nights Moses spent on top of Mount Sinai. Progressive interpretation of that teaching maintains that only part of the Torah was revealed to Moses himself, whilst part was revealed to a succession of Jewish generations.

Three events in recent history have profoundly affected the contemporary Jewish world: the 1967 Six-day War, the 1973 Yom Kippur War, and the persecution of Jews in the Soviet Union, who expressed the wish to live Jewish life freely and emigrate to Israel. Each evoked in Anglo-Jewry the awareness that Progressive and Orthodox Jews had a shared responsibility for Jewish survival. Few who lived through the fateful weeks of May/June 1967 could forget the tension spreading through the Jewish world when a massive combined Arab military force encircled Israel's borders, bent on her destruction. Suddenly institutional division appeared far less relevant, with the State of Israel and her population under threat.

Orthodox, Progressive and secular Jews queued outside Israel's embassies throughout the world to volunteer help in a time of crisis. The awareness that Jews, no matter what their theological differences might be, could and should co-operate and work alongside each other became even more acutely realized in the 1973 Yom Kippur crisis. On the holiest day in the

Jewish calendar a massive Arab military force overran Israel's borders. During the several crucial weeks in which Israel's defence force struggled to fight back the enemy, forcing it to surrender, Jews throughout the world panicked. Never before in her twenty-five years had Israel's survival been so much in the balance. In the months that followed, Israel's trauma was compounded by the deep isolation imposed on the country. One country after another, fearful of the effect on its national economy because of oil restriction, recalled its ambassador and cut links with Israel. Many thousands of Jews throughout the world demonstrated their solidarity with Israel in massive rallies, waving 'We stand by Israel' banners. In those dark days of the aftermath of Yom Kippur war the Jews in the Soviet Union were particularly isolated. The Soviet Union had stood firmly behind the Arab world for many years, and had supported the Arab force threatening Israel's survival morally, economically and militarily.

Following the Yom Kippur war the position of this group of Jews worsened. Application for exit visas was instantly refused by Soviet authorities, followed by persecution and removal of civil rights. The Refuseniks had only the Jewish world to turn to for support. The campaign to fight for the rights and the protection of their fellow Jews in the USSR was one for which Jews in Great Britain were prepared to set aside differences. Faced with cries for help from a group of Jews so utterly relying on their support, Orthodox and Progressive Jews shared a sense of common responsibility.

Rabbi Norman Lamm, a leading Orthodox rabbi, who, whilst firmly distancing himself from the Progressive's rejection of the divine authorship of the Torah, makes conciliatory noises to the non-Orthodox world, said:

> Reform, Conservative and Liberal communities are not only more numerous in their official memberships than the Orthodox Communities, but they are also vital, powerful and dynamic, they are committed to Jewish Survival.[7]

In the editorial in *Manna* in 1986, based on Norman Lamm's comments, Rabbi Tony Bayfield formulated a view which points the way to future co-operation between Orthodox and Progressive Jews. Bayfield calls for the establishment of

> Friendly, harmonious and respectful relationships and the working together, of all of us, towards those Jewish communal and global goals that we share and that unite us inextricably and indissolubly.[8]

Bayfield's as well as Lamm's comments highlight the challenge facing the Jewish world in the late twentieth century: to sustain Jewish communal life.

In the late 1990s the number of British Jews has decreased to below 300,000. In 1994 Rabbi Jonathan Sacks wrote *Will We Have Jewish Grandchildren? Jewish Continuity and How to Achieve It*. In it, he makes a cry from the heart: 'The immediate question is less whether Jews are at home in London or Jerusalem than whether they are at home in their Jewishness.'[9] In summer 1995, 'Missing Generation Work Party', a group of Reform Young Adults, deeply concerned with the falling away of increasing numbers of young Jews from organized religion, published their pamphlet *Beyond the Synagogue*. They plead with rabbis and lay leaders in Anglo-Jewry to make their synagogues and centres appeal to and inspire the younger generation. Would that Anglo-Jewry's religious leadership, Progressive and Orthodox, could respond to that appeal! In the 1990s Anglo-Jewry's parents, children and grandchildren consider 4,000 years of Jewish survival, and, realizing their essential position as a link in that chain of Jewish continuity, they feel scared.

Anglo-Jewry's decreasing numbers, as well as the disillusionment of the young, as evidenced in *Beyond the Synagogue*, give profound reasons for concern. Acceptance of a divide in Anglo-Jewry between Orthodox and Progressive Jews because of that which separates them in religious and ideological issues is no longer acceptable. The Jewish community is fighting for its future existence. Successful survival will only be the result of a fundamental change in the way in which Anglo-Jewry regards itself, and plans for its future. One of the most deeply felt grievances of young Jews in the 1990s is Orthodox and Progressive in-fighting.

The rabbis who witnessed the destruction of the Temple in Jerusalem, which foreshadowed a bitter exile for Judaea's Jews, lasting for many centuries, claimed that the tragedy was brought upon the Jewish people because of their internal divisions.

At the end of 1995, the Jewish world was shaken by one of the most traumatic incidents in recent Jewish history: the assassination, by a Jewish religious extremist opposed to Israeli-Palestinian reconciliation, of Yitzchak Rabin, Israel's prime minister. The Jewish people are struggling to come to terms with the tragedy, as well as with the horror of division between Jews in ideology and outlook leading to murder. We must hope that a dialogue between Jews from many different positions will lead to a setting aside of division between Orthodox and Progressive Jews.

What is needed is for concrete steps to make their dialogue possible. In a shrinking Anglo-Jewry there is no room for pride. Orthodox, Reform, Liberal, Conservative, even secular Jews have to join forces to return the disaffected Jews to the community. If the in-fighting between the various religious groups is a turn-off to these disaffected Jews, surely they are sending us signals which we ignore at our peril. During the Gulf War Jews throughout the world felt panicked almost as much as was the case during the Yom Kippur war. They feared a catastrophe of monumental dimensions, with Iraq raining down scud missiles on Israel, threatening to resort to germ-warfare on her population. Synagogues filled up with anxious congregants sharing in prayers for Israel's survival. In the midst of these tense times I was telephoned by the rabbi of the Bournemouth Hebrew Congregation. He wanted a service of solidarity with Israel to take place in his synagogue. He wanted the Reform rabbi to participate in the service. There was no problem in our shared participation in the service because the love and concern which Orthodox and Reform congregants shared for Israel set aside any theological differences between them.

Many years of quietly, patiently breaking down barriers between Orthodox and Reform Jews in Bournemouth had turned suspicion between them into respect, with the growing understanding that they shared a responsibility for Jewish continuity. The Jewish nursery school is open to Reform and Orthodox children and takes place in the Orthodox synagogue. The Day Centre serves the entire Jewish population in the town, and takes place in the Reform synagogue. In the 1980s the establishment of the Bournemouth Jewish Representative Council testified to the homogeneity of Bournemouth's Jewish community.

The first steps towards improving relations took place in the 1970s. Concern for the plight of the Refuseniks in the USSR led to the establishment of a Soviet Jewry Solidarity Committee. When Reform Jews volunteered to serve on the Committee, this was perceived as a revelation by the Orthodox members. It had never occurred to them that Reform Jews were concerned with collective Jewish concerns. When the wife of the President of the Orthodox synagogue with her niece joined the Reform rabbi's wife on a visit to Leningrad to meet Refuseniks, it sent a very powerful message to the entire Bournemouth Jewish population, Orthodox and Reform. The report back of the three ladies on their return to Bournemouth was electrifying. They had identified with the suffering of fellow Jews in Leningrad and realized strongly that denominational differences made little difference to the Russian Jews they met and to themselves.

Around the same time the Reform Synagogue decided to set up its own *Chevrah Kadishah* (Ritual Burial Society), having come to the conclusion that the *Taharah* ritual (washing and dressing of the dead) offered dignity and meaning to Jewish funeral rites. The Orthodox *Chevrah Kadishah* offered the support and encouragement needed for the setting up of the Reform *Chevrah Kadishah* to succeed.

In its own modest way the Bournemouth Jewish community demonstrates that 'where there is a will, there is a way', as far as communal co-operation is concerned. Of course not everyone in the community is in agreement. There are dissenters in both Synagogues, but they are in the minority.

'Where there is a will, there is a way.' This motto applies to Anglo-Jewry as a whole. For the sake of its future, please God, may its lay and religious leadership find the way to co-operation and dialogue.

Notes

1. Stephen Brooks, *The Club – The Jews of Modern Britain*, Constable 1989, 148.
2. Jonathan Romain, *Faith and Practice*, RSGB 1991, 5.
3. *Junior Encyclopedia Judaica*, Keter Publishing House, Jerusalem 1982.
4. Jonathan Sacks, *Traditional Alternatives*, Jews College Publication 1989, 83–4.
5. Ibid., 83.
6. Michael Curtis, in *Reform Judaism*, ed. Dow Marmur, RSGB 1972, 136.
7. Norman Lamm, *Manna*, Autumn 1986.
8. Tony Bayfield, ibid.
9. Jonathan Sacks, *Will We Have Jewish Grandchildren?*, Vallentine Mitchell 1994, 100.

Anti-Judaism in Christian Feminist Theology

Rachel Montagu

Like many Progressive rabbis, I have derived much intellectual stimulus over the years from inter-faith dialogue with Muslims and Christians. At inter-faith conferences there has been time to talk about the spiritual issues for which the synagogue merry-go-round of committees and services does not always allow space. As Rabbi Tony Bayfield says in the introduction to *Dialogue with a Difference*:

> Dialogue has not shaken my Jewish faith, but it has enriched it and developed it in many subtle ways. Dialogue has proved to be a setting with great potential for religious growth and clarification.[1]

In particular, I have gained from inter-faith dialogue with women. Women in Judaism, Christianity and Islam are all currently trying to work out how much of our tradition's attitude to women derives from Sinai, from the essence of Jesus' teaching and from Muhammad, and how much is cultural baggage from the intervening centuries which by long custom now seems to be written in stone. Jewish and Christian women are wrestling with inclusive language, with creating new rituals for events in the female life-cycle which until now have been liturgically unmarked. As a newly-ordained rabbi living in Cardiff with no rabbinic colleagues nearby and few role-models for women in the rabbinate, I derived considerable support from the local Women in Ministry group, where others were trying to answer some of the questions that perplexed me.

I also met many Jewish, Christian and Muslim women at the annual Women's Week at Bendorf.[2] But there and at other women's inter-faith meetings, I have suddenly had the sensation of biting into the fruit of wisdom and finding a rottenness within.

The search for a theology which makes women's concerns as central as those of men is one of the most important religious quests of the twentieth century. Feminist Christians trying to do this have often claimed Jesus as a feminist, citing his pro-women statements and actions. In contrast, they criticize the Judaism of Jesus' time, and often all Jewish teaching, as hostile to women, defining them as chattels while excluding them from the world of religious discourse and ritual. This is a distortion of Judaism, often based on very selective quotation. Judaism sometimes discriminates against women and sometimes affirms them, but it is usually only the negative material that is used by Christian theologians.

A good example of this is Jane Williams' article 'Jesus the Jew and Women,' which begins: 'It is now probably an accepted cliché that Jesus was "good with women".'[3] She then proceeds to quote most of the unacceptable clichés about women and Judaism. Judaism, she says, has a low view of women and blames Eve for 'The Fall'. However, 'The Fall' is not actually a Jewish concept. As Christine Trevett said in an illuminating lecture to the Jewish-Christian-Muslim Women's conference held at Woodbrooke, Birmingham in 1988, Christians need to define humans as 'fallen' because of their doctrine of salvation through Jesus. Jews do not, because they believe in repentance and prayer for the forgiveness of sins. While some rabbinic midrashim do censure Eve, others celebrate Eve as the crown of creation; they regard her, created from a human body rather than from the earth like Adam, as a more evolved life-form, and blame the first couple equally for their disobedience to God's command.

Williams also says that Jewish men bless God daily for not making them a woman.[4] The best comment I have encountered on this is that of Alice Bloch in her article 'Scenes from the Life of a Jewish Lesbian':[5] 'I am tired of feminist books that sum up all Jewish thought in that one stupid prayer . . . that has probably been invoked more times in this decade by Christian women to condemn Judaism than by Jewish men to thank God.' It has been dropped from the Reform and Conservative liturgy, and many Orthodox men change it quietly when praying from the traditional prayer book. In the documentary 'Half the Kingdom', Norma Baumel Joseph, Orthodox feminist and rabbi's wife, explains how their daughter persuaded her husband to stop saying this blessing.

Another canard is: 'Women themselves were the property of their fathers and husbands and could not own anything.'[6] In fact Jewish women became autonomous on the death of their husband, or on divorce.[7] In the rabbinic period they retained control of their property in marriage to an extent undreamed-of by women in the UK until the passage of the Married Woman's Property Acts 1870–93. It is interesting that Williams herself seems to realize that her remark is inaccurate; she says that rich women continued to manage their own property after marriage, without stating that this was the legal norm for all women. She defines Jewish spirituality as correct performance of the legal restrictions, which is not a view recognizable to Jews, but seems to owe more to the persistent stereotyping of Judaism as materialistic and legalistic documented by Sister Charlotte Klein in her book *Anti-Judaism in Christian Theology*. Klein demonstrates the process of transmission of inaccurate portrayals of Judaism from one supposedly scholarly book to another without anyone verifying the Jewish sources.[8]

Williams criticizes Judaism for restricting women to a domestic role and for not permitting them to read from the Torah. Women may have read from the Torah; the rabbis discuss the possibility, just as they certainly permitted women to offer sacrifices, not because they were obliged to, but because it would give them spiritual pleasure.[9]

Anyone who wants to read a first-rate introduction to both feminism and the importance of feminist theology in religion would do well to read Lisa Isherwood and Dorothea McEwan's book *Introducing Feminist Theology*.[10] However, it is marred by persistent hostile and inaccurate stereotyping of Judaism.

For example, 'Jesus showed signs of regaining the mutual relating that was evident in Goddess religion by calling God *Abba* or "Daddy". In this way he signalled that God was not the remote judgmental figure of the Hebrew scriptures.'[11] Many feminist theologians print versions of this statement (which would probably have surprised the characters of the book of Genesis, the prophets and the author of the Psalms, whose God is neither remote nor judgmental), originally made by Joachim Jeremias, a German theologian. In her excellent book *Anti-Judaism in Feminist Religious Writings*, Katherina von Kellenbach says that Jeremias retracted after being shown rabbinic parallels for the title '*Abba*' for God;[12] despite this, his original comment seems now to have taken on a life of its own. The notion of an ideal egalitarian Goddess religion destroyed by the birth of Judaism is described by Kellenbach as wishful thinking, and by Susannah Heschel as another deicide attributed to the Jews.[13]

Isherwood and McEwan say: 'In the social context of the time it is remarkable that women went to meetings, that they converted others, that they actively promoted the gospel and that they were publicly thanked for it.'[14] What are really remarkable are the assumptions many Christian writers make about the social mores of first-century Judaism. Going to meetings and converting others seem normal enough activities. The rabbinic *midrashim* speak of Sarah converting the women of their household to Judaism, while Abraham converted the men. There are no sources which suggest that Jewish women, like the women of Pericles' Athens, acquired a good reputation only by never being mentioned and never leaving their homes, and many which suggest that they were economically and socially active. Indeed the rabbinic sources contain many respectful statements about women; it is interesting that these are not cited more often.

Not only are the positive sources in Judaism often ignored, but even positive material may be quoted with a distracting air of amazement. In *The Case for Women's Ministry*,[15] Ruth Edwards claims that 'it is remarkable that Huldah and Deborah do not hesitate to say "Thus says the Lord" '. 'Remarkable' again. Given that they and other women are named as prophets, why is it so surprising that they prophesy?

When Edwards turns to the time of Jesus, she quotes rabbinic material selectively, for instance saying that the rabbis discouraged excess talk with women; she does not mention the story in which Beruriah, one of the learned women quoted in the Talmud, mocks Rabbi Jose for using more words than necessary when he asks her for directions. To ignore the rabbis' own irony and self-criticism is to distort.

Edwards obviously wishes to accentuate the contrast between Judaism and Christianity, and this influences her choice of sources. Why she thinks that this improves the excellent case she makes for ordaining women as priests is unclear. She includes a footnote reference to Bernadette Brooten's book *Women Leaders in the Ancient Synagogue*, but does not allow Brooten's recognition that archaeological and other evidence suggests that women had prominent roles in synagogues, and only prejudice has prevented scholars from taking titles like 'synagogue elder' in the feminine at their face value, to permeate her main text.[16] Nor does she make any allowance for the way in which rabbinic statements often exaggerate for polemical purposes. She also fails to recognize the extent to which life may have been different for Jewish women in the Diaspora and the way in which even within the rabbinic sources, descriptions of what women are actually doing often gives a slant different from that given by the rabbis' homilies.

One of the issues that comes up time and again in Christian feminist comments on Judaism is menstruation. The traditional Jewish view is described as an abuse of women by Isherwood and McEwan:

> The primitive church had disregarded the Jewish view on purity and impurity. But the established church had succumbed to the ancient prejudice, and it naturally followed that women were excluded from cultic functions because of their so-called 'monthly impurity'.[17]

Growing up Jewish I was never interested in the laws of 'menstrual purity'. In contemporary Judaism they have no relevance to spirituality or ritual, and because they are regarded as an extremely private matter by those who observe them, they are rarely discussed among Jews. The mediaeval rabbis did discuss whether a woman can pray or visit the synagogue during her period; the answer was invariably yes to the former and almost always yes to the latter. Jewish ritual is conducted partly in the synagogue and partly in the home, and women participate fully in all home rituals at all times. A married woman may not have sex with her husband during her period, until she goes to the *mikveh*, but her spiritual life continues unchanged – except in so far as married sex is regarded as a spiritual as well as a physical good in Judaism. (This may or may not be a good thing. Muslim women, who are exempt from praying during their periods, have told me that they find an occasional break from prayer refreshing.) A single woman's menstrual state is never of any consequence at all. The very words 'pure' and 'impure' are problematic, although always used to translate the Hebrew words *tahor* and *tameh*; the English has a moral connotation which the Hebrew does not.

It is sad but true that even some Jews believe that a woman cannot touch a Torah scroll during her period. The sources are explicit that nothing renders a Torah scroll impure. Even in Temple times, when impurity did bar both men and women from access to the inner areas of the temple, there were many ways of becoming impure, some of them obligatory; for instance, fulfilling the commandment to bury one's dead relatives. The whole community, both men and women, frequently moved in and out of the pure and impure state. In biblical times the book of Leviticus says that anyone who touches something used by a menstruating woman also becomes impure; this was dropped from post-biblical observance by the very rabbis who in other ways elaborated the purity laws. Menstrual impurity was anyway very minor compared with death impurity.[18]

Christians have often told me in tones of prurient revulsion how Judaism discriminates against women because of their periods. Monica Furlong claims that Judaism taboos both pregnant and menstruating women.[19] In fact, for Jews, pregnancy puts these laws into abeyance.[20] However, a pregnant woman is a sexually active woman, so this may be an example of the scapegoating of Judaism for concepts and practices in Christianity which it is hard for Christian women to acknowledge in their own tradition as described by Katherina von Kellenbach. For instance, Judaism has never mandated the different funeral rites for women who have died in childbirth detailed by Ute Ranke-Heinemann in her book *Eunuchs for Heaven: The Catholic Church and Sexuality.*[21]

Lack of space prevents me considering the other significant errors of fact about Judaism which litter the works quoted and many more.

One of the other problems in anti-Judaism is the extent to which it has conditioned even those who might not consciously wish to be negative about Judaism. Sara Maitland and Jo Garcia edited *Walking on the Water*,[22] one of the first anthologies of women's spiritual material published in the UK. It contains articles by both Christian and Jewish women, but the Christian articles, while deploring many of the church's attitudes to women, especially to their sexuality, are mostly determined to change Christianity and expand its roles for women and its respect for feminism. The three articles by Jews do not reflect this. Gail Chester robustly states that she rejects any statement that Judaism is more patriarchal than any other religion as disguised anti-Semitism, but she feels that feminists must reject all religion. Michelene Wandor writes of her mother's death as an atheist. Maureen Gilbert describes – with many gross errors of fact – Judaism as inherently discriminatory against women; she says her only reason for maintaining Jewish identity is ethnic attachment and fear of the next Hitler. All of the contributors are writing from their personal experience, which renders Gilbert's inaccuracies somewhat less offensive than they would be from a non-Jewish author, but I find it extraordinary that as late as 1983 no knowledgeable Jewish women were found who would parallel the Christian writers in wishing both to identify what was wrong in religions' past treatment of women and to build a different kind of religious future. I am sure the editors would not have deliberately intended their book to give the impression that Christianity offers feminists spiritual hope whereas Judaism does not, but centuries of Christian teaching that Judaism is a mere prologue to Christianity may have unconsciously influenced them.

Katherina von Kellenbach has just produced a definitive book analysing anti-Judaism.[23] She quotes extensively from the now considerable German and American literature of feminist theology, of which her knowledge is clearly exhaustive.[24] Her project obviously took considerable courage; she says that she was violently attacked by many German feminist theologians for even raising anti-Judaism as a question. She demonstrates an acute awareness of the implications of anti-Jewish statements which their authors might not have deliberately intended as such; her examples include Rosemary Radford Ruether, who elsewhere writes on anti-Judaism herself.[25]

Von Kellenbach concludes that lack of education about Judaism is the main cause of anti-Judaism, even among those German feminist theologians who tend to use more violent language about Judaism because of the emotional weight which anything to do with the Jews carries in Germany. Her book is a magnificent contribution to dispelling ignorance of the extent of the problem and lack of awareness as to what does constitute anti-Judaism.

The attempt to divorce Jesus' attitude to women entirely from his Jewish upbringing and beliefs, and to blame all subsequent sexism within the church on regressive Jewish influence (with perhaps a little Hellenism thrown in), is not universal. Daphne Hampson in her book *Theology and Feminism*[26] says that the process is dishonest and that a number of Jesus' comments on women accept the existing *status quo* of his community. She writes as a post-Christian. Within the Christian world, Mary Grey in her book *Wisdom of Fools*,[27] which tries to define a Christian feminist theology of revelation, says that Christian feminists must try to find a world-view which does not denigrate Jewish beliefs.

There is an increasing awareness within the community of feminist scholars that anti-Judaism is a problem. The 1989 conference of the European Society of Women in Theological Research gave space to this issue, and the papers presented at that conference were published by the *Journal of Feminist Studies in Religion*.[28] Nevertheless, noted feminist theologians have written deplorably prejudiced works since that conference. Despite this, I am glad to have had many discussions with Christian women where I have found only support and respect and knowledge of Judaism. There is much in Christianity that I have come to value because of dialogue. I am aware that I have often complained about anti-Judaism to those most willing to listen sympathetically, which usually means those least to blame for it in their own theology.

Jewish feminists do have clear problems in contemporary Judaism, just as Christian feminists have with twentieth-century Christianity. Our problems, however, are far short of those that many Christian women assume, and in many areas we probably have fewer difficulties than they do.[29] But this is an area where sharing is more useful than competing or blaming, which is precisely the difficulty caused by anti-Judaic comments and writings. Jewish and Christian women are both trying to generate a theology which values women as much as men. We have shared problems, and we have so much to offer each other in support and shared experience, yet that sense of a common task and value-system becomes impossible when having to correct prejudice and basic errors of fact. In her article in *Nice Jewish Girls*, Judith Plaskow says that the present situation reflects not sloppy scholarship but a negation of values feminists proclaim to be essential, such as refusing to project undesirable qualities on the other, as patriarchy has so often done:

> 'The real tragedy is that the feminist revolution has furnished one more occasion for the projection of Christian failure onto Judaism. It ought to provide the opportunity for transcending ancient differences in the common battle against sexism.'[30]

While writing of the anti-Judaic aspects of books I have otherwise found intellectually and religiously stimulating, I have a deep sense that by raising this topic, I am betraying spiritual women bravely engaged in the task of creating a world fit for heroines to live in. Feminist theology is a relatively new subject. Books published as recently as 1980 say that the author feels herself to be doing something without parallel or precedent.[31] The output of literature in the last fifteen years has been astonishing in both its quantity and its quality. Feminist theology is no longer so frail and new that it has to be protected from legitimate criticism. My hope in raising this issue is that Jewish and Christian women's energies can be combined to develop a theology of mutual respect in which we help each other to go further than either of us could go alone in the task of creating a world free of the blemish of disrespect for women emanating from religions who have everything to gain from the exercise of our spiritual and intellectual powers.

Notes

1. *Dialogue with a Difference: The Manor House Group Experience*, ed. Tony Bayfield and Marcus Braybrooke, SCM Press 1992, 6.
2. See Dorothea Magonet's editorial in *European Judaism* 1987/1 for a fuller history of the Jewish-Christian-Muslim women's conferences originated by Anneliese Debray at the Hedwig Dransfield Haus, Bendorf.
3. Jane Williams, 'Jesus the Jew and Women', in *Feminine in the Church*, ed. Monica Furlong, SPCK 1984, 86. I have quoted so extensively from this article because many untrue statements appear in rapid succession. The same ideas can be found in many other writers.
4. Ibid., 87.
5. Alice Bloch, 'Scenes from the Life of a Jewish Lesbian', in *On Being a Jewish Feminist*, ed. Susannah Heschel, Schocken Books, New York 1983, 174.
6. Williams, 'Jesus the Jew and Women' (n.3), 88.
7. Mishnah Kiddushin 1.1.
8. Sister Charlotte Klein, *Anti-Judaism in Christian Theology*, Fortress Press, Philadelphia 1978.
9. For a fuller discussion of this topic see Susan Grossman and Riva Haut (eds.), *Daughters of the King*, Jewish Publication Society, Philadelphia 1992, especially the articles by Susan Grossmann and Hannah Safrai.
10. Lisa Isherwood and Dorothea McEwan, *Introducing Feminist Theology*, Sheffield Academic Press 1993.
11. Ibid., 102.
12. Katherina von Kellenbach, *Anti-Judaism in Feminist Religious Writings*, Scholars Press, Atlanta 1995, 75.
13. Susannah Heschel, 'Current Issues in Jewish Feminist Theology', *Christian Jewish Relations*, the journal of the Institute of Jewish Affairs, London 19/2, 1986.

14. Isherwood and McEwan, *Introducing Feminist Theology* (n.10), 43.
15. Ruth B. Edwards, *The Case for Women's Ministry*, SPCK 1989, 32, 28, 25.
16. Bernadette J. Brooten, *Women Leaders in the Ancient Synagogue*, Brown Judaic Studies 36, Scholars Press 1982.
17. Isherwood and McEwan, *Introducing Feminist Theology* (n.10), 18, 44.
18. See Rachel Adler, 'Tumah and Taharah — Mikveh', in Strassfield, Strassfield and Siegel (eds.), *The Jewish Catalog*, Jewish Publication Society, Philadelphia 1973, 1677–71, for a further discussion of menstrual impurity and its relationship to life and death.
19. Introduction to *Feminine in the Church* (n.3), 7.
20. See Linda Sireling, 'The Jewish Woman: Different and Equal', in *Through the Devil's Gateway*, ed. Alison Joseph, SPCK 1990, 94, for a description of how she and her husband felt they were taking each other physically for granted during pregnancy, which they did not during their normal cycle of observance.
21. Ute Ranke-Heinemann, *Eunuchs for Heaven: The Catholic Church and Sexuality*, André Deutsch 1988.
22. Jo Garcia and Sara Maitland (eds.), *Walking on the Water, Women Talk about Spirituality*, Virago 1983.
23. See n.12.
24. I have therefore quoted only authors published in the UK not cited by her.
25. Rosemary Radford Ruether wrote *Faith and Fratricide: The Theological Roots of Anti-Semitism*, Seabury Press, New York 1974. She deplores anti-Judaism in her feminist theological books, yet von Kellenbach cites a number of her arguments which are clearly anti-Judaic. She and her husband Hermann Ruether have produced a book *The Wrath of Jonah* which violently criticizes Zionism: the connections to be made between anti-Zionism and other forms of anti-Judaism and antisemitism is a major topic in itself.
26. Daphne Hampson, *Theology and Feminism*, Blackwell 1990.
27. Mary Grey, *Wisdom of Fools: Seeking Revelation for Today*, SPCK 1993.
28. *Journal of Feminist Studies in Religion* 7/2, 1991. I am grateful to Sister Clare Jardine nds for making a copy of this available to me.

29. See Judith Plaskow, quoted in Kellenbach, *Anti-Judaism in Feminist Writings* (n.12), 79f.
30. Judith Plaskow, 'Blaming the Jews for the Birth of Patriarchy', in *Nice Jewish Girls. A Lesbian Anthology*, ed. Evelyn Torton Beck, Crossing Press, New York 1982, 254.
31. Carol Christ, *Diving Deep and Surfacing: Women Writers of Spiritual Quest*, Beacon Press, Boston 1980, xiii.

German Jewry Fifty Years after the Holocaust

Henry Brandt

Had this article been written five years ago, it would have described a very different picture from that today. The Jewish scene in post-war Germany may have been complex and disturbing, but at least it would have been expected. The change wrought in the course of recent years has been as profound as it has been dramatic. Jewry in Germany has altered decisively in the last few years, and it will never revert to what it was before.

Although I shall attempt to report fairly and objectively, I have – for the sake of honesty – to admit to a certain prejudice and bias. Having been trained at the Leo Baeck College and moulded by my tasks and experiences in non-Orthodox congregations in Britain, Switzerland and Sweden, I had acquired certain definite religious attitudes and convictions. Not that these were inflexible or immutable, but the broad lines of my understanding of Judaism in all its aspects had been set. This included an affirmation of the pluralistic option within it and hence the rejection of all doctrinaire approaches and claims to exclusive truths. For me Jewish belief and practice did not require an abdication of reason or scientific methods. Reverence for Jewish traditions and its wisdom of the ages does not stand opposed to a relevant and livable religious practice in every day and age. Thus armed and equipped, I assumed rabbinic office in Germany in 1983. What I found there, and that to which I had to accommodate were I to serve my communities, often led me to impatience and sometimes to the edge of despair. But then, a rabbi has to be there for his community and not the other way round. Yet, on the other hand, a rabbi cannot be expected to betray his fundamental beliefs and convictions. The choices are seldom that clear-cut. This lesson I had to learn rapidly and comprehensively, frequently the hard and painful way, a walk on a dangerous tightrope worth trying only if one thinks that the goal on the far side is worth-while. I considered that Jewish survival and continuity in Germany was and is such a worthwhile aim. Nevertheless, my report may at times reflect my subjective reaction to events and people.

One factor has been and still is of over-riding significance in the life and the shaping of the character of Jewish communities in Germany after the war: the Shoah – the Holocaust. Virtually every facet of communal – and to a marked degree of individual – awareness and activities has been shaped and determined by this grim, nay incomprehensible, reality. Not only were the early members and founders of Jewish communities in Germany at the end of the war themselves mainly survivors of the extermination and labour camps, they also had to face the bitter fact that they were living in the land of murderers and perpetrators. On one hand they had to justify their remaining in Germany before their own conscience, but more difficult and bitter was the necessity on the other hand to explain this to the violently critical and disdainful Jewish people and institutions in other parts of the Diaspora and, above all, in Israel. This inevitably led to the formulation of a host of defensive and apologetic positions, some sincerely held, others at variance with the true but hidden convictions of their proponents. On the part of Jews and many non-Jews in other countries there was also little readiness to lend an open ear and mind to these arguments. For some decades the Jewish communities in Germany and their members felt themselves to be the pariahs of the Jewish world. One of the resulting attitudes was the syndrome of the 'packed suitcases'. In simplest terms, this meant that in answer to the question why one was prepared to live in Germany came the claim of one's intention to leave as soon as something or another had been settled. The suitcases were, so to speak, already packed. These protestations remained current for a considerable time, even after it had become abundantly evident that they were utter fiction, as some erstwhile emigrants returned and a trickle of Jews from other countries – including Israel – came temporarily, or settled in Germany, although they had no prior connection with this country. The reasons for this development were clearly to be found within the realm of material possibilities and benefits. On the broader field of communal activities these considerations inevitably led to a predominance of political and material concerns. The special and precarious situation of the communities had to be kept permanently in the eyes of the authorities and the public, only too ready to deny, belittle or cover with silence the guilt and deeds of the immediate past. Particularly in this area, many individuals and institutions have rendered great services to the Jewish communities in Germany. Synagogues were built or restored, memorials erected and dedicated, communal institutions established, and social services put in place. The Jews in Germany would not let the memory of the victims of the Shoah be forgotten or levelled down. In this they were eminently successful. Thus was laid a foundation for the more open and forward-looking dialogues in many areas, which developed over the last quarter of a century.

It must be recalled that the size of the Jewish community in Germany after the war has always been very modest, much smaller than many people think. Even as late as the beginning of the 1990s, the number of registered members of the Jewish communities in the Federal Republic of Western Germany did not exceed thirty thousand. The fall of the Berlin Wall and the reunion with Eastern Germany brought no appreciable change in this figure. Some other development did, but about that I shall have to report further on. Berlin constituted the largest community, followed by Frankfurt and Munich. The 'intermediate' communities boasted around 1,500 members each, a sad reminder of devastation considering the numbers in those proud pre-war Jewish communities such as Cologne, Düsseldorf and Hamburg. Other major cities had memberships mostly in the lower reaches of three figures: Stuttgart, Hannover, Dortmund, Bremen, Mannheim and others. Then followed a fair number of minuscule communities with but a handful of registered members.

The inevitable problems created by modesty of scale were compounded by the heterogeneity in the composition of the memberships. Hardly any two communities were alike. There were differences of origin, experiences, cultural background and religious orientation and commitment. The composition of the earlier communities was largely determined by the chance of circumstance: who was liberated where and when, and which was the nearest centre of population, affording a possibility of survival and facilities for medical and economic help. However, in most cases a common denominator was that almost always the largest part of those Jews who joined forces to establish some kind of Jewish life, seed-beds for the later emerging communities with their formal structures, were of East European origins, often from Poland. This fact in consequence determined the religious attitudes and the liturgical forms current in the new communities after the war. In no case were they really a renewal of the former German Jewish communities. These were irretrievably destroyed. As the saying went – and still goes – there are again Jewish communities in Germany, but there are no more *German* Jewish communities.

The aforementioned factors naturally also determined the religious scene. For reasons good and bad religious life in the Jewish communities in Germany was determined by a compulsive status quo thinking. Although the number of genuine Orthodox Jews was extremely modest, the liturgical forms ordained for the places of worship, large and small, were mainly according to the East European ritual of pre-war years. With very few exceptions, hardly a trace remained of the traditions of the local communities from before the war. On the contrary, the prejudice against the German Jewry of yesteryear was widespread and often reached slanderous proportions. The rabbinic leadership was appointed with these considerations in mind. This proved regrettably easy, as virtually all surviving German rabbis – with very few notable exceptions – declined to return to the country of the murderers and their accomplices. The lay leadership, widely composed of people with limited religious knowledge and a level of observance to match, placed the emphasis of its endeavours in the administrative and political sphere. In these it was remarkably successful.

Synagogues were built and community centres established. Social services were put in place, state treaties for the financing of all these activities negotiated and concluded. However, real religious and educational concerns remained on the back-burner, with devastating results. In the fields of Jewish thought and religious education Germany became a virtual desert. These sins were covered by the magic figleaf concept of the alleged *Einheitsgemeinde* – the unified community.

The idea of the *Einheitsgemeinde* was not new. Originally it was supposed to denote a Jewish community in which the different main religious orientations found a place for their prayers and study under the umbrella of one community, which provided and cared for all. Its members could freely decide to which of the synagogues and schools to give their allegiance. Often people frequented more than one particular synagogue.

The new version of the *Einheitsgemeinde* was a unified structure in which all Jews could be members, whatever their religious point of view, but its religious orientation had to be exclusively Orthodox or, at least, strongly traditional. Any liberalizing or reforming ideas were summarily ruled out of court and considered virtual treason *vis-à-vis* the Jewish community. The only real exception was the Jewish community of Berlin, where the plurality of religious expression was retained. The argument of the *Einheitsgemeinde* and the perennial slogan *Immer schon so gewesen* ('It has always been like this') brought it about that synagogal liturgy as well as religious education remained in an uninspiring and unedifying strait-jacket of habit and convention. The only way in which people could make their negative reactions felt was to vote with their feet. This they did in great numbers. Only in recent years did dissent and opposition take concrete forms. A few small communities have consciously and courageously chosen a more modern way for themselves, and small but not insignificant groups have formed themselves inside as well as outside existing communities with the avowed aim of seeking religious forms and expressions more suitable to their needs and convictions. Even without the influx of new members from the East, the beginning of a mood for renewal and critical appraisal of existing structures has begun to be felt in Jewish Germany.

It is not surprising that Jews in Germany are more sensitive to any manifestation of antisemitism than anywhere else in the world. The memories of the Shoah are a constant reality in their consciousness, and everywhere one encounters monuments and reminders of the horrific inhumanity of the Nazis and their fellow-travellers. The Jewish community in Germany has been described by a number of sociologists as one which defines its identity by the Shoah and by a vicarious attachment to the State of Israel.

No one in his right mind and aware of his surroundings would claim that anti-Judaism no longer exists in Germany. Many are the signs and plentiful the evidence that ignorant and stupid prejudice against Jews is still fairly wide-spread amongst the people, many of whom have never encountered nor spoken with a Jew, apart from the television screen. There have been daubings of graves and synagogue walls, and the news about a few actual attacks against Jewish institutions have made headlines around the world. In fact, overt manifestations of anti-Judaism are not the prime concern of the community at present. Most Jews feel fairly safe and secure in their presence in Germany. A more serious and threatening factor is a more general xenophobia rampant in German society – and not only in Germany – directed in the first place against coloured people and Turks. But this type of frame of mind has always an accompanying element of anti-Judaism, and there is every reason to remain watchful and prepared. In parallel, a considerable body of philo-Judaism has also developed in Germany. For many people Jews can do no wrong, and if they do, good and proper reasons can be adduced for their conduct. One thing is clear: just like the antisemites, they too prevent Jewish life in Germany from developing towards normality, i.e. Jews are not considered citizens with the same rights and duties as all others.

For a number of years after the war the churches in Germany appeared to have been struck dumb by the events of the Nazi period. Many of their functionaries either could or would not recognize that their world had changed, never to become again what it was before. Their declarations of failure seemed pale and unsure, often failing to make specific reference to the biggest sin of all. Only the passage of the years brought a fundamental change in this area. Over the last thirty years or so, all the large German churches have openly and candidly examined not only their own conduct in the period of the Nazis, but also the antecedent history of the teaching of the church, which laid the seeds for the ultimate fall from grace. Since then a large number of resolutions and statements have acknowledged their guilt and failure and stressed the necessity to re-examine their stance towards Judaism. Theologically most significant was their stated recognition of the continuing election of the people of Israel as God's chosen people. Antisemitism was brandmarked as a sin. The study and knowledge of Judaism became an avowed and recommended aim for community work and, especially, in the curriculum of Christian seminaries.

Nevertheless a lot also remains to be done in this area. At this point in time one of the principal bones of contention is the activities of some small but active and vociferous missionary groups, which refuse to abide by the wider consensus that this type of activity is no longer acceptable, and seek easy prey amongst the recent arrivals from the former Soviet Union.

On the positive side one has to report that in all the major churches, high-powered commissions of Jews and Christians have been appointed to continue the work in the direction of a proper understanding and a new relationship between the two religions. Moreover the movement of the German equivalent of the 'Societies of Christians and Jews' has not lost its momentum, and now counts nearly eighty local branches throughout the country. They are linked by their umbrella organization, the *Deutscher Koordinierungsrat der Gesellschaften für christlich-jüdische Zusammenarbeit*, which usually stands under the patronage of the President of the Federal Republic of Germany. Its annual 'Week of Brotherhood' has become a fixed and firm item in the cultural calendar of the country. The national opening ceremony, lasting an hour and a half, always coupled with the award of the Buber-Rosenzweig Medal, presented for outstanding services in fostering inter-faith and inter-communal relationships, is transmitted live on the leading TV stations for the entire German-speaking region of Europe.

It remains to mention that topic which at present dominates all concerns of the Jewish communities in Germany, and taxes and strains their possibilities and resources to breaking point and beyond: the arrival of 40,000 refugees from the erstwhile Soviet Union. That for which one hoped and prayed every Seder night – the freeing of our brothers and sisters from Soviet bondage – has become reality, and now there are not enough places round the Seder table to accommodate them all. Within the last few years the membership of the Jewish communities in Germany has more than doubled; in some places the numbers have increased by up to 500%. Doubtless this is a momentous development full of potential and promise. Communities which teetered on the brink of dissolution are now facing the problem how to acquire new premises and personnel. Instead of the cemetery the need is now a kindergarten. However, there is a rub, a fly in the ointment. The 'Jews' who thus increase the numbers are seldom 'Jews'. I do not mean to convey that most are halachically not Jews – though this issue is also a constant headache; rather, they have virtually no awareness of the meaning and content of being Jewish. It is true that they had the notation 'Jew' in their identity cards, and because of that they often encountered disadvantages and discrimination, but this 'Judaism' signified their membership of an ethnic grouping within the rules of the Soviet Union, and not an adherence to a religious faith and committment. Generally of a high educational and professional standard, their knowledge of Judaism is absolutely negligible, if not non-existent. On the whole the Jewish communities in Germany are quite helpless in the face of this challenge. There are various courses and other instructive events, but the rigid structure described earlier on, with its attendant lack of flexibility, show them ill-equipped to deal with the problem. The response seems to be largely to convey to the newcomers the givens of the existing situation and practices, and to appeal to their sense of duty and gratitude to bring them to comply. It is noticeable that this is hardly the way to motivate particularly the younger and intermediate age-groups. Consequently, once the main material necessities have been obtained – living space, either work or social security payments, language courses and the like – many of the newcomers disappear from the horizon of the communities. The increase at worship in the synagogues is recruited mainly from among the older generation.

Contrary to what might have been expected in the prevailing social climate in Germany, there seems to have been no noticeable increase in anti-Jewish feelings or antisemitic incidents related to this immigration. It should, however, be recorded that the federal and the state governments have been impressively generous and accommodating towards this wave of Jewish arrivals, as most funding comes from these sources. One of their avowed aims was the deliberate strengthening of existing Jewish communities in Germany.

The reunification of Germany made the this goal really possible, although its beginnings go back to the period before. The economic problems which this momentous development caused, although they certainly increased the general social discontent – once the first waves of enthusiasm had waned – did not lead to any noticeable curtailments in the allocations for the reception and integration of Jewish immigrants from the erstwhile Soviet Union. Otherwise, the impact of reunification on the West German Jewish community was relatively negligible. The surviving Jewish congregations in Eastern Germany numbered no more than 200–300 members, most of whom lived in East Berlin.

Jewish awareness and knowledge were at a premium, and it is doubtful whether most of them would have survived for very long. Yet the dedication and stubbornness of a very small number of devoted leaders has to be mentioned with gratitude and admiration. But for them, the situation might have been tragically worse. In the light of later developments one must acknowledge that they ensured that now there is a future for these communities.

The full picture is, of course, considerably more complex than this brief description, but one could sum it up as follows: it is a struggle for percentages. Certainly not *all* will be lost, nor will *all* be retained within the orbit of the Jewish communities. The success or failure of each community locally and of the overall community in Germany generally will be measured by the percentage of new immigrants they succeed in keeping within the ranks. The bottom line is: a virtual miracle has happened and the promise is there for all to see. Perhaps the foundation is being laid for a new German Jewry.

From USSR to FSU – From Oppression To Opportunity

Robert Shafritz

This article is based on reports compiled by rabbis, most of whom have received *semichah* (rabbinical ordination) from the Leo Baeck College, among other travellers to the Former Soviet Union (FSU). It covers approximately the twenty years between 1975 and 1995. As this period witnessed the collapse of the Soviet state, I follow current practice in referring to its former territory as the FSU, even though the latter has no political reality of its own. For most British based Soviet-Jewry groups, the new phraseology acknowledges the collapse of Soviet power and the change in historical circumstance. For the Jews who still reside in the region, however, it marks a radical change in their existence opening up the passage from oppression to opportunity.

In March 1985, when Mikhail Gorbachev became the leader of the Soviet Union, I was spending the third year of my Leo Baeck College training in Israel. Very few Jews were allowed to leave the USSR. State-sponsored antisemitism suppressed almost all Jewish activities. It was the time of the Refuseniks. Little could I have imagined that only five years later, as a result of Gorbachev's accession to power, the Moscow City Council would grant official status to Congregation Hineni, the first Progressive synagogue in the FSU; moreover, that after receiving rabbinical ordination and taking up my first post at the West London Synagogue, I would be invited to Hineni to officiate at the service of dedication of its new home, Polyakov House. I accepted the invitation and departed for Moscow.

The service took place on 30 November 1990 in the presence of Jews from right across the religious spectrum. Members of the Orthodox, Chasidic, Refusenik and secular communities were all represented, as were some non-Jews as well. With Chanukah approaching, I focussed the service on the theme of re-dedication. A light was kindled by the youngest member of the community present, and this act articulated in a symbolic way the rebirth of Jewish life extinguished for several generations in the FSU.

A solemn occasion, the atmosphere in Polyakov House was filled with expectation. The expectation burst into joyous rapture when, just as the service was about to finish, in walked Ralph Goldman of the American Joint Distribution Committee, to hand over to the congregation its first Scroll of the Torah. Ralph Goldman was the 'angel of God' who transported the Scroll all the way from New Jersey, USA for the occasion. Electricity and excitement filled the air as it was presented to the Congregation's President, Zinovy Kogan. Smiles could be seen on every face, and it was as if the burden of the past had been lifted away at that moment. All the participants and everyone who had heard about the service acknowledged its historical importance for Jewish life in the Soviet Union. For me personally and my wife, Aviva, who had accompanied me to Moscow, the service was deeply moving; the moment when Ralph Goldman entered the hall remains indelibly printed on my memory and, I am sure, on the memories of all of those present.

I was not the first among my rabbinical colleagues from the Reform Synagogues of Great Britain (RSGB) to travel to the FSU. At the height of the Refusenik era, some fourteen years earlier, many had travelled to the then USSR to lend support to the Refusenik cause. The programme of travel carried on for a couple of years and operated in conjunction with British based Soviet-Jewry groups, the '35s' and the National Council for Soviet Jewry. With the founding of Hineni the programme of rabbinical travel was re-launched, only this time under the banner of the RSGB affiliate 'Exodus' (now 'Exodus 2000') and co-ordinated by the World Union for Progressive Judaism (WUPJ) in Jerusalem.

The re-launched programme saw rabbis from both the Reform and Liberal movements travelling to the FSU. Between March and June 1990, Rabbis Eimer, Silverman, Kraft, Soetendorp and Borts travelled to Hineni to help lead services, teach Judaism and provide organizational and pastoral support to its members. With the help of the UK rabbis Hineni celebrated its first wedding and batmitzvah. None of the rabbis was under any obligation to give of him- or herself. Each rabbi, nevertheless, responded individually with time and commitment to the calls for help, the one coming from the group of Moscow Jews who formed the nucleus of Congregation Hineni, the other from within him- or herself. Rabbi David Soetendorp describes the nature of the 'call' and the spirit in which the journeys were undertaken, when at the end of the report on his journey he says: 'To Jews who present themselves to us from the background of the Soviet Union's spiritual barrenness of seventy years with the statement – *Hineni* (Here I am!) – there can only be one response from us rabbis in the West, and that is our resounding – *Hineni*!'[1]

The seventy years of 'spiritual barrenness' have nevertheless taken their toll of Soviet Jewish life. The impact of these years has been felt both on personal and institutional levels. Let me consider the personal one first.

The seventy years of oppression have inflicted pain and death on generations of Jews and robbed whole families of an inheritance. While in Moscow in 1990 Aviva and I stayed in the flat of Maya D. On her bookcase was a large sepia photograph of Maya's family. Aviva recounts their story as Maya D told it to us:

> There sit Maya's mother's family in 1918 in Riga. Her grandparents are in the centre, surrounded by their five grown-up daughters and various sons-in-law, including Maya's parents . . . Her grandfather was in the lumber business; they were comfortable. And what became of them all? The part of the family which remained in Riga was killed by the Nazis. Two sisters and a brother-in-law who moved to Moscow were killed by Stalin. A cousin was killed fighting as a soldier in the last war. Her parents, she and her brother were the only ones who survived. The history of loss, murder and premature death in Maya's family has its counterpart in almost every Jewish family in Russia.[2]

Then, with Gorbachev's accession to power and the liberalization of political life which followed, the floodgates opened. Jews poured out of the FSU in their hundreds of thousands. Those in Israel and the West applauded – the dreams of freedom and return were fulfilled. And yet, life for the Soviet Jews remained hard. Aviva continues the story of Maya D's family:

> Maya had a son and a daughter and two granddaughters. Until last year she lived in her three-room flat with her husband, her son, daughter-in-law and granddaughter. Her husband died a year ago. Last summer her son and his family went to Israel. Now she is on her own in the flat. Her daughter and granddaughter live nearby. They do not want to leave the Soviet Union. Maya is torn and sad. Should she go or should she stay? Many Jews are staying. Many are going. Families are being torn apart. It's very painful.

So even the opportunity to leave has brought with it the pain of separation, loneliness and loss. The single institution left holding Jewish life together in the FSU, the family, has again been torn apart – this time, however, not by war, nor by a mad dictator, nor even by assimilation but, and herein lies the irony, by the hope for a better future in the land of Israel!

Turning now to the impact of the last seventy years from the institutional point of view, they have prevented the development of workable Jewish institutions. The oppression has stifled the training of leaders, without which, of course, communities find it difficult to grow and enhance Jewish religious, social and cultural life. Let me explain just how this problem presents itself, for it will probably prove crucial to the future development of Judaism and Jewish life in the FSU.

The WUPJ, which I mentioned earlier as the organization co-ordinating rabbinical travel to Congregation Hineni, has spear-headed the development of Progressive Judaism all over the FSU. Moscow was the first 'stop', so to speak. Since the founding of Hineni the seeds of twenty-five Progressive communities have become firmly rooted in the FSU, from Kiev and Minsk in the West to Omsk and Birobidzhan in the East. The communities share the feature of attracting all types of Jews, many between the ages of twenty and forty, but especially those only beginning to discover their Jewish roots. At the same time, they suffer from the same weakness – the absence of an institutional infrastructure. With people emigrating to Israel or other destinations regularly, the communities cannot train or 'reproduce' leaders fast enough to replace those who depart. Developments in the Ukrainian city of Cherkassy highlight the matter.

In September 1992, Rabbi Joel Oseran, the Education Director of the WUPJ, travelled to Cherkassy, a provincial city of about 300,000 inhabitants situated a few hundred kilometres west of Kiev. The Progressive congregation there had been founded in 1991 by Ludmilla Pomeranskaya, a professor of mathematics, after attending High Holy Day services at Hineni. Since then the congregation has grown and moved into a rented facility for Sabbath and festival services. Ludmilla herself went to Jerusalem to learn about Progressive Judaism and took part in WUPJ seminars in the FSU. She started the congregation's religion school as well. She taught most of the Hebrew lessons and was helped by her family as well as by other members of the community. She served as the main source of inspiration for the community's religious and cultural development. In her own son Michael's words: 'The dream of her life was to return to Judaism.' She returned, but not alone. Ludmilla's charisma, her love of Judaism and, in particular, her dynamic leadership brought her family and other Jews along with her. So why the visit by Rabbi Oseran?

Rabbi Oseran visited Cherkassy to establish contact with the congregation's new leaders. Ludmilla, the guiding light of this fledgling community, had decided to emigrate with her family to the United States in the summer of 1992. Ludmilla's sudden departure highlights the problem of continuity of leadership to which I referred above and which plagues all new communities in the FSU. Without continuity, where are new leaders to come from?

This is not a new problem. It has surfaced before – for example, during the Refusenik era. Rabbi Oseran articulates it in a report he compiled for the WUPJ in January 1989 after a fact-finding mission to the FSU:

> As Jewish leaders grow in awareness in Hebrew skills and communal activity they ultimately receive exit visas and leave . . . It is truly a mixed blessing – no one can deny that a Kosharovsky or a Zelochenick do not deserve our unbridled joy and support for leaving – and yet what happens in the continuity of Jewish life in the communities they leave behind? How many Jewish leaders can keep springing up to take over? And for how long before they themselves must leave?[3]

Ludmilla's departure raised the very same questions, this time in the context of a developing new community. What would happen to the continuity of Jewish life in Cherkassy? Fortunately, a new leader emerged in the person of Marina Boguslavskaya. But how many Marinas are there with the talent, time and commitment to step in at such short notice and fulfil leadership roles?

The problem of leadership continuity has not gone away, and it does not look as if it will for some time to come. Nevertheless, Rabbi Oseran traces the cause of this phenomenon to an institutional weakness in Jewish communal life in the FSU – the absence of an 'infrastructure of continuity'. He makes the point in the same report from which I quoted above:

> . . . until such a time as each community has a more organized communal structure which institutionalizes Jewish activity and creates an *infrastructure of continuity* [my italics] – until such time as communal leadership will not rest on special personalities but on positions of leadership – until that time the problem of leadership continuity will continue to pose a serious threat to Jewish cultural and religious life in Russia . . .

The absence of any infrastructure of continuity is the 'institutional' price the Jews have had to pay for the seventy years of oppression. These years choked the very life out of the Jewish community, leaving it leaderless, worse, without the infrastructure to train new leaders should the need arise. The Jews, however, saw no need to train new leaders, to develop the institutions to train them, for such a need presupposed a future, and under Communism the Jews *qua* Jews had none.

Seen from personal and institutional standpoints, therefore,

Jewish life has been marked, if not marred, by seventy years of oppression. Since Gorbachev, however, religious freedom has provided Jews with the impetus to rid themselves of some of their historical baggage. They have exchanged oppression for the opportunity to learn about Judaism, and they have been supported by Jews from abroad. I gave examples earlier of rabbis from Britain travelling to Hineni to officiate at services, teach Judaism and support congregational development. Let me give one last example to show just how the situation has changed, where Jews of the FSU have begun to seize new opportunities reaching far into the future while at the same time lightening for themselves the burden of the past.

A number of Jews have always been able to leave the USSR, even under the most oppressive dictators. Moreover, they have always managed to continue studying and learning about Judaism, even if only in secret and illegally. What they have never had the opportunity to do, at least not until now, is to train to become leaders to serve their own communities without going abroad. The WUPJ in November 1993 established the Institute of Advanced Jewish Studies in Moscow with this sole purpose in mind – to train Jews from the FSU to become leaders of Progressive communities and create an infrastructure of continuity so that communities need not collapse should a leader depart. Several Reform and Liberal rabbis from Britain along with Israeli and American colleagues have taught courses at the Institute. A two-year programme, the first in the classroom studying Judaism, the second in the field working in developing Progressive communities, the Institute invites individuals to train to become Jewish communal leaders. Never before has such an opportunity presented itself. At one and the same time, the programme seeks to resolve the problem of leadership continuity, the inheritance from the past, and to enhance Jewish communal life. The training at the Institute takes place exclusively in the FSU and embodies for the Jews there a rite of passage – from dependence on Jews from abroad to self-sufficiency at home.

It is too early to predict the impact that the Institute and its graduates will have on the development of leadership in FSU communities. The first group of students to have completed the course have only recently graduated to positions of communal leadership. Be that as it may, the establishment of the Institute is the first clear sign that Jews of the FSU understand that without the institutions to train their leaders Jewish communities have little chance of survival or of enhancing the religious, social and cultural life of their members.

The Progressive Jews of Europe had to respond to a similar situation after the Second World War. With the annihilation of European Jewry and the destruction of the single most important Progressive rabbinical training institution in Berlin, the Hochschule für die Wissenschaft des Judentums, Progressive Jews in Britain founded the Leo Baeck College to train rabbis to serve their communities and, as it has turned out, ones in Europe and the FSU as well; three students from the FSU are now training for the rabbinate at the College. Obviously, the circumstances surrounding the establishment of the Institute in Moscow differ significantly from those surrounding the beginnings of the Leo Baeck College. The need, however, remains the same. If the success of the Leo Baeck College is in any way the measure of things to come, then the audacity and daring to establish such a training institution in Moscow will have been well worth the effort.

From the outside we in Great Britain look on at the rebirth of Jewish life in the FSU and, in particular, the development of Progressive Judaism there with interest but also with uncertainty. We see the impact the seventy years of oppression have had on individuals, their families and institutions. Individuals have been stripped of a religious identity, families torn apart, and institutions cut off. Tainted by the mistrust and cynicism of the Cold War, we perceive the rebirth at best as precarious because of the years it will take Jewish institutions to become well-established, at worst as life-threatening and dangerous because of the upsurge in chauvinistic nationalism and antisemitism. We ought not to forget, however, that the opportunity belongs to Jews there. We may support them in *their* quest and participate in *their* opportunity. Often we will even gain from such participation. But we ought not to allow *our* cynicism, *our* mistrust, *our* complacency or *our* ideology to interfere with *their* opportunity and new-found hopes, lest we undermine *their* purpose and give *them* the wrong signals about the importance of Jewish life and the contribution it can make to healthy communal living.

Let me conclude with the following observation. Within a few years of Gorbachev's accession to power the Refusenik era came to an end, and with it years of oppression. The Jews of the FSU entered a new era, one no longer characterized by 'spiritual barrenness' but rather by hope and opportunity; one no longer dependent upon super-power political trade-offs, but rather upon building viable Jewish institutions based on mutual respect, support and independence. Through institutions such as the Leo Baeck College, Exodus 2000 and the World Union for Progressive Judaism, Jews in the UK have responded with a quiet and determined activism to the resounding *Hineni*! (Here I am!) of those in the FSU, those who have mustered the courage to identify themselves positively as Jews and as part of the greater family of Israel.

Notes

1. Rabbi David Soetendorp, unpublished report entitled *Report of a Visit to Moscow May 17–May 22, 1990*, Bournemouth, June 1990, 12.
2. Aviva Shafritz, 'The First Steps', *Manna*, Spring 1991, 5.
3. Rabbi Joel Oseran, unpublished report entitled *Report of the World Union For Progressive Judaism Fact-Finding Delegation to the USSR: December 21, 1988–January 11, 1989*, Jerusalem, 13 January 1989, 4.

THE NEEDS OF THE PEOPLE

The everyday tasks and dilemmas modern rabbis face

The needs of the people here in Britain are addressed by those writing in the section, headed by Lionel Blue, who reveals the simple formula for his astonishing success in communicating God over the airwaves at a time in the morning when, for most people, God is furthest from their thoughts. Elizabeth Sarah highlights another far-reaching development, the recognition of sexual diversity. She presses for a radical approach to sexual ethics, albeit based on traditional sources. For many years Douglas Charing has been involved in another revolution, teaching non-Jewish children about Judaism. He describes the major changes that have occurred in religious education in schools and the enormous social impact this will have for the next generation. Jeffrey Cohen also calls for a new awareness in his field of speciality, mental illness, talk of which often has the tabu status that sex once held. Chaim Wender tackles a subject that is leaping to the forefront of the Jewish agenda – ageing. With the proportion of elderly members of the community increasing rapidly, he puts forward a series of proposals to deal with it constructively and caringly. What happens next is confronted by Julia Neuberger, who considers the approach of death and the ethical dilemmas that modern medical techniques present. Combining her knowledge of Jewish teachings and experience in health work, she tries to suggest ways in which we can not only live well, but die well too. Sylvia Rothschild follows the same theme from a slightly different perspective, homing in on how Judaism itself has to adapt new rituals both for those dying and for those mourning. She emphasizes that death need not be viewed as a defeat but is another of the stages in the cycle of life, and is to be treated as positively as all the other ones.

Radio Religion

Lionel Blue

I got on to the radio by accident. They were doing a sort of Down Your Way programme at a synagogue where I used to take services. So I was summoned back from the continent where I was taking a wedding. On the late night boat all the rich chocolates and smoked salmon I had consumed so recklessly regurgitated into the waves and I arrived back in London very late, very grey and very wan. So when they asked me the first question, I could only repeat a most unsuitable joke the ship steward had told me, and when they asked me another, I heard myself in horror saying something even more unsuitable. It is a common situation when one dreadful statement follows another and you can do nothing about it. That was me! Well, no matter, I thought. I would soon be returning to the continent, so what difference did it make if I had made a fool of myself with the BBC?

To my surprise, I received a letter about three weeks later asking me if I would do a 'godslot' on the morning programme. I don't think it was called Thought for the Day then, but a title more committed and pious. I realized later that by sheer accident I had stumbled on the secret of radio religion. It is very simple. Radio is an intimate medium, and if you are prepared to say what you really think, and not what other people think you ought to think, or what you think other people think you ought to think, it works! What you say does not have to be the profoundest or holiest thing ever uttered, but it has to be your own. There's the rub! How do you preach radio religion? The answer is a boomerang. Are you prepared to risk being yourself: your real self, not your minister self, nor your political self? If you are, the way is open. If not, the role-playing is evident and destructive. Radio is intimate and demands honesty.

Your radio congregation, after all, are also themselves. They are not clothed in their creaky sabbath best, smiling politely at fellow members of the faithful, and trying to look good before God (the result is often indistinguishable from constipation). They are in bed, doing whatever they are doing, in the bathroom, the loo, or swearing blue murder in a traffic jam when your vignette on salvation or eternity hits them. It is important always to keep your radio congregation and its circumstances in mind. A colleague asked me why I didn't instruct them in the Jewish problem or quote them Talmud. At that time of the morning, when they are worried about what's going to hit them during the day? To give them another problem when they are undermined by the problems life throws at them and they want to dive back under their duvet again! Radio religion forced me to deal with where people are in life, not where I would like them to be. Unfortunately a lot of establishment religion is about where people ought to be, with too little help about getting from they are to where they ought to be.

It is wise to remember that your radio congregation has a power your normal congregation does not possess. Or rather, it has it but is too timid to use it. The only person I know who ever had the guts was Sister Louis Gabriel, also known as Dr Charlotte Klein, but then she was a strict Jewess before she became a nun. 'Father,' she would say severely in impeccable Prussian-nuanced English, 'What you are saying is simply not true!', and she might then walk out. Fortunately, says the trade unionist in me, few of the faithful have that self belief! But I admired her. Now if you are at the other end of a transistor, it is only too easy to extend an arm, twiddle a knob and blot out the sermon for ever.

So be careful! Concentrate not on what you want to say but on what your listeners need to hear. Your words may not be the holiest or the most mystical ever uttered, but they do have to be relevant. They have to be part of the same world as the bedroom, bathroom, loo, kitchen and traffic jam. Like a lot of the Talmud, in fact! Bonhoeffer agonized over the division between the religious ghetto and the life of the boulevard. Since your 'godslot' is embedded in a fast news programme, detailing the life of the boulevard, you do not theologize about the gap; you just grit your teeth and close it before your listeners switch you off. It is an excellent discipline, because religion and reality are growing steadily apart, to the impoverishment of both.

This means that preaching, old style, is cut. It is neither the time nor the place to show off your learning with great gobbets of law and theology. And also do not quote scriptures too much either. What, no scriptures? Yes, I mean no. No undigested scriptures, because your listeners either do not share the same scriptures, or more likely they have no scriptures. They come from all faiths or none, mainly none, and as far as the latter are concerned, scriptures are only old books. They have a point. It is fascinating listening to the struggles of a minister in a contemporary pulpit trying to relate the goings on in Moab to modern times, or the complicated home life of the patriarchs to the mores of Hampstead Garden Suburb.

So where is the authority for what you say? You cannot say 'the prophets say' because your listeners probably do not recognize any prophets, and the same goes for assorted sages, mystical, rational or whatever. At first you feel theologically naked without them, but then you take courage and start to speak out of your own personal experience, however slim it might be, and that carries conviction. The traditional scriptures do matter, but only if they have integrated themselves into your life and become part of your personal scripture. In this situation doubts are precious. If you are honest about your doubts, then your faith, however slight, becomes credible. To make too many claims for your faith results in a switch-off. Your listeners are too accustomed to the overkill of commercials, and take preventive mental action. In this respect religion is no different from any other end-product.

On the radio it also faces the same test. Not many are bothered about the provenance of what you say. That is an in-person's problem. Their problem is 'Does it work?' The wise words can be extracts from the Gita, the Koran, the Zohar, the Tanya or What The Stars Foretell. They are judged, not by respectability or antiquity but by their effect when your partners walked out on you, or you are trying to keep your self-respect in a dole queue, or wondering about the metaphysics of happiness on a package holiday. 'By their fruits ye shall know them' is of course from the New Testament, but I'm sure the same sentiment is echoed in the recesses of rabbinic writings.

Your product – religion – has to fulfil the same tests as any other product, and you have to back the claims you make for it. Now religious claims in the past have been inclined to go over the top, ending up in a froth of poorly documented wonders. And the suspicious modern listener might doubt his trip to heaven and suspect being taken for a ride or on a trip to cloud cuckooland. Which is why the claims made in a godslot should be sober and tested out in the speaker's experience. Take prayer, the best example of DIY religion! What does it give if you are a secular listener prepared to give it a go? Well, in my experience, prayer does not give security or the answer to the problems of the cosmos – at least it never has for me. But though it has not changed the external world to suit my convenience, it has changed me, and I am part of that world. It has not given me security, as I have said, but it has given me courage, and helped me cope with the next step ahead. If courage is what you want, on you go. If you prefer magic, and that is what most of us secretly would like, it is better to consult the adverts in specialist journals.

But though radio religion cannot give the answers people secretly want, it can face up to the questions they are shy of asking because they might seem too secular or frivolous. Now official religion has considered for a long time the answer to 'How can I be good?' But in a hedonistic society, the more immediate question is 'How can I be happy?' I do not think we should look down our nose at such a question, or be spiritually snobbish about it. The metaphysics of happiness concern all human relationships, all the holidays we take, and the plans we make. Since happiness is not synonymous with objects but is largely a value we ascribe to objects, it also has a spiritual component.

Radio religion taught me a lot. For one thing it cut me down to size. Yes, it builds up your vanity, of course, but you soon realize that you are also part of the entertainment industry as well, subject to the sell-by date of fashion. This makes you come face to face with humility as surely as a few laps round the liturgy on the

High Holy Days. It also taught me that preaching is a two-way business. Although you are alone with a microphone, you have to employ all your imagination to the reality that lies beyond that mike. The strange thing is you empathize it, you feel it, as well as reading reply letters. I think all preachers should be as attentive to their listeners as the radio practitioner.

Above all you realize that wisdom is two-way. You are not only giving to them, they are giving to you. Now the old idea of revelation was, imaginatively speaking, rather snobby. From some effects, God revealed his truth from above to the awestruck ignoramuses below. But in a democratic, scientific (or pseudo-scientific) age, another way of seeing revelation is required. And from the unpretentious little godslots on the radio and the modest enquiring replies, I have learnt that it seeps up too from below, from the hard-bought wisdom and life struggles of seemingly very ordinary people. Like Anne Frank or Etty in fact. That was a lesson of the Holocaust, confirmed in the correspondence sent to me by the BBC.

It's a humble truth, and radio religion has always been humble. It is classed as 'entertainment', just as jokes are regarded as light. But jokes are no joking matter, and such religious 'entertainment' provides the daily spiritual fare for people on buses, in hospital, awake with worry at nights, and at a bar in Blackpool. In fact more people listen to such little sermons than ever before. A Pause for Thought on the Terry Wogan show may well be heard by more people than all the congregations in all this country's synagogues and churches on a sabbath added together. And heard with interest and appreciation. And yet many moan that this is an irreligious country in an irreligious time. Perhaps they are not looking for the Spirit in the right place! Perhaps they have not tuned in to his (or her or its) new wavelength. Perhaps they are, theologically speaking, still pre-FM and internet!

Towards a New Jewish Sexual Ethic

Elizabeth Sarah

Sex lessons in the Torah

It is significant that very little is said directly about sex in the Genesis narratives concerning the creation of humanity, save for the assumption that it is *heterosexual*, *monogamous* and geared to *reproduction*. Elsewhere in the Torah, however, in both narrative and legal texts, we find a number of teachings about sex which, together with Genesis 1 and 2, have become the basis of Jewish sexual ethics.

The most extended treatment of sex is contained in Leviticus 18 and 20, where the focus is on prohibited sexual acts – those between family members; a man and his neighbour's wife;[1] a man and a menstruating woman;[2] two men; a man or woman and an animal. In all these cases, with the exception of bestiality, where initiation of the act by both sexes is conceived, the individual male is the *subject*; the individual female is the *object*. And this perspective is reinforced in all the other references to sex in the other legal texts in the Torah: a bride must be a virgin (Deut. 22.20); a father is prohibited from making his daughter a prostitute (Lev. 19.29); sex out of wedlock is not punished as long as the woman is an unbetrothed virgin and the man who lies with her, marries her (Exod. 22.15–16; Deut. 22.28–29).

Interestingly, however, in two key *narrative* passages dealing with exceptions to the taboo surrounding incest, the active role is taken by women. Following the destruction of Sodom and Gomorrah, and the transformation of Lot's wife into a pillar of salt (Gen. 19.26), Lot's two daughters, left alone with their father, get him drunk on successive nights and lie with him, to ensure they have offspring (19.30–38). In another case where the commandment to be fruitful is at stake, Judah's daughter-in-law, Tamar, childless because Onan has spilled his seed rather than produce a child in the name of his dead brother, Er (Tamar's first husband), conceals her true identity with the garments of a prostitute and entices her father-in-law to lie with her so that she may conceive (Gen. 38).

These two exceptions highlight the hierarchy of values implicit in the system of sex laws outlined in the Torah: ultimately, the imperative of reproduction is so important it may even over-rule incest tabus. What is more, *ethical* conduct as such is a secondary consideration. The primary principle underlying the rules of sexual behaviour is the maintenance of *social order* and the preservation of the *separateness* of the people of Israel. The laws regulating sexual acts in Leviticus 18 and 20 are set in the context of the book's concern with *kedushah* – with *setting apart:* the offerings to be made on the altar from the remainder of property, the priests from the people, the people from the other nations. As the preamble to the sex rules in Leviticus 18 indicates, ethical issues are less relevant to the laws regulating sexual conduct than the need to ensure that the people do not follow the ways of Canaan or Egypt, but rather walk in the way of God (18.2b–4).

But one rule in Leviticus 18, by contrast, does seem to emerge from a predominantly ethical concern. At verse 18 we read:

> And you shall not take a woman to her sister, to be a rival to her, to uncover her nakedness, beside the other in her lifetime.

While there are no laws against bigamy in Torah, and indeed bigamy was only outruled for Ashkenazi communities in the late tenth century by the ban of Rabbenu Gershon ben Judah, and remains an option (in theory) for Sephardim within the religious Courts of Israel to this day, the rule against marriage between a man and his wife's sister seems motivated by consideration of the wife's feelings and the need to preserve the integrity of the relationship between two sisters. As such it has much more in keeping with the next chapter, Leviticus 19, where the need for right conduct in social relationships is stressed again and again. Indeed, the link in ethical tone between this rule and the chapter sandwiched between the two dealing with prohibited sexual acts, makes the apparent contrast between the *ethical* preoccupations of Leviticus 19 and the *separatist* agenda of 18 and 20 even more marked.

But the juxtaposition of the chapters is not accidental. Rather, it suggests that just as the sex rules should be understood in the context of the imperative of setting the people Israel apart from the other nations, so they should also be understood in the context of the ethical regulation of social relationships. And yet, in fact, to this day, Jewish law has failed to consider the implications of this juxtaposition for sexual ethics.

Sex and love: a new combination

At the heart of Leviticus 19, a chapter dealing with correct ritual practice and ethical behaviour towards the poor, the stranger, the disabled, the elderly, one's neighbour, lies the famous dictum 'You shall love your neighbour as yourself. I am the Eternal' (19.18). According to Rabbi Akiva, a leading second-century scholar, this commandment was not simply an important rule, it was 'the great principle of the Torah' (*Sifra* 89b). What does that mean? The *first* principle. The *underlying* principle. You shall love your *neighbour*. Who is your neighbour? The person who lives *next* to you; the person who is *like* you. You shall love your neighbour as *yourself*. You shall love yourself – then you will be able to love your neighbour. And what is love? It is not merely an emotion; it is an act, a commitment. The phrase 'You shall love your neighbour as yourself' is part of a section of laws dealing with acts of justice, with the myriad material ways in which we must fulfil our responsibilities towards our neighbours and towards God.

None of the various laws relating to sexual behaviour both in Leviticus and elsewhere say anything about love. The word is not even used in connection with the story of the first relationship at the beginning of Genesis. And yet there are many love stories in the Bible: Jacob and Rachel, Samson and Delilah, David and Jonathan, Ruth and Naomi.

And then there is the great book of love, *Shir HaShirim*, The

Song of Songs, traditionally attributed to King Solomon, the child of David's union with Bathsheba, another legendary lover. In contrast to the Garden of Eden narrative, Arthur Waskow points out that '(t)he sexual ethic of the Song of Songs focuses not on children, marriage, or commitment, but on sensual pleasure and loving companionship.'[3]

The Song of Songs provides a welcome reminder that sex is not just about *who* can do *what* with *whom*; it is about love and the joys of physical desire and intimacy. Fortunately, post-biblical codes, while primarily concerned with the reproductive imperative, generally validate pleasure and so include both the 'right' of wives to experience sexual satisfaction (*Ketubot* 61bff.; 47b–48a) and the permissibility of a wide range of sexual practices – including both oral and anal sexual activity – if it is desired by the couple concerned (Maimonides, *Mishneh Torah*, Hilchot Issurei Bi'ah 21.9).

But the implications of love – as understood in the context of Lev. 19.18, and of loving companionship – as described in The Song of Songs – are not part of the framework of the rules governing sexual conduct. The reasons for this derive from the fact that despite the acknowledgment of women's capacity for sexual pleasure, the rules of sexual conduct are primarily concerned with what *men* do.

Significantly, of the various ethical rules delineated in Leviticus 19, only that concerning the command 'You shall love your neighbour as yourself' deals with the relationship of *peers*, of *equals*, of *equal men*. All the others involve ensuring right conduct between those whose relationship to one another is *asymmetrical*: the person with property *vis à vis* the one who is poor, the Israelite *vis à vis* the stranger, the able-bodied *vis à vis* the disabled, the young *vis à vis* the old. Similarly The Song of Songs is unique in its egalitarian treatment of the lovers. In its pastoral paradise, love and desire is expressed equally and actively by both partners. Indeed, it is the passionate female voice present in the poem which has led some scholars to suggest that the text is probably the work of a woman.[4]

For the spirit of Lev. 19.18 and The Song of Songs to infuse the sex laws would require a huge conceptual shift. It would mean treating both women and men as active *subjects*, peers, equals. It would mean perceiving sex, not as a series of acts perpetrated by one party on the body of another, but as a means of expressing a *relationship*. It would mean seeing the expression of love and desire as one of the *primary purposes* of sexual activity. It would mean recognizing all relationships, whether heterosexual or homosexual, with or without children, as *variations* on the theme of human partnership and evaluating them all according to the identical criteria of *love, equality* and *reciprocity*.

The commandment to 'love your neighbour as you love yourself' provides the ethical framework for a code of sexual behaviour. So what happens when we apply the criteria of love, equality and reciprocity to the sexual prohibitions outlined in Leviticus 18 and 20? Clearly all relationships in which the *inequality* of the parties is an inherent feature, for example relationships between adults and minors, are unacceptable. As far as other relationships are concerned, a clue to whether or not they fulfil the criteria emerges from the specific sexual terminology employed in the texts. There are a number of linguistic expressions for sex in the Torah, of which the most common are *to know – lada'at* and *to lie down – lishkav*. Both of these terms are morally neutral. The words themselves do not convey the nature of the sexual encounter, positive or negative. By contrast, the expression *gillui ervah*, 'uncovering nakedness', which is used in Torah exclusively in cases of incest and in reference to sex with a menstruating woman, suggests not only sexual intimacy, but *vulnerability* and *danger*. Within the world-view of Torah, blood is a powerful substance, and contact with it is tabu. From the vantage point of the present day, the danger associated with 'uncovering nakedness' has more to do with the potential for exploitation involved in 'uncovering' a person's 'nakedness'. In the words of a contemporary rabbi quoted anonymously:[5]

> Very simply, it means making a person completely vulnerable, and then not taking care of them in their nakedness.

The implications of this interpretation are clear. Whether or not one abstains from sex during menstruation, most Jews today would probably not put sex with a menstruating woman in the same category as sex with a family member, where the issue of exploitation is much more readily apparent. However, there would probably be general agreement that there is a *potential* for exploitation in *any* sexual context.

But the perspective of Torah appears to be much narrower. Interestingly, the expression 'uncovering nakedness' is not used in Torah in connection with the other categories of prohibited sexual behaviour outlined in Leviticus 18 and 20 – adultery, sex between men and bestiality. In these examples, the more neutral term 'lying down' is employed.[6] Clearly none of these cases entails the danger either of blood contact or a built-in asymmetrical power dynamic. Indeed, in the case of two men lying down together, perhaps there may be an implicit assumption that the *independent male subject* is not in a position to exploit his *equal* – another male. But, at a deeper level, 'uncovering nakedness' refers not only to *who* is involved, but to *what* is involved: even if the parties concerned are equals, any sexual encounter which entails exposing and exploiting another person's vulnerability is 'uncovering nakedness'.

Towards an inclusive, egalitarian Jewish sexual ethic

In recent years, sexual ethics has once again become a topical item on the Jewish agenda – largely in the context of the need to rethink Jewish attitudes towards same-sex relationships.[7] But other issues have also prompted new debate: sexual activity on the part of teenagers;[8] sex out of marriage;[9] the incidence of extra-marital relationships; the growing phenomenon of 'serial monogamy'; the general diversification of family patterns.[10] The challenge of an inclusive, egalitarian approach rooted in love and reciprocity is that it may be seen to turn heterosexual marriage, monogamy and child-rearing into options among a wide range of other alternatives rather than the essential components of the *model* Jewish family arrangement.[11] On the other hand, the reality of Jewish relationship patterns today *is* diverse. And indeed, as David Biale has argued,[12] contemporary concerns, like pre-marital sex, are actually not new issues at all and have always been a feature of Jewish life, more or less sanctioned and accepted at different times. An inclusive, egalitarian approach makes it possible to apply ethical criteria to the broad *spectrum* of relationships and does not give *any* individual or group the licence to live outside the law and engage in irresponsible, exploitative or dangerous sexual behaviour.

And so, within the parameters of love and reciprocity, it is possible to specify a range of core ethical values which may be expressed in a *variety* of different relationships. In his article. 'Rethinking Jewish Sexual Ethics' in *The Reconstructionist* (July/August 1989), David Teutsch lists twelve 'values' which may be seen as 'central' to Jewish sexual ethics regardless of whether the relationship is between 'two women or two men' or 'a woman and a man' (11): 1. Procreation; 2. Meaningful relationships; 3. Freedom for consenting adults; 4. Strong families; 5. Fidelity; 6. A stable community; 7. Protection from violence and abuse; 8. Good health; 9. Honesty; 10. Privacy/ modesty; 11. Physical pleasure; 12. Caring(8–10).

Ironically, of these values, procreation alone – the first sexual imperative of the Torah – is clearly *not* a possible feature of all relationships: there are loving, committed heterosexual couples who cannot have children and those who choose not to. Equally, within same-sex relationships, some partnerships include children, others do not.[13] Just as an inclusive, egalitarian approach should inform our understanding of what constitutes a valid intimate relationship, so our definition of *family* needs to be expanded to encompass a variety of different 'familial' living arrangements, including: heterosexual and gay or lesbian partnerships – with or without children; 'communal' families encompassing single adults and/or couples – with or without children; and one-parent families.[14]

The impressive *Report of the Reconstructionist Commission on Homosexuality*[15] includes a 'discussion of values fundamental to Reconstructionism', which provides a further contribution to the development of a new approach to sexual ethics. Here in a treatment of fifteen different values, we find a number which do not appear in Teutsch's list: human dignity and integrity; *kedushah*/holiness; equality; inclusive community; democracy; learning from contemporary sources of knowledge;

'You shall surely pursue justice'. Clearly from the teachings of tradition to the insights of modern scholarship, there is a host of resources out of which to construct the specific details of a Jewish sexual ethic based on love and reciprocity. Contrary to the fear that an inclusive, egalitarian approach will prove too permissive, the reality is that it is extremely challenging and demanding for all Jews – heterosexual, lesbian and gay alike.

Embracing diversity: kedushah *today*

An inclusive, egalitarian approach may have its roots in 'Love your neighbour as yourself' and encompass a wide range of Jewish values, but is it really in harmony with the predominantly separatist spirit of Judaism? After all, among all the observances which function to reinforce Jewish *separateness*, none expresses this value more completely than *kiddushin*, the marriage ceremony in which the couple, likened to the first human beings in the Garden of Eden, are 'set apart' for one another.

The philosophical framework of Jewish thought is characterized by the making of clear, unequivocal distinctions. At first sight the values of equality and inclusivity seem at complete odds with this dynamic – particularly when it comes to including same-sex relationships and treating them as equal. But in essence, *kedushah, setting apart*, is paradoxical. The bride and groom are set apart *to be joined* with one another.

What is more, not only are separated elements essentially part of one another, but unity is *rooted* in diversity. Towards the end of each of the three daily services, there are two complementary prayers known as the *Alenu*. In contrast to the *particularistic* tone of the first prayer, the second one includes the *universalistic* 'hope' that 'all the inhabitants of the world will perceive and know that to You every knee must bend and every tongue swear loyalty . . . On that day the Eternal will be One and known as One'. The vision of universal unity is a coming together of all the different people. It is a *union of different parts*.

There is increasing evidence of different Jewish constituencies taking an active part in Jewish life today. This is particularly true of those who have been most excluded in the past – lesbian and gay Jews. Many Jewish lesbian and gay couples have participated in Jewish ceremonies celebrating their relationships, particularly in the United States, because they are committed to living Jewish lives and are determined to include themselves in the Jewish community.[16] Hopefully, before too long, those who wish to sanctify their relationship before God and in the presence of their community will also have the option of having ceremonies included as variations of Jewish marriage.[17]

The Jewish concept of holiness sets apart and embraces different elements and remains at the heart of Jewish sexual ethic. Homosexuality is different from heterosexuality. Female sexuality is different from male sexuality. Each individual relationship is different. And each relationship is also part of the rich texture of possibilities for human love and as such should be subject to the same ethical rules. Ultimately, that is what an inclusive, egalitarian approach to sexual ethics is all about.

Notes

1. See also Ex.20.13.
2. See also Lev.15.19ff.
3. Arthur Waskow, 'Down to Earth Judaism: Sexuality', in Jonathan Magonet (ed.), *Jewish Explorations of Sexuality*, Berghahn Books 1995.
4. See Sybil Sheridan, 'The Song of Solomon's Wife', in ead. (ed.), *Hear Our Voice. Women Rabbis Tell Their Stories*, SCM Press 1994, 64–70.
5. See Sharon Cohen, 'Homosexuality and a Jewish Sex Ethic', *The Reconstructionist*, July-August 1989, 15f.
6. Note that the reference to bestiality in the case of a woman and an animal says 'You shall not stand before a beast . . .' (*lo ta'amod lifnei veheimah*).
7. See *Homosexuality and Judaism. The Reconstructionist Position. The Report of the Reconstructionist Commission on Homosexuality* (January 1992), and an early attempt to grapple with the issues by the Reform Synagogues of Great Britain, the pamphlet *Jewish and Homosexual* (1982).
8. See 'Sex. And What Should I Tell My Teenager?', *Manna* 26, Winter 1990.

9. Hyam Maccoby, *The Independent*, 12 September 1987, for a discussion of the sources on pre-marital sex. See also *Foresight*, the journal of Progressive Jewish students, September 1990, special issue on *Love and Sex*.
10. See *The Jewish Family Today and Tomorrow*, a pamphlet published by the Reform Synagogues of Great Britain in 1983, for an early attempt to confront 'Social change, its effects on the family and the implications for Jewish life'.
11. See Waskow, 'Down to Earth Judaism' (n.3), and the response to his view by Daniel Landes, 'Judaism and Sexuality', in the same volume.
12. See David Biale, *Eros and the Jews*, HarperCollins, New York 1992, for a full treatment of Jewish attitudes to sex 'from Biblical Israel to Contemporary America'.
13. See Ariel Friedlander, 'Hundreds of Kids', *Manna* 48, Summer 1995, for a sensitive treatment of Jewish teaching and attitudes on fertility and infertility.
14. See *The Jewish Family Today and Tomorrow* (n. 10), 5.
15. See n.7. See also the study materials for a course designed for synagogue study programmes, Robert Gluck (ed.), *Homosexuality and Judaism. A Reconstructionist Workshop Series*, The Reconstructionist Press 1992.
16. See for example Leila Gal Berner and Renee Gal Primack, 'Lesbian Commitment Ceremonies', in Debra Orenstein (ed.), *Jewish Women on Life Passages and Personal Milestones*, Jewish Lights Publishing, Woodstock, Vermont 1994; Paul Horowitz and Scott Klein, 'A Ceremony of Commitment', in Christie Balka and Andy Rose, *Twice Blessed. On Being Lesbian, Gay, and Jewish*, Beacon Press, Boston 1989.
17. In March 1996 the Central Conference of American Rabbis, which represents 1750 Reform rabbis, voted to support same-sex marriage.

Judaism in School Classrooms

Douglas S. Charing

The 1944 Education Act intended Religious Instruction to be solely on the Bible and Christianity, and for the whole ethos of Christian education in schools to be an extension of the church. Parents had the right to withdraw their children from these lessons, especially if they were Roman Catholic or Jewish. The same Act demanded that Local Education Authorities should be responsible for producing an Agreed Syllabus for Religious Instruction in their areas. One of the committees involved was drawn from members of the Church of England, and another brought together people from other Christian denominations. In the words of the then Archbishop of York: 'Their (teachers') responsibility is great, for the future Christianity of our nation largely depends upon the nature of the religious teaching which is given in our schools.'

Twenty years later minor changes were introduced, the best example being the new Agreed Syllabus of the West Riding. This progressive educational authority was the first in the country to appoint an Adviser in Religious Education, who introduced a page in the syllabus entitled 'Jewish Children and their Religion' and another page called 'Immigrant Children and their Religion'. This was perhaps the beginning of the teaching of comparative religion. However, this was still a matter of comparing other religions with Christianity, but from a Christian perspective. The 1970s saw a much greater change. First, the terms 'religious instruction' or 'religious knowledge' were dropped in favour of 'religious education'. The subject was viewed as an opportunity no longer to indoctrinate pupils in a particular religion, but rather to educate them about various faiths. This was the birth of teaching a multi-faith religious education, and a change from comparative religion to world religions. The first new Agreed Syllabus reflecting these changes was produced by the City of Birmingham.

There was an attempt to teach about Judaism in some schools during the 1960s, but this was usually confined to what was regarded as the Judaism at the time of Jesus, and dealt with topics such as Passover, the Temple and the synagogue. Material on Judaism was very sparse, but one of the earliest pioneers to inform schools about today's Judaism was the then Education Officer of the Board of Deputies, Myer Domnitz. With very little funding, he produced many leaflets and wrote the first book on Judaism for schools published by a commercial publisher In the 1970s a number of organizations interested in multi-faith education were created. These included the Standing Conference on Inter-Faith Dialogue in Education, chaired by Rabbi Hugo Gryn of the West London Synagogue, and the Shap Working Party on World Religions, in which Rabbi Gryn was also involved. Around the same time, the Christian Education Movement, which had a major involvement with schools, began producing material on religions other than Christianity. In 1974, the Jewish Education Bureau was founded in Leeds by me and was the first organization to promote the study of Judaism as a world religion within a framework of multi-faith religious education.

Judaism has been and has remained the most popular non-Christian religion taught in schools, especially at Primary level. This cannot be because of the number of Jews in Britain, seeing that Islam is clearly the largest non-Christian religion in the country. There are a number of reasons for the situation. First, both Judaism and Christianity share the Hebrew Scriptures, the Old Testament for Christians. Since most teachers have some form of Christian background, there is a feeling of familiarity about the Jewish religion. Secondly, there has been a Jewish presence in Britain for many centuries, and some Jews have a high profile. Thirdly, some teachers have built up an interest in Judaism by visiting Israel. All these factors contribute to making Judaism the most popular religion after Christianity.

This does not mean that Judaism is well understood by teachers. Indeed, it has often been argued that the Judaism taught is through Christian eyes and through the Bible alone, without reference to the post-biblical literature, such as the Talmud, the work of the early rabbis. Such an approach would also largely ignore the importance of Jewish ethics. That is why in the 1960s the Judaism taught was the 'at the time of Jesus' variety, and usually limited itself to looking at the areas already outlined in this article. So in a way Judaism, which appears on the surface to be the easiest religion to teach, in actual fact can be the most difficult, until the teacher sees it through Jewish eyes rather than through Christian ones.

The teaching of Judaism in today's schools is taken more seriously, and most teachers want to do it justice. It is not only in the classroom that pupils are learning about Judaism. A growing number of schools, even infants, are visiting synagogues, and these educational outings can be very helpful in explaining Jewish belief and customs in the very place where Jews worship, study and congregate. Some pupils, especially those engaged in GCSE or 'A' level Religious Studies, attend a Sabbath service so they can experience at first hand a Jewish act of worship and its atmosphere, which cannot be gained by reading books or even watching a video.

Teachers will be guided by their local syllabus as to what they cover, but usually a study of Judaism will include the Sabbath and some of the festivals, life-cycle events, synagogue and prayer, sacred books, and the role of Israel. Pupils also learn about both Orthodox and Progressive forms of Judaism, and older children will study a little about the history of Anglo-Jewry and its current situation. Even Jewish pupils will extend their knowledge in this way, and possibly become prouder of their Jewish heritage, at an age when many youngsters have rather negative attitudes towards religion, including their own.

One area where Religious Education teaching has helped other subjects is in the sensitive area of the Holocaust. This has been tackled over the years within Religious Studies GCSE and 'A' level. It is only recently that it has been included in the history curriculum, and there is also an increased interest in English, as in the teaching of Anne Frank's *Diary*. The 'Anne Frank in the World' exhibition which has been staged in many cities and towns throughout Britain in the past twelve years has also encouraged the study of prejudice, racism and antisemitism, and helps to make pupils more aware of diversity and multi-cultural issues. Some schools have invited Holocaust survivors to speak to pupils. This has been a most rewarding experience for both pupils and survivors, and hopefully will make children grow into tolerant adults, sensitive to the needs of minorities and open to religious and cultural pluralism.

There is a need for good resources if one is hoping for good teaching and good learning. Such resources can be divided into materials, places and people. Some teachers may opt for teaching Judaism for the simple reason that resources on Judaism are good, easily available, and plentiful. This is mainly due to the large number of Jewish publishers, especially American, who produce well-written and often colourful books for both children and adults, often at an attractive price. Most of these publications, whilst written primarily for American Jews, can easily be used by non-Jewish non-Americans. In the past two decades, a number of British publishers have made an important contribution to multi-faith books.[1] These books are highly colourful and user-friendly and help pupils of all ages understand a living faith and its people.

In the last twenty years, Religious Education Resource Centres have been set up in many cities and towns throughout the country. Here teachers and other interested people can discover books and other items such as videos, posters and artefacts on the world's religions. Often most of the items can be loaned, or advice is given on where they can be purchased. Courses for teachers also take place at these centres. The largest are in London, Birmingham, and York and the National Welsh Centre in Bangor. The centres constantly update their material so that all new publications on the subject are on display, including a wide range of journals, many of which are published by the various faith communities. One of the most interesting centres is the Interfaith Education Centre in Bradford. Here, in addition to the usual members of staff, they also employ a number of people from some of the faith communities who visit local schools and are available to consult with teachers about that particular faith. Although the Centre does not employ any Jewish member of staff, mainly because there is a very small Jewish community in Bradford, it does call on local Jews, including the present writer, to speak on Judaism on many occasions. This also includes visits to one of the two Bradford synagogues. There is another special aspect to this centre, in that each faith has its own room. It also has excellent relations with its local faith communities.

People must also be regarded as an important resource, and a growing number of the various faith communities are making themselves available to talk to groups of teachers and pupils. This may be at their place of worship where they can guide visitors through their synagogue, mosque or temple, or they may be willing to visit the school and make a presentation there. Children will often enjoy listening and learning from a visitor, and this is an important area in making RE a lively and exciting subject. Some schools, of course, will be located many miles from a non-Christian community, so it may not be possible for such a visit to take place. Some of these schools are nevertheless willing to make a long journey and find the end result very worthwhile, and a useful link between the school and a community.

Those teachers, especially Secondary trained, who have majored in Religious Studies have an advantage over others. However, a growing number of Primary schools have appointed one teacher to be RE co-ordinator, and they are, through courses, learning a great deal about world religions. Children of all ages often ask very searching questions, and although no one can expect a teacher to know all the answers, good quality in-service courses will go a long way in providing many answers to these questions.

Another way of promoting a lively RE is, in the case of Judaism, to participate in a Judaism day. The Education Department of the Board of Deputies offers one in London, whilst the Jewish Education Bureau runs such days in Leeds, Manchester and London. These days are geared towards older pupils, college students and teachers. The day will usually comprise a synagogue visit, a Jewish meal, a trail, and a visit to the Jewish Museum in either London or Manchester. If they remember very little else, at least some pupils will remember for a long time eating Jewish food!

RE in the Primary school is often taught by way of themes. Thus, for example, 'Festivals of Light' will include a study of the Jewish Chanukah and the Hindu/Sikh Divali, as well as the Christian Christmas. On Chanukah, pupils will hear about the story; learn a song; play dreidle, the spinning top; and possibly make and eat latkes, the potato pancakes. Probably Chanukah, Passover and Purim are the most popular Jewish festivals studied in schools. Stories generally are a good way of presenting a religion, both for children and adults. Judaism has plenty of stories for all ages.

It is helpful when teaching about a religion to use terms in use within that community. So for example when teaching Judaism, it is good to refer to the kippah rather than the skullcap, or the tallit rather than the prayer shawl. This will not present a problem even for very young children.

The 1988 Education Reform Act included much on RE. Two areas were considered by some to be controversial: first, that the majority of the time should be given over to Christianity; secondly, that all pupils should learn something about other faiths. Some felt that the former was turning the clock back to the period before Britain became a multi-faith society, and that perhaps some people would use the situation for indoctrinating rather than educating. With regard to the latter, some people did not wish to learn about any other faith, especially if they lived in what they considered as a white Christian area or a predominantly Muslim one.

Whilst many Jews who had children in the state system welcomed a multi-faith approach, others, including the former Chief Rabbi, Lord Jakobovits, did not. Indeed, the former Chief Rabbi was instrumental in the House of Lords in defining the Act. His opinion was that a course on comparative religion opposes both Jewish and Christian interests, and that Jews and other non-Christians have no business to help to deprive Christians of their religious heritage. He further felt that teaching about various faiths without any commitment would turn the nation's children into confused pagans. He argued that minorities should continue the practice of withdrawal from RE lessons and assemblies, and also be entitled to request worship and instruction in their own faith when the numbers warranted this. His views would be shared by a number of Christians and Muslims, but they do appear to miss the point of what RE in schools is all about. It is not the task of the school or the teacher to teach a religion from a doctrinal point of view. This surely is the business of the faith communities themselves. RE in school must be open, even critical, and available to all pupils, learning together about faiths other than and as well as their own. Also, bearing in mind that not every pupil has a faith in our increasingly so-called secular society, RE in schools is to help pupils become aware of what makes other people tick religiously. They should learn to respect other peoples religious practices and beliefs. This way our young people, the adults of the future, will learn to live at ease and in peace with their neighbours, whatever their faith and the colour of their skin. Adult members of the faith communities can also play their part.

Another aspect of the Education Reform Act was for Local Education Authorities to set up a Standing Advisory Council on Religious Education (SACRE). Here members of the various faith communities can appoint a person to represent them, and they will then have a voice on the quality of RE provided in their local schools.

The following is what good RE should be all about. It is brought to the attention of all teachers attending courses at the Bradford Interfaith Education centre:

Our first task in approaching
another people
another religion
another culture
is to take off our shoes
for the ground on which we stand is holy
else we may find ourselves treading on someone's dreams.

Notes

1. These include Douglas Charing, *The Jewish World*, Macdonald 1983; Arye Forte, *Judaism*, Heinemann 1995; Clive Lawton, *Passport to Israel*, Watts 1989; Christine Pilkington, *Judaism: An Approach for GCSE*, Hodder Educational 1991; Sybil Sheridan, *Jewish World*, McDonald 1986.

A Jewish Response to Mental Illness

Jeffrey Cohen

> 'All the gates are locked except for the gates of wounded feelings'[1] (Baba Metziah 59b).

This statement from the Talmud poignantly highlights the anguish which is so often felt by those who experience mental illness or see it in their family. Because of the stigma and fears associated with mental illness, both the person with the disease and the family feel isolated and shamed. They often speak of the feeling of being a pariah, of feeling excluded. Of all the parts of the body, the mind is the least well known. It is as if a line has been drawn across the neck and everything below is researched, but the mind is left alone. It is only at the end of the twentieth century that any significant money has been applied to brain research.

Mental illness is a term used to describe a group of disorders causing severe disturbances in thinking, feeling and/or relating to others. Often the result is a substantially diminished capacity for coping with the ordinary demands of life. It can be a permanent condition, or a temporary one. In the case of the latter, a previously well-adjusted individual may have an episode of mental illness lasting weeks or months, and then may go for years without another bout, and perhaps never have one again. Others may become ill periodically. Between episodes they may be perfectly well. During those times it is both unfair and unrealistic to label them as 'abnormal', while those who have recovered from their illness resent being treated as different ever after.

Mental illness is, at best, an equal opportunity disease, knowing no distinction according to wealth, social class or education. One in four families knows the pain when someone in their family experiences serious and prolonged mental illness. One in ten people experience some form of mental illness in their lives, the most pronounced form being clinical depression, which is a biological disease like diabetes. Studies presented at the 1995 American Psychiatric Association's Annual Meeting show that in contrast to the situation in the general community, where women seem to suffer more than men, depression is just as prevalent among Jewish men as with Jewish women. It is suggested that this is due to the lower consumption of alcohol among Jewish men, for alcohol seems to be used by many to mask the symptoms of mental illness, at least temporarily. The study went further in suggesting that among those Jews who move more into the mainstream of society there is an increase in the use of alcohol and drugs, with the result that there may *appear* to be a lower prevalence of depression among some Jewish men.

I think of my time in a congregation. If the suggestion of one in four families being affected by prolonged mental illness is correct, how does that reflect back on the one thousand families who made up the congregation? At the time I was aware of half a dozen families who were open about their family member having a mental illness. I can perhaps identify another ten who were not so open. I cannot believe that the research studies can be so far out that instead of the two hundred and fifty families who should have been identified as having someone with a mental illness there were less than twenty. Since that time I have been able to verify what I had suspected: that the shame was so great that they could not even speak about it. Where had they gone, and could they be enticed back into the community? These are the challenges which face us when working with persons with mental illness.

The first onset of mental illness is at an average age of eighteen to nineteen years old. When a family has a child with mental retardation it is identified early in the child's life. They make adjustments in the expectations they have for that child. It is different for the family who experiences mental illness. The child has often developed through the normal stages of development with perhaps only some minor hiccups. The parents develop dreams, and what good Jewish parents do not have dreams for their child? Then suddenly they are faced with this disabling disease and the loss of their dream. It is a loss very similar to a death. For many family members, it is almost impossible to accept.

Not too long ago I was sitting with a member of my family who suffers from schizophrenia. His first experience of this disease was as a doctoral student at Harvard University. Now he is almost unable to concentrate for more than a few sentences, and the only job he can hold down is occasionally re-cutting ties to keep them somewhat in fashion.

In our conversation, he challenged me about how and why this had happened to him. We have all heard the same question with other diseases such as cancer and muscular dystrophy. He was obviously asking me more than just the straight biological 'why?'. It would have been easy to answer in terms of genetic predisposition and chemical imbalances. Any physician or psychiatrist could have given him that data.

I had to offer something different – a religious response. Obviously it was not because of some sin committed, or bad parenting, or weakness of character. At first I had no answer for him, for I had no theology of illness. It was through the writings of Elliot Dorff,[2] Louis Jacobs[3] and J. David Bleich[4] that I could offer some thoughts and some solace. Over the past decade, more has been written on the topic, often from the viewpoint of the family.

Writers point out that mental illness is not something new. There are so many examples contained in our literature, beginning with the Bible. Think of the melancholy which envelops King Saul (I Samuel 16. 14–23). There are many times in the Psalms of David where we would also describe David's condition as one of depression. It is an on-going theme throughout Chasidic literature. Many of the rebbes are described as suffering from melancholy. Others had fanciful flights and delusions of grandeur. Some exhibited mania, living far beyond their means or building large courts.

Theologically, we all struggle when these diseases occur. It is obviously not a struggle between the *yetzer ha'ra* (the inclination for evil within us) and the *yetzer ha'tov* (the inclination for good within us). We think of the world as created by God, but left in human hands. Yet the biological process which leads to mental illness is something over which the person has no control. Our happiness, longevity, successes and failures cannot be predicted or guaranteed. Chemical imbalances and genetic predisposition to mental illness are unfortunate realities of this imperfect world.

The causes of mental illness are not fully understood. The evidence shows that the brain's neurotransmitters do not function properly, because of a chemical imbalance in the brain. This is comparable to other imbalances that cause illnesses in other parts of the body. In addition, there are other factors which may contribute in vulnerable people including heredity and stress, and the use of 'recreational drugs'. Never is mental illness, as I have defined it, caused by dysfunctional families, nor is it evidence of weakness of character.

Of course, there are different types of mental illness. They differ in their symptoms, their degree of severity, and their effects on each person's life. However, in all cases the effect is not only on the person but also those around him or her, particularly the family. It also has an impact on the work environment. Moreover, the cost to society in terms of lost wages, demands on health-care systems, social-service needs and benefit support are enormous. In the United States, the amount has been estimated to be in the hundreds of billions of dollars.

Since the causes of mental illness are not fully known, there is little effective prevention. Nevertheless, proper treatment through drugs may substantially improve the functioning of persons with these illnesses, and in some cases they may completely recover.

When spending time with persons with mental illness I am often reminded of the Talmudic story of the four rabbis who entered the garden of mystical knowledge (Hagigah 14b). One died, one lost his mind, one abandoned his faith, and one emerged enriched. Just as they experienced different outcomes, so there are different possible outcomes for the person experiencing mental illness. Some recover completely (about one third of people who experience schizophrenia only have one episode); some can be part of society with the help of medication (functioning perhaps at a lower level); some remain chronically ill (as medications are developed, less and less remain hospitalized); and some never return from their own world to be part of ours.

Ask almost any Jew about the Jewish contribution to psychiatry and he or she will respond with a list of names including Sigmund Freud, Alfred Adler, Melanie Klein and Mortimer Ostrow. These all represent the psychoanalytic approach. Few of us could also name those who have contributed to the biological study of psychiatry, including Kurt Goldstein, Leslie Cohen, Stanley Rapoport, Eli Robins and Sam Keith.

The actor George Burns is not known as a theologian, yet there is an on-going theme in many of his films that, while God created the universe, God lets things progress, including genetic change. Many find comfort in this portrayal of a God who does not control us, but lets each of us get on with our own lives and wants us to develop, both for our sake and for the sake of others.

Rabbinically and theologically we are challenged to bring all of God's children into the community of Israel. The Jewish community has done an excellent job over mental retardation and developmental disabilities. But we have been quiet when these values have been applied to persons with mental illness. It is only when we confront the stigmas of our society that we will start to bring nearer the messianic vision that our congregations be a 'house of prayer for all peoples' (Isa. 56.7) without discrimination.

I think of the scene in Yentl where the young rabbinic student is delighted at the bride who has been selected for him, but is also afraid that the wedding might not take place. He carries a stigma with him. His brother has committed suicide and the potential bride's family must not find out, for perhaps the illness is in his genes and the match will be called off. How would we counsel someone in a similar situation in today's world? I am sure that we would not have the same view of suicide as those a hundred years ago. Now we know it is not 'catching' or a hereditary disease. Instead we recognize that suicide is often an outcome of extreme depression, where the person has no sense of anything except absolute nothingness.

We must acknowledge the distinction made by Rabbi Nachman of Bratslav (1772–1810) when he spoke of the difference between *r'fuat ha'goof* (healing of the body) and *r'fuat ha'nefesh* (healing of the spirit).[5] In modern medicine a distinction has emerged between curing, which hospitals attempt to do, and healing, which is a holistic care model focussing on the four dimensions of a person: physical, intellectual, emotional and spiritual. Synagogues need to think of their reactions too. Members of a community – be it rabbis or congregants – often struggle to find an appropriate response to families who are living with mental illness. The following prayer acknowledges some of the difficult experiences they can have.

> Lord, I have done all I can to help . . . It seems that it has been all in vain. He/she still remains afraid of things that only he/she understands. Dear God, you know how hard it is. I am so very tired. Sometimes I feel that I can take no more. I need Your help to keep me from despair. I thank You for Your love when I feel so alone. Help me to find the strength to deal with this illness. Help me to learn from each event I face. Help me to have the endurance to continue looking for solutions for my loved one's situation.

One of the challenges in working with persons with mental illness is trying to find appropriate tasks for them in the congregation. There are always places where they can contribute. Perhaps it is handing out prayer books and prayer shawls at services; perhaps it is operating the mailing machine in the office. Many other examples are possible. The real challenge is to make these individuals visible and productive, so that they feel included, and that the synagogue is 'a place of prayer for all peoples' and not just for others.

In addition, the rabbi and other communal members can serve in a number of important ways: being a source of information and referral; letting the family know they are not alone; avoiding being judgmental; refraining from offering simplistic solutions to complex problems; being supportive of the entire family, including brothers and sisters who feel neglected or helpless. The pastoral care should also include those members who come to services infrequently, as these are the people who may feel the most isolated; it should encourage the family to continue to be a part of congregational life and not feel that they have no place because they are 'different' or have a problem.

In the Book of Genesis, we read the story of the three angels visiting Abraham and Sarah and promising them a son and heir despite their old age (Gen. 18.1–16). The story is a critical turning-point in the life of Abraham and we tend to concentrate on the unexpected good news that he and Sarah receive from the messengers of God. Perhaps more important is what Abraham was doing at the time. According to the rabbis, he is recovering from his recent circumcision. Abraham is sitting at the tent door in the heat of the day when he looks up and sees three strangers. He welcomes the travellers without hesitation and does not ask their background or status; he is welcoming without preconditions. Likewise, we are challenged to open the doors of our synagogues to all and to offer a place in our homes just as Abraham did.

In the episode that follows immediately afterwards, we read: 'Shall not the Judge of all the world judge justly?' (Gen. 18.25). The story revolves around how the people of Sodom and Gomorrah treated strangers, or visitors. The rabbis suggest that the punishment of destructions was meted out because no hospitality was given by those townspeople. Hospitality takes many forms. The most obvious is that given to the wayfarer. So many of those who experience mental illness are also 'strangers within our gates', for even if we once knew them, they are strangers to us now. Some of that change is due to their experiences with mental illness; some is just the normal growing process each of us experiences. Our challenge is not to be like the people of Sodom and Gomorrah, but to offer hospitality and openness to each person who enters our doors.

Those with a mental illness suffer from 'wounded feelings' in a double sense – both because they find it so difficult to function fully, and because they are hurt by the reactions of others. They demand a better response, and we are the ones to give it.

Notes

1. The original Hebrew term – an *ona'ah* – refers to someone whose feelings have been hurt because of some injustice.

2. Elliot M. Dorff, 'The Jewish Tradition', in *Caring and Curing: Health and Medicine in the Western Religious Traditions*, ed. Robert L. Numbers and Darre Amundsen, Macmillan, New York 1986.
3. Louis Jacobs, *A Tree of Life: Diversity, Flexibility and Creativity in Jewish Law*, Littman Library, Oxford 1985.
4. J. David Bleich, *Mental Incompetence and Its Implications in Jewish Law, Contemporary Halakhic Problems*, Volume 1, KTAV, New York 1982.
5. See Simka Weintraub, *Healing the Soul, Healing the Body*, Jewish Lights, Woodstock 1994.

Ageing and the Role of the Synagogue

Chaim Wender

According to Age Concern there are over ten million people in the United Kingdom of pensionable age (i.e. men aged sixty-five and over, and women aged sixty and over). This is 18% of the entire population, and in the first thirty years of the next century the figure is expected to rise by five million to 26%. The number of people over fifty years of age is higher still, with the Association of Retired Persons declaring that there are already some eighteen million individuals in this category.[1]

The situation is even more pronounced within the Jewish community. The latest available statistical and geographical study issued by the Board of Deputies of British Jews states unequivocally that 'the Jewish population is ageing'. An illustration of this is a table on comparative age structures, which compares the age ratios of the estimated Jewish population of Great Britain with those of the general population for the same period. It indicates that the Jewish population shows an excess for all the age cohorts over fifty-five. Yet another table, pertaining to 'Population Projection for the Jewish Elderly 1985–2005', indicates that, given the declining size of the general Jewish population here, the proportion of the elderly will rise dramatically.[2]

Surely such a significant and growing population must be considered, heard and addressed. This imperative is both demographic and moral.

Biblically and theologically, Jewish tradition views old age as the proper completion of the divine plan. It believes that old age can be rich and productive. It holds Moses as an ideal, who 'was a hundred and twenty years old when he died; his eye was not dim nor his natural force abated' (Deut. 34.7).[3]

The commandment to 'honour your father and mother' (Exod. 20.12) was interpreted by Jewish tradition as indicating that honour, deference and respect should be given to all the elderly.[4] This general attitude was most clearly stated in the Holiness Code of Leviticus: 'Thou shalt rise up before the hoary head, and honour the face of the old' (19.32).

It is also worthy of note, in citing Num. 11.16, that in ancient Israel the elderly were highly regarded and served in leadership roles within the Jewish community.[5] The venerable title of *z'kenim* (literally 'elders'), which carries the meaning of both advanced years and wisdom, was based on the concept that with age there will often arise the wisdom that emerges only from experiential knowledge.

However, in spite of that ideal, the Hebrew Scriptures also include the recognition that old age may be accompanied by physical infirmities. In this connection, the imagery of Ecclesiastes (12.1–7) is certainly relevant:

> Remember your creator in the days of your vigour,
> Before the evil days come,
> And the years approach of which you will say,
> 'I have no pleasure in them';
> Before the sun becomes dark,
> And the light, and the moon, and the stars;
> And the clouds return after the rain;
> On the day when the guardians of the house tremble,
> And the strong men are bent . . .
> And those that look out shall be darkened in the windows . . .
> And the sound of the bird is faint . . .
> And the terrors are on the road . . .
> Because man is going to his eternal home.

In so speaking, the author of Ecclesiastes recognized such physical infirmities as loss of vision, hearing impediment, propensity to falling, and tremors in the limbs, which sometimes afflict the aged.

The psalmist's fear of loneliness and rejection also continues to have poignant meaning for some in our own day, namely, 'Cast me not off in the time of old age; when my strength fails, forsake me not' (Ps. 71.9).

In the classical rabbinic literature, we also find evidence of great respect for the aged. This regard, held by the early rabbis, was not only for the learned elderly, but also for those who were not learned; not only for the Jew, but also for the non-Jew. For example, the Talmud relates that Rabbi Yochanan used to rise up before the non-Jewish aged, saying 'How many troubles have passed over these old people' (Kiddushin 33a).

By the same token, in the commentary to the Book of Genesis, Bereshit Rabbah 63.6, it is asserted that 'He who welcomes an elder is as if he welcomed the divine presence'.

Even those whose intellectual faculties have deteriorated were to be treated with the same dignity as an elderly scholar. Thus: 'Be careful to honour the old who have forgotten their learning because of advancing years. Remember that the broken fragments of the first tablets were also kept in the Ark of the Covenant alongside the new tablets' (Berachot 8b).

On a sadly realistic note, the Talmud includes this observation: 'People often say, "When we were young we were considered adults in wisdom, but now that we are old, we are considered as babies"' (Baba Kamma 92b).

Far more recently, Rabbi Abraham Joshua Heschel formulated a response to such perennial concerns in a paper he delivered at the 1961 White House Conference on Ageing in Washington, DC: 'A revision of attitudes and conceptions is necessary. Old age is not a defeat but a victory, not a punishment but a privilege. In education we stress the importance of the adjustment of the young to society. Our task is to call for the adjustment of society to the old.'

I have come to appreciate this from my own personal experience too. My maternal grandfather, Julius Michael Keller, was the principal of a Jewish day school in Revere Beach, Massachusetts for thirty-five years, and I was deeply moved by his wonderful spirit. I recall that, as I was growing up, his health was always poor, but his optimism, his love of life and of people, his wisdom and warmth were such that, in spite of frail health, my image of ageing was always positive, thanks to the power of his personality.

When I was doing graduate studies at the Hebrew Union College in Cincinnati, I found that I had some free time during the weekends. Accordingly I spoke with the director of a local Jewish home for the aged, and asked how I might be of service. He indicated that volunteers were always welcome, to come along to visit and simply befriend the residents. So we would chat, and we would play chess or draughts or a hand of cards. The visits all seemed to be appreciated, but I found myself feeling that I was given at least as much as I gave, if not more.

Two of the residents at that home particularly stand out in my mind. One was an elderly gentleman who required a walking frame. He said to me, 'Chaim, I have some new shoes. We're about the same size, you and I. I only wear slippers to shuffle along here. I'd like you to have my shoes.' I was genuinely moved by his kind offer, but I felt uncomfortable with the prospect of taking the man's shoes. So I refused. I thanked him, but I could not do it.

Another day, a lovely lady in her eighties said to me, 'I want you to have some handkerchiefs that I will embroider with your initials. Would that be all right?' I knew that she suffered from arthritic hands and that her eyesight was very poor, with cataracts and thick spectacles. So I thanked her, but I felt I had to turn down the offer, fearing that each stitch would cause her hands to ache and strain her eyes. All of that took place twenty years ago, but in retrospect how I wish that I had accepted their generous gifts. It was their way of giving, and I had denied them the ability to reciprocate the friendship that had developed. I now know what I did not realize then: that we live as we give. Whatever our age, whatever our state of health, we want to give, to feel useful and be needed.

Whilst studying at the Leo Baeck College, I encountered one of the most significant and positive books on ageing that I have ever read, *The Generation Jigsaw*. The author, Dr Irene Gore, was initially involved in studying the biological aspects of ageing, but came to be concerned with personal and social attitudes as well.

One problem she raises which is pertinent to the Jewish community is that of stereotyping:

> Our stereotype of an elderly person as someone who is unable to manage much, who is less able or capable than a younger person, also leads us to assume that the last thing fit older people need or want is to be stretched, physically and mentally. So we end up with such time-wasting and totally unstretching pursuits as bingo in old people's clubs. The provision of such an amenity is based on an assumption, which ignores the fact that the potential for doing new, interesting and meaningful things is possessed by as many elderly people blessed with sufficient intelligence as by younger people equally blessed. As long as we refuse to recognize that older people are people who do not become mental defectives at the stroke of age sixty-five, so long shall we offer them time-wasting sops, instead of opportunities for using their time to some purpose. As in other contexts, expectations tend to fulfil themselves, and the more we expect of people, the more they prove to be capable of extending themselves.
>
> There are always two strands in the type of needs that have to be met: first, the needs of the physically, mentally or socially disadvantaged older people; second, the needs of the more fortunate, the physically and mentally fit, older people. The confusion which often arises because 'the needs of the elderly' are lumped together, without a clear distinction being made between these two strands, has perpetuated a stereotyped view that *all* older people *inevitably* need *care*. No. They all need *thought*, some need care, and others need opportunities for redeveloping their own resources and using them.[6]

Prior to reading that text, I had been under the impression that the best counselling approach for dealing with older adults was simply a matter of listening with attention and caring in a rather passive way. However, subsequent to this, my views altered. I came to believe that the approach to dealing with older adults should be considerably more active, providing challenging opportunities and encouragement for their continued personal growth.

The synagogue has a long and proud history as a genuinely caring institution. What might contemporary congregations offer to enhance the quality of life for their older members?

In 1993 I helped produce a pamphlet on ageing for the Union of Liberal and Progressive Synagogues.[7] It included a suggested action list for synagogues to consider implementing:

1. Formulate a statistical profile of the age groupings of your membership with a view to determining the percentages of those who are over sixty, over seventy and over eighty.
2. Support your synagogue's current programming for older adults, such as Friendship Clubs.
3. Sensitize your membership to the array of emotional and spiritual needs that may be experienced by those who are no longer young or working in a society that places so much value and emphasis on youth and work. Implement ways of affirming the ageing process in your congregational life. For example, special events and worship services may be held honouring older members; public blessings may be offered in celebration of retirement or grandparenthood; and oral history projects involving your members of long standing may be organized pertaining to their reminiscences about the earlier years of your synagogue or of Jewish life as it used to be.
4. Promote a more inclusive attitude to all of your synagogue's activities. Roles can be found for your older members in many ways, such as teaching in the religion school; helping with the synagogue library or office; as committee or council members; with the choir; helping to arrange transport to synagogue functions for those who require it; and as friendly visitors to other older adults who are home-bound or hospitalized. Recognize the vast potential of this resource of time and talent.
5. Organize adult education seminars on retirement planning, on making the home safer as you grow older, on how those who live alone can obtain personal emergency alarm buttons.
6. Assess your synagogue's facilities for those who may have need of audio-induction loop systems for the hearing impaired; large-print prayer books for the visually impaired; ramps for wheelchair access and toilets for the disabled.

7. Synagogues should have the necessary information to provide reference to caregiver respite services and support groups (including the Alzheimers Disease Society), day care centres, hospices and appropriate agencies (such as Jewish Care).

The need to cater for an increasingly elderly Jewish population in a challenging and fruitful way was reinforced by the ULPS document *Towards 2002*. It also highlighted how 'the older generation is a greatly under-used resource of knowledge, experience and expertise that could be of infinite mutual benefit in congregational life'.[8] As a result, a National Task Force on the Older Generations was set up, of which I was the first co-ordinator. Its agenda has been to progress from consciousness-raising, through identification of needs, to concrete proposals and action. The object is to help to empower an increasing proportion of our membership, whose needs and capabilities are all too often overlooked and under-estimated.

Let me end with another story. Several years ago, during a flight to California, I had occasion to sit next to a couple in their fifties. After conversing with them for a time, I overheard the wife remark rather sadly to her husband, 'I know all too well I am ageing . . . the mirror doesn't lie'. In a silent response I mused, 'It may not lie, but it reveals merely half-truths. The inner spiritual beauty, so manifestly apparent to the human heart, remains quite concealed to its all-too-narrow view.' It is incumbent on us all to see beyond the limited confines of outward appearance, searching always for the hidden good within ourselves and those around us.

Notes

1. Age Concern, *Older People in the United Kingdom*, May 1994, 1.
2. Stanley Waterman and Barry Kosmin, *British Jewry in the Eighties. A Statistical and Geographical Guide*, Board of Deputies for British Jewry 1986, 8–15.
3. See further Lindsey P. Pherigo, 'Perspectives on Aging: Jewish, Roman Catholic and Protestant', *Quarterly Papers on Religion and Aging* Vol 1, No 2, Fall 1984.

4. John H. Westerhoff, *Living the Faith Community*, Winston Press, Minneapolis 1985, 28.
5. Irwin Fishbein, 'Judaic Care and Counselling of Older Persons'; *Dictionary of Pastoral Care* (unpublished manuscript).
6. Irene Gore, *The Generation Jigsaw*, Allen & Unwin 1976, 116, 125.
7. Rabbinic Conference of the Union of Liberal and Progressive Synagogues, *Where We Stand on Ageing*, ULPS 1993.
8. Officers of the Union of Liberal and Progressive Synagogues, *Towards 2002*, ULPS 1994, 24.

Attitudes to Life and Death in Judaism

Julia Neuberger

When I look at Britain from the vantage point of someone Jewish, British, of refugee origins on one side, and strongly involved in healthcare, I am struck by the fact that there is still a real problem in the way we die in this country. For many of us will be cared for by palliative care specialists – nurses and doctors – and will die at home or in a hospice. Others of us will die in pain, in the midst of acute care, or uncherished, at home or in a nursing home or wherever, wondering why we had not made an end of ourselves. That is despite the fact that Britain leads the world in modern hospice skills, despite the fact that our hospice movement is admired the world over, and that our percentage of people dying in hospital is falling gradually, a statistic (though it is still around 55%) which is envied by many other societies, and particularly by the Americans, with their 80% of hospital deaths,[1] and still rising.

But people in modern Western societies have expectations now of dying pain-free, and increasingly feel that they should be in control of how and where they die. Our sense of natural justice, of the natural order of things, would suggest that they are, of course, quite right. But Judaism does not hold such views to any great extent, and it has been an issue for me all my rabbinic career to try to reconcile traditional Jewish attitudes to life and death with both the desirable modern hospice philosophy of dying pain-free, with one's emotions as resolved as they can be, and with the expectation of being able to say 'No more treatment' when one has had enough.

The modern hospice movement, despite its medieval origins, was founded in Britain by a woman of great vision and strength of Christian belief, Dame Cicely Saunders, OM. For her, the fact that people were dying in pain was quite unacceptable. At least part of her revulsion was related to her Christian faith: the journey to the afterlife should be a good one, and the good death was a goal much to be desired. Meanwhile, for committed Christians caring for the terminally ill, there is much to be gained spiritually from helping to alleviate their pain, in order to allow them to focus on their end – and on the next life.

One might argue, of course, that there is in Christianity a tradition which argues that suffering ennobles the spirit, and that the person of spiritual experience is the one who has suffered, emulating Jesus both physically and spiritually. In the same vein it is fair to say that in most other circumstances Judaism has a marked aversion to suffering, and regards all avoidable suffering as to be got rid of at all costs. But in this one crucial area many Christian traditions believe in controlling pain, even if that means shortening life, whilst Judaism regards any life-shortening for whatever reason as unacceptable, and feels we must simply put up with the pain.

There is one notable exception, when the maidservant of Rabbi Judah ha-Nasi, the Prince, the supposed compiler of the Mishnah, the first codification of Jewish law, decides that his pain is intolerable and should be stopped. His students were praying for his life to be spared. She dropped a jar she was carrying, causing them to stop praying briefly. As a result their prayers were interrupted and he slipped away (B. Talmud, Ketubot 104a). His suffering was over, and she was never condemned in Jewish tradition.

But on the whole the emphasis is on life preservation rather than allowing someone to die well. Indeed, it is about extending life, and wishing to live longer at all costs. Hence we say to a mourner who has just lost someone dear to them 'I wish you long life!', which is often the last thing they want at that moment. Indeed, longer life is often the reward for acts of repentance and charity. For instance, when God said to King Hezekiah, 'Set your house in order for you shall die . . .' (II Kings 20.1–2), Hezekiah turned his face to the wall and prayed, reminding God of the good things he had done and the things for which he deserved a rethink of the sentence of death. On that occasion he recovered, and God added an additional fifteen years to his life. This was a definite reward. There is no sense there that he might not have wanted an additional fifteen years. One *must* want it, for it is God's gift, and God's creation, and it is not for human beings to destroy it, or even wish it away. Despair is unacceptable. One has to keep the light of desire for life burning.

All this may be related to the fact that, on the whole, in the Jewish tradition, we do not die well. We rage and we storm. For us, for the Jewish tradition as a whole, life, *chayyim,* is the greatest blessing. *'L'chayyim'* is the toast to which we raise our glasses. Integral to our value system is the rabbinic teaching that one may, indeed must, break all but three of the commandments and prohibitions of our legal system in order to save a single human life. (The exceptions are the prohibitions on murder, incest and idolatry.) Within the Mishnah, the legal code define from the end of the second century, we read:

> 'One single man was created in the world, to teach that, if anyone has caused a single soul to perish, it is as if he has caused the destruction of a whole world. If anyone saves the life of a single person, it is as if he has saved a whole world' (Mishnah, Sanhedrin 4.5).

Add to that the belief in traditional Judaism that God has decreed the time of each individual's death, and that at the beginning of the ten days of penitence, on Jewish New Year, a book – the Book of Life – is opened in which, if God feels we have done well, our names are inscribed for another year, and the importance of life – *this* life – becomes entirely clear. The New Year greeting is not only 'Happy New Year' but also 'May you be inscribed in the Book of Life.' Indeed, one can avert a decree of death by charity, repentance and prayer – if they are all sincerely meant (and that traditionally is what King Hezekiah did).

In some Jewish folk-traditions you can avert a sentence of death by changing the name of the sick person: after all, the names are written in the Book. This is why in most Ashkenazi (European) Jewish traditions Jewish children are never named after a living grandparent, because to do that would be tantamount to writing the grandparents out of history.

Life is God's gift, and the emphasis is quite clear that we must value it, and do anything we possibly can to preserve it. Hence doctors, physicians, are held in the highest regard (which is not always the case in all modern Western societies, as professionals are losing respect) because they are thought to have been given the power to heal by God. In the Talmud – at the end of the fifth century CE – we read: 'The school of Rabbi Ishmael taught: And the words: "And he shall cause him to be thoroughly healed . . ." (Exod. 21.19) are the words from which it can be derived that authority to heal was given by God to the physician'[1] (B. Talmud Berachot 60a). And in Ecclesiasticus (Ben Sira 38.1–2) there is further evidence of adulation of the doctor: 'Honour a physician according to your need of him, with the honours due to him. For the Lord has created him.'

So the doctor, the physician, is able to cure – one hopes – and to preserve life. In this line of thought, he becomes a semi-divine creature beyond the ordinary man or woman, because through him life can be preserved. The corollary to that status must be that a physician who deliberately actually ends life is committing the greatest of sins, not only breaking trust but actively going against what it is God wants him or her to do – preserve life. Therefore a physician who was actively involved in euthanasia and was an observant Jew would have to square within him- or herself the sense that he was deliberately negating God's wish for him, God's purpose for him, and the role for which he was created by God.

For in the Jewish tradition, we do everything, put ourselves through everything, in order to save life, including amazingly unlikely interventions, with small chance of success, that one might argue are too much. We must make every effort. So intellectually, following that reasoning, there should be nothing off-putting about a death in intensive care, intubated, uncertain of whether it is day or night, surrounded by machinery and expert carers. That is the last-ditch attempt to save life. And yet it is often deeply disturbing, as is the giving of some forms of drugs which are so toxic in themselves that, despite the fact that they may give one a little hope of a longer life, most people ask themselves whether it is worth it. There is no doubt about the reply to that question in the Jewish tradition. We are obliged to try. It becomes purely rhetorical. Yet sometimes the peaceful death seems more attractive, particularly for those of us who feel we have had a good long life already.

After all, the traditional measure of our days is seventy years, and eighty in exceptional circumstances. The majority of us will outlive eighty by some years, yet we might have our doubts about whether we wanted to do everything, make heroic efforts, to preserve our lives if we were terminally ill in our late eighties.

That particular conundrum is one with which Judaism has still got to get to grips. Those who want heroic treatment in their late eighties should not be denied it on the basis of cost, say, or it being somehow inappropriate, but equally, our own tradition should not force us to have treatment which we do not want. Indeed, one can imagine many Jews, just like others, all too pleased to sign an advance directive in which they state that in certain circumstances they do not wish further treatment, if they are in a state where they cannot make decisions or give consent themselves, such as in a coma.

This is very different from euthanasia, for which there can be no argument in the Jewish tradition. The desire simply not to strive officiously to keep alive is very different from euthanasia, from the deliberate taking of life, yet it goes against a strong strain in the Jewish tradition: of trying everything to preserve life. And that requires some new thinking, and a series of *responsa* (answers to hard questions where a rabbinic authority gives a series of legal views) which are positive about advance directives, arguing perhaps from the age point, or from the modern capacity to keep alive almost indefinitely in many circumstances.

Yet, should it be that someone is dying and cannot be healed, that same Jewish tradition which is so life-affirming begins to fail us. For we are not, on the whole, well-disposed to the relief of suffering. We read, for instance, in a rabbinic collection (Ecclesiasticus Rabba v.6): 'Even when the physician realizes that the end is near, he should order his patient to eat this and drink that, not eat this and not drink that. On no account should he tell him that the end is near.' So we cannot even be honest!

Or, in the commentary to our legal code, the Shulchan Aruch, we read: 'It is forbidden to cause the dying to pass away quickly; for instance, if a person is dying over a long time and cannot depart, it is forbidden to remove the pillow or cushion from underneath him.' We do not, traditionally, make the going easy. The quality of life of the terminally ill person is not rated highly in our tradition. The idea of the good death is utterly foreign to the Jewish view.

But one might reflect on why that should be. First, if human life is valued so highly, there is a clear reason to value every last moment of it, even if it is deeply uncomfortable, or one is in intense pain. So quality has to give way to quantity, because the fact of life, rather than how it feels, is what matters. That in itself throws an interesting sidelight on all the moves for euthanasia, let alone the calls for advance directives, which so many Jews have found to be anathema.

But, second, and perhaps even more importantly, if tendentiously, many Jews are what Christians might call a bit 'shaky' on the afterlife – and, since we know what we have in this life, we tend to feel it is as well to stick with it as long as possible. For although Orthodox Jews assert as an article of faith in their daily morning prayers that they believe in an afterlife, the nature of that afterlife is fairly unspecified. Rabbinic statements that all of this life is a prelude, or an anteroom, to the world to come, are relatively late, dating from the period of the beginnings of Christianity, with little evidence of earlier traditions. The obsession with what happens to us after death is not an early one in Judaism, nor is the idea that there will be physical resurrection, which is Talmudic (end of the fifth century CE) rather than biblical, and may be in response to the fact that ideas about resurrection were gaining popularity in other faiths.

The belief that dates to the biblical period, amongst Jews, is in the biblical Sheol, the shady place where nothing much happens and where all is colourless. And, though that does not produce *fear* to any more notable extent amongst Jews than amongst anyone else, what it does produce is the determination to hang on to life, often perhaps for too long.

But if one looks further, at the way we look after the bereaved, other contrasts appear between Judaism and other traditions. For where Judaism scores highly is in its attitudes to bereavement. The rituals mirror what psychologists tell us are the normal stages of grief. The immediate time after a death is involved with rituals surrounding the body, sitting with it, reciting psalms, and then washing it, and wrapping it in a shroud. The funeral, traditionally a burial, which the community does for itself, with spades full of earth landing on the coffin lid with a resounding clang, is bitter, but it brings home the reality of the death to the bereaved. Orthodox Judaism does not allow cremation, but many people who are not Orthodox have no problem with having a cremation, which has fewer of the obvious rituals which affirm that the death has taken place – no spadesful of earth landing on the coffin lid, no pauses on the journey down to the grave to recite psalms, and so on.

Nevertheless, the stages of grief are still marked. For after the funeral comes the *shivah*, seven days of mourning, with evening prayers in the home every night, with mourners and friends coming to pay their respects, bringing gifts of food (there is always food in the Jewish tradition), encouraging the bereaved to talk about their loss. By the end of seven days the chief mourners are exhausted, delighted to see the back of their callers, glad to see them go. It is the end of a stage. Then come the *shloshim*, the thirty days, of lesser mourning, but no parties, no celebrations, and daily prayers at the synagogue, which continue into the next stage, the eleven months before the consecration of the tombstone, when the year of mourning is technically over, and life – as much as it can – goes back to normal.

That system is undeniably humane, helpful – though some people actually find seven days of *shivah* too much – and designed to comfort the living. It is for the living, and not the dead, whilst the dying person is all too often regarded as a failure, not someone who can make it, and therefore not someone to be given enormous attention, other than prayers for the well-being of the soul.

But there is a lesson there to be learned from the maidservant of Judah ha-Nasi, the maidservant who stopped the ardent disciples praying long enough for her master's soul to slip away and for him to die. His suffering was over. It is that example which has involved so many Jews in the modern hospice movement, and particularly in the North London Hospice, originally designed as the first inter-faith (as opposed to non-denominational) hospice in the country. It has the capacity to recognize the customs and beliefs of all faiths, but it has a commitment to alleviating suffering. It does so by skilled medical and nursing care, and by profound spiritual care as well. And it provides aftercare, too, to the families of those whom it has cared for in their dying days, weeks and months. It seems to me that we can learn the lesson of Judah ha-Nasi's maidservant, and help people to die well, whilst encouraging those who are left to live well. That would seem a proper form of respect for life, and entirely in keeping with our life-affirming tradition. Indeed, we should be able to say *'L'chay-yim'* to such an endeavour, to such a goal. And that way we should all be able to die well, at the end of a life lived to the full, but maybe dying without pain sooner than might have been the case if we had gone to the last ditch with active interventions. And would that in the end be against Jewish law?

Notes

1. Sherwin B. Nuland, *How We Die*, Alfred A. Knopf, New York 1994, 255.

Part of this chapter was previously published in Julia Neuberger, *On Being Jewish*, Heinemann 1995 and 1996. Permission to reprint has been granted by Heinemann.

Working with the Dying

Sylvia Rothschild

When schoolchildren on their visits to the synagogue ask what are the best and what the worst parts of my work as a community rabbi, the answers fall into the same area: the privilege and the pain of being with the person who is wrestling with impending death can be one of the most fulfilling and most challenging experiences, as well as one of the most frustrating and infuriating. As a rabbi one is often allowed a closeness to, and a level of trust from, the terminally ill person and his or her family that is breathtaking in its responsibility, and one has to find ways to be listener, guide, human individual and representative of the tradition all at the same time.

Each individual is concerned about different matters, but there are general issues which surface, and which I believe must be confronted and considered by rabbis working with the dying and with the bereaved.

The Jewish tradition must begin to confront the total pain of the individual who knows that he or she will soon be leaving life. How one begins to deal with such pain, which inevitably echoes inside all of us too, is something not yet deeply explored within Jewish texts or rituals.

This total pain is made up of a variety of physical, emotional and spiritual factors. Terminal illness is linked to the world of physical pain and the fear of the loss of control and human dignity that may lead from it. Often a desire is expressed to take into one's own hands the decision to end that pain by causing the life to end. There is also the fear of what the future might hold, both in this world and in the world to come: for some the fear of annihilation, for others some unresolved scenario of punishment.

Many have a real anxiety about leaving behind their beloved ones without enough support. Others worry that their life has had no meaning, and that the opportunity to create from it as it were a work of art is fast diminishing. Yet others reflect on what will now for ever remain unfinished.

There is often sadness and anger about all that is left to do which may not now be done, and there is the pain, too, about the perceived need not to be completely honest about the dying. Where there is a sense of societal disapproval about how one chose to live one's life and make personal choices (the diagnosis that indicates AIDS, for example, or the smoker with lung cancer), it can make the dying process even more poignant. How can one assert one's personality and desires when these very factors are 'blamed' for bringing about the end of life prematurely? In the value judgments which ensue, it is difficult to separate the right of individuals to live their own life up to the end from the way they exercised that right earlier.

Families and friends will sometimes not allow the thought of death to be aired at all, as if the denial of the process will somehow prevent it. The anxiety of the people closest to terminally ill individuals can easily be translated into 'compassion' for them. The confusion of feelings which arises in those who care about the dying person – fear, guilt, worry and pain – is often too deep for them to disentangle. Far easier not to have to confront it while the beloved yet lives. Far nicer to let them live in optimism, rather than enter the shadowy uncertain world that the carer is currently inhabiting.

Both sides may at some level know that the relentless process of death is present, yet neither side wants to speak it, to make the other unhappy in the certain knowledge that they will not be able to take the unhappiness away. So they may end up struggling with their private pain in their separated worlds, fearful of risking the pain of the other, fearful of their inner confusion of feeling dishonest and constrained, unable to say the things they really want to say. The question must always be asked, and the answer is particular in each life, 'Which alternative honours the individual person as a living, needing human being more?'

Everyone coming into contact with the dying person is

concerned for that individual to have what has become known as a 'good death'. The question ultimately has to be, 'What is a good death for that individual, and how do we hold the space so as to allow it?'

In Jewish tradition there is a term for a person considered to be mortally ill – the *gosses* – defined as one who is sinking or dying. It is a category which we in modern times might define as terminally ill, yet the ambivalence that Judaism displays about the process of dying is revealed here: we are told that 'the *majority* of those believed to be in a dying condition (*gossesim*) really die' (B. Talmud Gittin 28a). In other words, there is a reluctance to accept the inevitability of the process, and the strong imperative is that one should in no circumstances ever assume death is likely, and so take away hope.

This ambivalence towards confronting the reality of impending death leads to enormous convolutions in the rabbinic literature. For example, the terminally ill person is to be advised to look over his affairs and see if he has any debts or credits outstanding – but he is to be reassured that this is only a precaution, and that it does not mean that he is about to die (Shulchan Aruch Yoreh Deah, ch. 335). Another example is the *vidui*, the confession by the dying person, who is to be told, 'Many have confessed and then not died, just as many have not confessed and died'. If he does not know what to say in his confession, then he is instructed to say, 'May my death be an expiation for all my sins', but this is not to be done in the presence of women and children in case they should cry and break his heart (Shulchan Aruch Yoreh Deah, ch. 338.1).

While the imperative to life has always been one of the most powerful factors underwriting the survival of the Jewish people, it has caused real problems in working with the Jewish dying. It has meant that we have been unable to create or formalize many useful rituals which would help to express religiously the spiritual pain of those who are diagnosed as being terminally ill. So the search for meaning in life is often forced to take place outside any established Jewish tradition.

Any dying person needs to be listened to, responded to, accepted and loved, reassured that there is indeed a meaning, and helped towards finding it for themselves. For that process to begin, the acceptance of the likelihood of impending death has to take place, without hope being taken away, but instead being reframed into a more usable hope than that afforded by denial. The total pain that envelops the dying person can be alleviated to some extent by addressing in a sensitive way some of the roots of that pain.

One traditional method to focus the self is the writing of the ethical will, a document in which the individual, whether dying or not, periodically examines his or her life and searches for the underlying principles which give it value and meaning, and which they want to bequeath to their families. In this way both the need to gain understanding about one's life and the need to share that understanding so as to pass something of oneself on after death can be addressed. It can be a deeply moving and very powerful experience to act as scribe for people composing their ethical will, and they too are often made both more hopeful and more accepting as a result of having found their words. An anthology of ethical wills[1] makes painful but creative reading, and their opening quotation from *The Testament* by Elie Wiesel is one of the most powerful I know in confronting the death of a loved one: 'My father is not dead. My father is a book, and books do not die.'

We have few other traditional ways of acknowledging the process of dying without removing hope. Like all community rabbis, I have been faced with finding ways to respond to each dying individual differently and appropriately. Like many of them, I have been frustrated by the strictures which apparently require me to deny to the dangerously ill the fuller picture of their condition. However, like most, I take my own cue from that of the dying person, who frequently 'knows' his or her own state, and is searching for a way to make sense of that knowledge in the loving presence of another human being.

When involved with people who do not want to know the severity of their condition, then one can be a loving presence by respecting that wish. I can hold no brief for a blanket response – just as all human beings will live their life as they are, so too they must be true to themselves in their dying. The most delicate encounter as a pastoral rabbi must be with those who do not yet know the danger of their condition, and when uncertainty hangs over whether they would want such information or not. My own feeling is that one can only wait, and hope that time clarifies the uncertainty. Badly given or badly received news is more likely merely to shock, and so cloud individuals as to prevent them from engaging at all.

As long as the will to live is not crushed or denied, it seems to me that any ritual that is meaningful to the dying person can be valid. Preparation for death is not alien to the Jewish tradition – one only has to read of Moses surveying the future he will not share from Mt. Nevo (Deut. 34. 1–8), or Jacob's death-bed blessing of his sons (Gen. 48. 1–49.33) to know that these were deaths that came at the end of a period of informed reflection. Indeed, the rabbinic homily which comments upon the death of Moses tells us that when Moses realized that the decree of death had been sealed against him, he drew a small circle around himself, stood in it, and said 'Master of the Universe, I will not move from here until you void that decree' (Deut. Rabbah 11.10). He went on to argue with God about who would take over his task as leader, to demand time to bless the Israelites, and so on. Eventually he became reconciled to his dying, and was rewarded with the good death – he died at the kiss of God.

In the scriptural and rabbinic texts, Moses displayed all the textbook signs of human beings confronting their own mortality. He was angry, resentful and sad. He denied the reality of what was happening to him and then tried to control it. He sought for meaning, and he sought for more time. He bargained and implored. Yet finally the imagery of his dying is peaceful and intimate, while yet being appropriately emotional: 'God kissed Moses and took away his soul with a kiss of the mouth, and God, if one might say so, wept . . . the heavens wept . . . the earth wept . . . and when Joshua was looking for his master and did not find him, he also wept and said, "Help, Lord; for the godly man ceases and the faithful fail from among the children of men"', (Deut. Rabbah 11.10). The description of the reaction of Moses to the decree of his death, and the responses of the world around him, ring true to this day. Yet while rabbinic commentary has even God weeping, the process is not altered, and dying comes to be seen as both inevitable and proper.

Preparation for our own Jewish death could include such rituals as creating our own personal blessings for our children as did Jacob; or recording the family tree as far back as our living memory allows (complete with stories of what those people were really like), so as to ensure that in this post-Holocaust era the names of our ancestors are not blotted out. We might communicate significant events and insights from our own lives which, once we are gone, would otherwise be lost.

We might study Torah with a friend, as David did, on the basis that, according to one tradition, the Angel of Death does not approach one who is studying Torah (B. Talmud, Sotah 21a). We could follow Isaiah's advice to Hezekiah to set our house in order (Isa. 38.1; II Kings 20.1–2). Setting one's house in order can imply a variety of actions, from putting one's papers and estate in order, through to doing that which we have up till now left undone, and to mending our relationships with other people. The process of dying must be one of completing and finishing a life, keeping such a process in character with the essential person, while balancing it with the need to create a sense of wholeness. Fractured and dysfunctional families can be healed through the 'good death' of one of their members; other apparently solid families can be torn apart by the words and actions of one individual as a member faces their dying. It is an easy legacy to leave behind guilt and anger in others, particularly as these are likely to be prevalent emotions in the dying person. Some social inhibitions are stripped away, and simmering rivalries or bitternesses may emerge among the people close to the terminally ill, as well as within the dying person. One only has to read some ethical wills to see the need to control or take revenge from beyond the grave; one only has to witness family arguments to see the opportunity that was lost to say what was really important – words like 'I love you', or 'It isn't important any more', or 'I forgive you', or even 'You were right'. However it is done, relationships that were important enough to create pain when something went wrong must be thought about, and if possible some healing must take place. People out of touch should be contacted and given the opportunity to meet, even if only by letter. Wills should be thought about, and their consequences explained. Our urge to be remembered and to continue impacting on family and friends must be framed positively.

We might plant a tree for the generations that come after us – or, if that is too difficult, ask a friend or relative to do so for us. We might rename our dying self (not for the rather superstitious tradition that it might confuse the Angel of Death, who would then not find the named soul it is looking for), but to celebrate our life and our special identity, making overt the meaning we have found, the person we have become by the end of our time on earth. We could create a new ritual, inviting the companionship of the prophet Elijah who has always inhabited the liminal space between heaven and earth, a ceremony which marks the transition from this life to the next, just as the havdalah ceremony on Saturday evening denotes the end of the Sabbath and the beginning of the working week. Alternatively, we could compose a ceremony of farewell, making sure that we are passing on something of ourselves to those who come after us. A biblical precedent is Aaron's death on Mt Hor, where Aaron stripped off the robes of the priesthood and his son Eleazar put them on. In similar fashion Moses laid his hands upon Joshua and passed on to him his authority shortly before he died.

We could in some way invoke and reflect the Patriarchs and Matriarchs, and also the Sages, whose deaths were continuations of the lives they had lived, whose tears were for the loss of all the life that could have been, rather than for the life that was actually ending.

Traditional structures in Jewish ritual and liturgy often delineate the process of three discrete and sequential stages: creation, revelation and redemption. There is much that we could do to recognize and express our knowledge that being with the dying means that we too stand on the threshold of the world to come. Creation has occurred, redemption is yet to come. It is the revelation, the understanding and assimilation of the meaning of each life, which our tradition must address in innovative rituals and liturgies.

Within the area of the spiritual pain, the search for meaning, we are only beginning to find ways to open up pathways that might help. The area of physical pain, whether actual or feared, is one about which the imperative towards life also has much to say. It is forbidden to hasten a death in any way, by removing the pillow from a dying person or with any activity done with the *intention* of causing the death (Shulchan Aruch Yoreh Deah, ch.339). However, if there is anything external which is delaying the death, such as a clattering noise outside, or the sharp taste of salt on the tongue of the dying person, then one can act to remove these distractions, as this is said to be not a direct act but only the removal of a hindrance. Behind this distinction lies the idea that there is a proper time for the soul to depart, and that both untimely death and prolonged life are equally unacceptable in the Jewish tradition.

So how do we hold the space for a person to die a meaningful death? We reframe the process so that the dying person is in a position not where there is nothing more to be done, but where everything possible is being done. The 'everything possible' would, in this case, not be the striving to keep alive, but the facilitating to set the house in order. Accepting the inevitability, and setting hope within the context of what is achievable, will promote it. It is, I think, the task of the Jewish community to provide a pastoral *sukkah*, a sheltered framework in which the terminally-ill person can begin to name and work towards the achievable hopes, helped by skilled palliative care. Each person's life is different, and so is his or her death. There can be no generalized 'good death'. But 'faith in life and in death are basically one and the same, and much can be done to create a climate in which both the dying and their survivors can reach towards acceptance and even creativity'.[2]

The traditional Jewish imperative is to life. And if we work with the dying so that their last weeks are focussed on closing their lives appropriately, while living their days most fully; and if we help those around them both to love them and to learn to let go, is that not fulfilling the ancient imperative within a modern context?

The Chafetz Chayyim said that it is not difficult to die as a Jew; the difficulty comes in living as a Jew. In truth they are the same thing. Working with the Jewish dying is really all about working with the Jewish living, the individual with a terminal diagnosis, his or her family and friends, and community. The terminally-ill may not continue to live for very long, but the quality of the life that is left to them must be the most meaningful that it can be. And as individuals complete their days, they leave their indelible mark on all those around them. Rarely is a dying person isolated from a community of family and friends; rarely is a death unmarked. A pastoral rabbi, in facilitating a good death, is an agent for good Judaism, and will affect not only the dying individual but all those who care about that person. We cannot afford to ignore the wider meaning of the good death.

Notes

1. Riemer and Stampfer (ed.), *Ethical Wills. A Modern Jewish Treasury*, Schocken Books, New York.
2. Cicely Saunders, 'On Dying Well', *The Cambridge Review*, 27 February 1984, 49–51.

THE PAST IS STILL PRESENT

The diverse influences modern Jews have inherited

The Jewish approach to contemporary issues is always conditioned, although not restricted, by the teachings and experiences of the past. This is highlighted by the third section, beginning with Jonathan Magonet, who takes a look at our use of the Hebrew Bible as a whole. He outlines an approach that neither accepts it uncritically nor dissects it clinically, but uses the text to give a meaningful message that is both religious and realistic. This is illustrated by Howard Cooper's Noah, who finds himself facing a modern crisis, reacting with ancient impulses and leaving an eternal message. A wider perspective is provided by Sybil Sheridan and Michael Hilton; the former makes a foray into New Testament scholarship and relates John's Gospel to the Jewish theology of its time, while the latter breaks new ground in delving into the Christian influence on Jewish life, as seen in the choice of *haftarah* readings in synagogue. Reuven Silverman takes us to a later period to consider the theology of Baruch Spinoza, who, despite being condemned and ostracized by the Jewish community of his day, remains highly influential and has been remembered long after his detractors have been forgotten. Michael Leigh brings us to contemporary times with his reminiscences of the early days of the Leo Baeck College.

The Book of Many Voices

Jonathan Magonet

The Hebrew Bible is fundamental in the fashioning of the Jewish consciousness over millennia. It needs no introduction from me! And yet we have travelled such a distance since the Enlightenment altered radically our way of experiencing reality and led us to question seriously the nature of all spirituality, and above all the inherited religious classics, that some clarification of the nature of its potential impact on us, and the demands it makes, is required. Ultimately, the Hebrew Bible is not something to be talked *about*, but to be read, studied, meditated upon, prayed and lived with – for only when one tries to be on intimate terms with it does it yield its secrets, insights and strengthening power.

The Bible is not simply a 'book' but, if anything, a library of books, recording the ongoing conversation between our people and our God – a conversation acted out in the private and public experiences and dramas of history. It is a conversation conducted with words and with actions and events, in which myth, legend and historical fact blend with theological and philosophical speculation on the nature of humanity, its relation to the cosmos, the nature and purpose of society, the significance of the life of an individual nation and the vast historical tides of the rise and fall of empires. Because it is a library, many different voices are recorded in it – ranging from the most seemingly naive narratives to the subtle philosophizing of a Kohelet (Ecclesiastes) or the soaring poetic drama of a Job. Yet in this diversity there remains the unity of lives committed to living with the implications of the private and national consciousness of a covenant with the God of creation, the ruler of history, the master of life and death, justice and mercy.

This underlying unity is reflected in the very way the collection of writings is assembled by our Sages – the *neviim*, prophetic books, and *ketuvim*, 'writings', forming successive layers of garments around the core of Torah, the 'five books of Moses'. Like the layers of an onion skin they surround the central core, and, if one may carry this image further, successive generations up till our own time have added skin after skin – the rabbis who composed the midrash, the deeper exploration and interpretation of the received text; the *m'farshim*, the medieval commentators, who began to bring systematic clarification of the books of the Bible, drawing on their own received tradition and also the latest knowledge available to them in fields like grammar and comparative linguistics, philosophy and natural sciences; mystics who sought the secrets behind the images and words, behind even the very letters of the Hebrew alphabet; the preachers and teachers who brought to life the tales and sayings, simple and obscure, as they sought to reach the hearts and minds of their contemporaries, to give them purpose and meaning, strength and comfort in the complex, often tragic, circumstances of their lives in exile; the poets who played with biblical words and phrases, welding them into songs to be chanted in synagogue as the annual cycle of feasts and fasts came round; and the scientists, critics, theologians and polemicists, apologists and ideologists from our own disparate post-Enlightenment Jewish world. All of these have a share in the ongoing dialogue between the Jewish people and our Scripture. So the study of the Hebrew Bible perhaps offers the most direct introduction to the myriad worlds, physical and spiritual, in which Jews have lived in the millennia since the closure of the canon.

The Hebrew Bible is our heritage as Jews, and yet we have tended to relinquish the task of interpreting it to others in our time, except for issues directly relating to Zionism and the State of Israel. The predominant approach to Bible study over the past two centuries, one that has radically altered everyone's perception of the issues to be addressed, is that of the historical-critical school, which has tried seriously to go behind the received text and penetrate to the presumed historical 'core' of the Bible. It has used the tools of reason, logic and scientific method that have marked the triumphant progress of materialist philosophies in the secular world. Today it is fashionable to dismiss and debunk these achievements, now that we see the limitations of such an approach, particularly in the area of the spirit, and yet the scientific advance has forced religious people to examine very carefully the borderline between superstition and faith, between the truth of revelation and the human agents of transmission, with their fallibility and bias.

Though the particular approach is new, such challenges are not, for each generation has had to confront Scripture with the greatest available knowledge and values of its time, and the Bible itself gives evidence of the struggle with rival ideologies and world views. Yet the contemporary scientific approach has had a far more radical effect in questioning the fundamental assumptions of biblical faith, and in undermining a traditional, unselfconscious loyalty to 'the word of God'. The price has been high. Though strictly an analytical tool, the 'higher criticism', instead of leading to some higher truth, has also introduced its own dogmatism. The cruder analytical methods of the nineteenth century, often recognized as a disguised form of antisemitism, were also aimed unconsciously at removing God from the divine throne. Texts evaporated before our eyes into numerous contradictory substrata, oral traditions, theological schools and sub-schools. Much of this analysis was based on questionable assumptions about the nature of literary texts and an oversimplified, evolutionary view of the development of culture and systems of belief. Even when such presuppositions have been challenged or discounted, these 'assured results of scholarship' have continued to exert an influence in secondary fields of study and in popular literature, perhaps because, unlike other scientific disciplines, there are no dramatic consequences to these theories that might force us to revise them.

However, there is another side to the scientific approach to the Hebrew Bible that has affected popular, and also Jewish, views, The remarkable discoveries in the field of archaeology, the breaking of the codes of early languages, the revelation of the scope and quality of ancient Near Eastern culture before and during the biblical period, have given new dimensions of credence, if not to the theological truth, at least to the factual, cultural background of the Bible. Popular opinion swung between over-simplified acceptance of these two views: either the Bible was just a mass of literary 'forgeries' or complex strands of rival schools of thought clumsily edited by politically motivated redactors and thus to be given little credibility, or archaeology was seen to 'prove' the existence of the patriarchs, the miracles and so on.

The Jewish responses to these fundamental challenges to the authority of Scripture can be roughly categorized in three ways: one is a process of denial of their implications and a closing of ranks around certain traditional views – though since this is a defensive reaction it tends to prevent any creative or innovatory thinking; the other extreme is the acceptance of the 'demythologizing' of Scripture as part of a process of Jewish assimilation to contemporary secular culture; between these extremes is a process of accommodation, amongst 'conservative' and 'progressive' Jews, that has shifted the emphasis from the literal acceptance of the divine nature of revelation to a contemplation of the human nature of its reception.

Despite all the above challenges, the Bible remains a 'best-seller', with a whole variety of new translations and editions appearing. Some of them reflect a new 'ecumenism' and the desire to bring to bear the best of scholarship alongside the insights of tradition, particularly Jewish exegesis. Again, they reflect a kind of polarization between 'fundamentalism' and 'academic' approaches. However, what has radically changed the approach to the Hebrew Bible among Jews is precisely the availability today of the Hebrew language as a tool for study. Clearly this means most to Israelis for whom the Bible is an integral part of their education – though one may question whether the type of learning required for school curricula does not have a negative effect on the average Israeli's enthusiasm for it. Beyond the language issue, the Bible is an essential ideological tool in establishing, and debating, the authenticity of the Jewish claim to the 'promised land'. The fascination with archaeology is but one popular manifestation of the depth of this concern.

The study of the Hebrew Bible in its original language is extremely important for our grasp of the richness, flexibility and nature of the language, and the form and content of the biblical message. For language colours thought, and the very process of engagement with biblical Hebrew syntax, with its different time sense, the interrelationship between ideas and the words that convey them, the parallelism of its poetry, the precision of its narrative style, the dramatic simplicity and forcefulness of the prophetic idiom, begins the process of assimilation to its modes of thought, its way of expressing its view of reality, its experience of the transcendent, which is vital to any Jewish spiritual enrichment. We are enabled to step out of our contemporary cultural conditioning into other modes of experiencing reality, and are thus 'softened up', as it were, to approach with greater insight and sensitivity the ideas our tradition seeks to convey. For ultimately, behind even the problems of the language itself, we are entering into a dialogue with a different symbolism, a different metaphor for expressing reality, and it requires great imaginative powers, and a readiness to go beyond literal meanings, to reach behind the metaphor and the idiom of another society and culture and mode of experience.

For this task we are often poorly equipped in terms of the formal tools at our disposal. Moreover, today's materialistic climate leads to a mistrust of 'religious classics', particularly given the curiously moralizing tone of so many of their interpreters and devotees (a tone usually missing in the original) and the artificially pious way in which they are intoned in our religious establishments. And yet this very estrangement sets us free to begin afresh when we approach the Hebrew Bible, particularly in its own language, and bring to it all the experience and maturity we have, all the skills we possess in the areas of life where we have knowledge, education and other competences. And perhaps, too, in the twentieth century, when we have become particularly sensitized to the problems of discovering the truth behind the rhetoric of political and commercial propaganda, we may already know how to read beneath the surface. Certainly the Bible, if it is to be taken seriously in its own terms, demands much subtlety, and indeed an awareness of the life-and-death issues that are ultimately at stake in the commitment to its exploration.

There is hardly room to do more than touch on a few elements which mark the uniqueness of the biblical view and might prove helpful in our concern with our own spiritual enrichment. For example, one of the most outstanding and yet most abused features is the remarkable self-critical nature of Israel's view of itself as expressed in the Hebrew Bible. Whether we have a narrative passage describing God's anger, or an editorial reworking of the historical annals of the kings of Judah and Israel, or a prophetic lament about the imminent downfall of Jerusalem, there is to be found that same thread of awareness of the gap between the ideal society required by the covenant with God and the reality of private and public selfishness, of justice surrendered to political expediency. Alone of all the monuments and literature of Ancient Near Eastern civilization, the Bible contains this rigorous self-examination, and hence the possibility of renewal, of survival after destruction, of humility before the remarkable potential within human beings for awesome achievement and stupendous arrogance, folly and destructiveness. What has often been paradoxical in Jewish history is how that self-criticism has been used by those who claimed to inherit our Scripture as proof of our unworthiness – not realizing that any claimant to the covenant is immediately tried with the same demanding vision, and inevitably found wanting.

It is no wonder that the Bible calls Israel an *am kashey oref*, a 'stiff-necked people' – yet Israel's stubbornness, disobedience and backsliding in the face of God's demands after accepting the covenant have nevertheless provided the Jewish people with the strength to remain loyal to that covenant in the face of our own failures, and the attempts to seduce us or force us to accept a different ultimate loyalty. The Bible assumes a divine perspective on all human achievements, ambitions and loyalties, on the transience of the life of the individual, of societies, nations and empires, and on the inevitable reckoning to which each and every one is called. So it makes a plea for individual and collective mutual responsibility while at the same time documenting the infinite variety of ways in which human beings can and do evade and pervert this responsibility. It chronicles the need for a process of self-purification and cleansing, by the individual and the society, so as to cope with these delicate but crucial problems.

One effect of the biblical materials is to challenge our conventional thinking about the nature of events and issues. The real point may actually lie elsewhere, and be more subtle and more profound than our own contemporary perspective might suggest. If we bring to our study of the Bible our knowledge, insight, compassion, love and faith, the exercise of these values will have consequences for our actions in the world. And if sometimes the result is the revelation of our own 'nakedness', our loneliness and helplessness in the world, this is also a truth we have to face. Adam and Eve, after eating the forbidden fruit, became aware that they were naked, a biblical metaphor for weakness and helplessness. They tried to cover this awareness with fig-leaves, just as we cower behind our power, our possessions, our technology, our slogans, to no avail. These surface solutions provide temporary shelter at the price of our enslavement to them. Adam and Eve must be expelled from Eden once they recognize this reality. But they do not go out entirely naked and undefended. For in the biblical story it is God who offers them the clothing that they need.

If I have moved suddenly into metaphor and allegory, it is partly because it is hard to resist the evocative quality of these primal stories, and partly because it helps to make the transition to a brief additional note on the introduction the Bible offers to post-biblical Jewish creativity and spirituality. If the rabbis said that there are 'seventy faces to Torah', they meant that the possibilities of interpretation and reinterpretation are inexhaustible. A late tradition, one that is itself dependent on Christian models, suggests four headings under which such exploration was possible, the initial letters joined as a mnemonic in the Hebrew word *PaRDeS*, 'orchard'. The four consonants stand for *Pshat*, the plain or commonsense meaning of a particular word or phrase; for *Remez*, the 'hint' or 'allusion', the 'allegorical' reading; for *Derash*, the deeper searching of the text, the filling of gaps in meaning or application, leading to halachah, literally 'walking', the way of law and direction, but leading also to aggadah, literally 'narrating', all other matters ranging from legend to ethics, parables to practical wisdom; and lastly for the word, *Sod*, 'secret', the esoteric, mystical meanings.

If we are to capture again the hearts and souls of today's Jewish societies so that these traditions can speak again to us in the idiom of today, there is a new midrash that has to be written, harnessing the greatest minds of our own time to the rediscovery and reclamation of our tradition so that it may speak afresh to this generation. This should not be merely a sentimental reminder of past achievements, or a pastiche of a forgotten life-style, but a recapturing of that seriousness of purpose, that richness of creativity, of wit and understanding that characterized the real strength of our way of reading the Hebrew Bible. 'Turn it and turn it again, for everything is in it.'

Writing this article brings to mind a moment, probably during my own studies at Leo Baeck, when I visited a sale in the East End of London that marked the closing down of a Jewish bookshop. A very persuasive Professor Chimen Abramsky encouraged me to buy two old midrashic texts. I remember that as I left, I felt an overwhelming sense of responsibility towards them – as if they had been entrusted into my care as the last person who had to ensure that their teachings were handed on. If that did not happen literally, it has been my concern to ensure that Bible, Midrash and Parshanut (commentary) have a major part to play in the teaching of the College, despite the fact that the latter two in particular have been something of 'Cinderella' disciplines in the field of academic Jewish studies. To this day they are hardly taught at all in the UK. In this commitment I can detect time and again the influence of Dr Ellen Littmann, who taught me Bible, and Professor Nachama Leibowitz, with whom I had the privilege of studying in Jerusalem, as indeed have so many Jewish Bible scholars of my generation. Both in their own way taught the discipline of Jewish Bible study, but more than that they conveyed their love for the texts and the engagement with them of generations of Jewish scholars and teachers.

It was from another source entirely, however, that I learnt that Bible study is part of a dialogue process – a two-way engagement with the text itself, the teachers of the past and the students with whom we are ourselves engaged. That lesson came in a paradoxical way, given the Jewish experience of this century, from my engagement with the annual Jewish-Christian Bible Week that I have helped to organize for almost thirty years at the Hedwig Dransfeld Haus in Bendorf, Germany. It was here for the first time that I learnt that people come to the Bible and to Jewish teachers with real personal questions. The Bible is both text and pretext for a deeper engagement of the whole person, and for ever rescues the study of the Bible from its own traps – including the worship of the word alone or the tradition of teaching. Franz Rosenzweig expressed this experience by saying that now he does not simply try to answer the question posed by someone, but the person who poses the question. And that, too, is what the study of the Hebrew Bible is about.

The Hebrew Bible has not only characterized our own view of the world, but has found its vindication in our history – a transcendent vision of reality that nevertheless sends us back to earn our bread in the mundane reality of daily life, to take our place in the cosmos. It was neatly summed up by the medieval Spanish poet Solomon Ibn Gabirol: 'Plan for this world as if you were to live for ever; plan for the world to come as if you were to die tomorrow.' Any concern with the spiritual revival of the Jewish people must be aware of this polarity of our experience, even if the nearest thing to a transcendental reality that many Jews can accept is the historical experience of our people and its survival. On even this limited view, Bible as a key element of our national heritage is an essential starting point for study. Beyond that, like the other reality to which it points, and to the experience of which it testifies, it is there to be met whenever we wish to approach it with the humility, longing and hunger that have been the mark of the stiff-necked, God-intoxicated Jewish people.

The Last Temptation of Noah

Howard Cooper

Even before the Disaster I felt misunderstood. I only wanted a quiet life: to come home after work, relax and rest. After all – and this used to be my private joke, though it feels pretty grim now – that's what my name Noah means: rest.

Apart from my work and my family I couldn't really be bothered with anything else. I didn't have many interests, not even much ambition. I used to sit in the office during the day and dream of the journey home, opening the door, playing with the kids, helping them with their homework. In the evening I'd switch on the TV in order to switch off my thoughts, those terrible thoughts that kept coming, waves of them, more and more insistently over the years. All I ever really wanted was a rest – from the pressures that we all suffered. Just a rest from it all: the bills, the relatives, the dinner parties. Rest: it was all I wanted. Honestly.

Oh yes, I was known for my honesty. Even those who didn't like me said that I had integrity. They used other words too, which sounded good, words like 'upright', 'blameless', even (God help me) 'righteous'. But I never trusted them – not the words, not the people. Words had lost their solidity, their truthfulness, long before. In those days words meant their opposite.

When that TV presenter interviewed me (near the end this was, after I'd made all the fuss), he was the one who called me 'righteous'. But I could hear in the tone of his voice how he really meant 'self-righteous', how the compliment disguised the attack. And who knows, maybe he was right, maybe I did begin to feel a bit self-righteous. Because I *did know* what was going to happen. I wasn't taken in by all those words: freedom of opportunity, economic growth, individual choice . . . I could see what was going on, all that heartbreak beneath the surface, and what was going to happen if we didn't change. I did know it would end in disaster; but I didn't know *just how bad it would turn out.* I didn't, honestly . . . I can tell you don't believe me. It's all right – I'm used to that. Nobody ever believed me then, either. Before.

You see, I worked in industry, middle-management. Agricultural and forestry equipment the firm made. When it expanded we went into animal feed, fertilizers, that sort of thing – quite a broad spread – even livestock eventually. We were successful too: public company, safe investment, high annual returns, particularly good Third World market, what with all the problems they kept having. I was responsible for overseas sales. Quite an irony really when you think about it, considering what happened.

I was able to laugh more in those days too. Earlier on that was. I used to enjoy having fun: a good party, that sort of thing. I don't think I ever entirely lost my sense of humour – but I kept noticing things I'd prefer not to have known about.

I'd read a report here, hear a programme there, bits and pieces of knowledge on the periphery of my consciousness. First we had that string of warm years: 1980, 1981, 1983, 1987, 1988 – the hottest since records began, they said. It didn't bother me really: I was only worried about getting a bit of sun on our holidays. And where I went it rained anyway. But the statistics were global ones: it was beginning to warm up rather dramatically. Only a few degrees over a century didn't sound so much, but researchers in one country began to see the changes in plants and trees, and then another group at the other side of the world discovered that the world's beaches were eroding. These were just a couple of the warnings of the impending crisis.

I did mention it to a few people at work – after all, it could have had implications for our sales – but they just shrugged and said that these kinds of reports are not reliable, they come and go, you know how it is . . .

And although I didn't really know how it was, it was easier at the beginning to change the subject and ask what home computer they thought I should buy. It felt safer ground.

But then the dreams started. All that water imagery, all that flooding, swimming, drowning, seas and swimming pools, struggling to keep afloat – every night a new variation on the theme. My analyst told me that this was archetypal symbolism: the struggle of the Self to emerge from the Sea of Consciousness. I changed my analyst.

And all the time I knew that something else was going on, something much bigger than me. Everyone had heard about the 'greenhouse effect', how carbon dioxide in the atmosphere acts like glass in a greenhouse, letting the sun's rays through to the earth, but also trapping some of the heat that would otherwise be radiated back into space. We were burning all that coal and oil and gas, more and more of it, year after year – and the planet was heating up. Then there were those other gases: like the ones in those take-away cartons. Some firms changed them, others said the evidence was inconclusive (though of course it merited further study). But that still left aerosol sprays and even fridges – and I liked ice in my gin and tonic.

The problem was that I didn't have any answers. I only had fears and questions and intuitions – and they wouldn't go away. But it was that presentation I did at the shareholders meeting that finally wrecked me. I spoke about the rain forests we were destroying (indirectly of course: our firm only sold the equipment); I gave them all the facts and figures, how the earth was such a fragile interconnected ecosystem (yes, by then I'd learnt the jargon), that what the inhabitants of planet earth were doing was quietly conducting a giant environmental experiment. Were it to be brought before any responsible local council for approval it would be firmly rejected as having potentially disastrous consequences.

At the meeting all this earned a variety of responses: anger, boredom, though a few people seemed rather subdued afterwards. Perhaps it was naive to expect anything more – after all, I'd just bought a new car as well. I didn't want to change my lifestyle either. I was comfortable, I admit it. But we all were then – at least in the circles I mixed in.

Getting the push after that speech was actually a blessing in disguise. I devoted myself more and more to trying to get people to see what was going on around them all the time. I got involved with political groups, environmental groups, religious groups. I even started writing letters to *The Guardian*.

I gave the same speech wherever I went. 'The climate that has allowed the growth of civilization and agriculture – and to which all our crops, customs and structures are adapted – is virtually certain to disappear. The world will become warmer than at any time since the emergence of humanity on earth. This threatens to take place over the next forty years. Humanity will find it hard to adapt, particularly in a world fragmented by national boundaries and competing interests. Harvests *will* fail more drastically the cities we live in *will* go under water.'

People began to hate me for what I was saying. They used to avoid me, fear me: fear what I was saying, I suppose. A poet had written 'Humankind cannot bear very much reality', and it was true. I didn't blame people – I couldn't bear it either. My wife began to catch me talking to myself. I was trying to keep myself sane, keep myself from the madness of knowing that something was *inevitable* – that was the word the experts used – unless we worked together. Funnily enough, I did have faith in humanity then. I believed that people could change, with help and encouragement. And groups of people working together – communities – could do a lot. But first we had to realize that we'd taken a wrong direction; we had to turn from what's best only for ourselves, our family, our community, our nation.

Near the end I realized that we needed to pray too – though at first I was more sceptical about that. Religion had always felt a bit too cosy and comfortable: too much security was on offer. And I certainly had no security to offer anyone. I used to take myself off for long walks and look at the mess around me: the squalor, the poverty, the drugged ones, the violence, the neglect, the corruption, the decay.

I saw the goodness, too, in people I met, the beauty in small things. I could see infinity in a grain of sand and feel eternity in an hour. But over all, on these walks, I felt the inferno, the 'moronic inferno', as one of those clever Jewish novelists called it: the levelling down of contemporary life where people found themselves in that chaotic state, overwhelmed by all kinds of outer forces – political, technological, military, economic – which carry everything before them with a kind of disorder in which we were supposed to survive with all our human qualities. Who really had sufficient internal organization to resist, let alone to flourish?

It wasn't possible to go on that way. And in their hearts and souls, people knew it. It wasn't just me: I really was just an ordinary person. In my generation I was nothing special. I knew it. Later on, long after the Disaster, when they told those stories about me, things got changed somehow. It was true that I became whole-heartedly committed to speaking the truth I experienced, sharing my vision of what I knew was going to happen. But if I'd lived in a less corrupt time, nobody would ever have heard of me. Even the rabbis acknowledged that, later.

I could never explain properly those intuitions I'd have when I was off walking. I just knew in the end that I had changed and that others could change, too. It was very simple. I had an inner voice I just had to trust. Everyone had that voice deep inside them. It was obvious. But in those days so many temptations drowned out that knowing voice, so many possibilities of seduction away from our still and silent truth.

I once made a list, half-jokingly, of what I thought we needed to remember to be fully human, to be what we ought to be in this world. I jotted down seven things – it surprised me there were so few. I sent them on a postcard to a friend, and she wrote back saying I sounded like some kind of religious nut. It sounded, she said – she was very cynical though – as if I was walking with God when I went off on my expeditions round town. I wasn't hurt by this. Well, not really. It stayed in my mind though, that phrase, 'walking with God'.

Later on, when they told those stories about me, they seemed to think it was a compliment: that somehow this was an uplifting, desirable experience for a person to have. Actually it was hell.

I'll tell you the list, but before I do I want to say that I've gone against most of them in my time. There were so many temptations then, not even a saint could have resisted them. And I was no saint. But I do know there are some things that just have to be. If we're going to make it through this time. And call it walking with God if you like.

First, there has to be a system of justice. Real justice allows a society to function and the individual to retain dignity. And a system of political and legal justice means that the disadvantaged are protected from abuse – the abuse from power, money or class.

Secondly: murder – it's not on. We have to deal with our violent feelings in some other way. And leading on from there, thirdly: robbery, theft, is out, too. We have to find an alternative way of channelling our greed, and our envy of what others have.

Nor can incest be allowed. That wise professor from Vienna eventually uncovered just how much we do secretly want to express our sexuality inside our family. But we just can't have our mummy or daddy or children or siblings in that way. We've got to find someone else to do it with. And that reminds me of what happened after the Disaster. We were in such chaos. There was just our family, and my middle boy Ham did something to me which I can *never* forgive him for, that bugger, God damn him! But that's another story.

Yes, the fifth on the list is blasphemy. It's no use my letting rip like that. I still have to find a way of getting rid of this anger.

The sixth thing I listed I called idolatry. It was a handy word, it covered a lot of things. Actually I was thinking of all those adverts on TV, and all those colour supplements offering me happiness on every page. We were drowning in luxury in those days: so many divinely decadent choices. We knew it couldn't go on for ever, but we worshipped production and consumption. I loved buying things – it made me feel so secure, so good about myself. Crazy, really, looking back.

Last on my list, number seven, sounds strange now, though at the time it made sense. I called it 'not eating flesh cut from a living animal'. You see, I wanted something on my list that captured the essence of evil: that degraded the one who performed it and caused pain and terror to the victim. I suppose I could have chosen another image, another way to express this. Towards the end people came up with worse things, believe me.

Anyway, I thought out these seven things during my walks. Afterwards, people saw them as the natural religious basis vital to the existence of any human society. I suppose I'm rather proud of that. They even called them after me: 'the seven laws given to the descendants of Noah'.

Right. I'm nearly finished now. I just want to tell you what happened in the end, when the Disaster came.

I saw it all so clearly: we'd reached the point where the rate of environmental change in my lifetime was going to be many times the maximum that our planet's eco-system could endure. There was no escaping this fate unless a radical transformation took place. One day I saw it all so clearly that I grew really desperate. I felt more hopeless than I'd ever done before. I felt closed in, with this great weight around me. I'd built it myself, this mental structure I'd constructed from all the evidence I'd gathered. It was like a vessel of doom I lived in. I was going crazy inside it. I was in complete despair.

I just wanted to be left alone. The understanding I had was too much for me. I felt hundreds of years old. It felt completely hopeless. I felt overwhelmed by . . . helplessness, that's the word: I was completely helpless, like a baby. I couldn't do anything more. I had no strength left.

And I started to cry. It'd never happened before. After all, I was a man. But I did, I broke down, in front of my family: all of them were there – my wife and my sons and their wives. And I wept and wept. Tears of bitterness. Tears of remorse. Tears of anger. Tears of grief. I cried and I cried and I just . . . floated away.

It's hard to describe now. The sadness just flooded out of me. It went on and on, all those years and years of frustration and pain trapped inside – it all welled up and spilled out. The tears just seemed to pour out of me – it felt like days – for the sadness of it all, and the pity.

The rest you know of course. It's history – of a sort. It's in the books, though I know people argue over the details. Nothing ever was the same again.

Though there was one helpful moment: when I saw that rainbow. Yes, I know it's only the reflection of the sun in moist atmosphere, but I'd never really looked at one before. Really *looked*, I mean. That one time, though, soon after the Disaster, I saw those seven colours arched above me, translucent and glorious and shimmering. And I suddenly remembered the seven laws I'd jotted down on that card, and it was my conceit, I know, but I felt there was some connection between those seven basic norms for how we are to live together and those seven basic colours in which the world is enveloped.

There was a harmony at that moment: seeing how the natural world and our human world reflected each other's inner grace. And at that moment I knew, I knew as clearly as if I heard a voice speak it in my ear, I knew that this disaster could never be again. Not ever. It felt like a promise. If I were a religious man I'd call it a blessing. Never again – such relief, I can't tell you.

'While the earth remaineth, seedtime and harvest and cold and heat and summer and winter and day and night shall not cease.' The words just formed themselves in my head. It would never happen again. That's all there is to say.

Oh, I almost forgot. The last temptation of Noah. You want to know the very last temptation? It was after it was all over and we had to pull ourselves together and start again. That was hard. We didn't know where we were, where we were going, what we were doing. Everything had gone. We survivors felt so helpless so much of the time. And the hardest part was that we kept remembering how it'd been before: so comfortable, so secure – you'll never know. That was the worst part: I couldn't help but remember it.

I became very morose, self-pitying. I just wanted to forget, to forget how it'd been. And, I admit it, I started to drink. They never tell the story this way, but this is how it was. They always make me out as the father of vineyards and winemaking, but I'm telling you: soon I was drinking all the time – I just wanted to blot it all out.

And that was the last temptation: the temptation to blot it all out, to forget the knowledge I carried, the understanding I had, the lonely experiences I'd been through, the intuitions I'd borne all these years. I tried to drown myself in drink: another flood.

But it wasn't to be. It seems that my destiny is to remain aware, to remember, to remember when others have forgotten. Death is the only release from the burden of consciousness. But meanwhile, crying out when others keep silent, my work is just given to me to do, wherever I happen to be. The rest, as they say, is nothing.

John's Gospel through Jewish Eyes

Sybil Sheridan

A member of my synagogue once attended a calligraphy class. On looking at the other students at work, he noticed a nun carefully illuminating the words 'In the Beginning'.

'Ah,' he said, 'Genesis!'. She turned round surprised. 'No,' she replied, 'the Gospel of John!'

Those simple words – 'In the beginning' – which open the two biblical books are the first of many indications that the Prologue to St John's Gospel (John 1.1–18) is in fact a midrash on that first chapter of Genesis.

A midrash is an explanation – an exposition on a specific biblical text. It serves to illuminate biblical verses, extend them and broaden their meaning. All this, the prologue to St John's Gospel does, and while the conclusion the writer draws may not be theologically acceptable to the Jew today, the method he employs is in every respect Jewish.

We cannot know for certain what the Judaism of the early Christian period was like. The texts of classic rabbinic Judaism were written down almost a century later, and though they probably remain faithful to their oral forbears, they offer only a limited view of Judaism. Theirs is the faith of the Pharisees who emerged triumphant out of the ashes of the destroyed Temple. Of the Sadducees, the Essenes, and the various Jewish messianic sects in the Palestine of the period, relatively little is known. Still less is known of the many Hellenistic Jewish groups that derived from Alexandria and with whose forms of Judaism the writer of John's Gospel would have been most familiar.[1]

But the Prologue demonstrates such close knowledge of biblical, rabbinic and Jewish philosophical thought, that if the author were not himself a Jew, then he must have been a Greek engaged in an intense dialogue with those Jews around him. He wrote the Prologue, not for the conversion of Gentiles but for those very Jews that he knew.

> In the beginning was the Word,[2] and the Word was with God, and the Word was God. He was in the beginning with God; all things were made through him, and without him was not anything made that was made. In him was life, and the life was the light of men. The light shines in the darkness, and the darkness has not overcome it . . . The true light that enlightens every man was coming into the world. He was in the world, and the world was made through him, yet the world knew him not. He came to his own home, and his own people received him not. But to all who received him, who believed in his name, he gave power to become children of God; who were born, not of blood nor of the will of the flesh nor of the will of man, but of God. And the Word became flesh and dwelt among us, full of grace and truth; we have beheld his glory, glory as of the only Son from the Father . . . And from his fullness have we all received grace upon grace. For the law was given through Moses; grace and truth came through Jesus Christ. No one has ever seen God; the only Son, who is in the bosom of the Father, he has made him known.

Let us go through the passage, examining the various points of contact between this text and Jewish tradition, beginning with . . . 'In the beginning'.

Genesis

> In the beginning God created the heaven and earth. And the earth was unformed and void, and the darkness hovered over the surface of the deep and the spirit of God hovered over the waters (Gen.1.1–2).

The opening passage of Genesis is so familiar that it is automatically brought to mind when you start reading John. But instead of the familiar 'God created' you are confronted with the words 'was the Word'. What is this? The Word instead of God? This is deliberate. It is precisely John's message. The Word replaces God, because the Word is God. The verb also changes from the transitive verb of creation to the intransitive verb of being. That the word 'was' actually has no beginning is also important, because there is no way of measuring how long the 'was' was, before anything actually happened in creation. You have here the introduction of the Greek notion of a pre-existent universe rather than a created one. But that does not make it any less Jewish. The Jews had already taken that idea on board for themselves. In the second verse of Genesis we are told that the earth was 'unformed and empty' (or messy and unfurnished, if you follow the Greek Septuagint that John would have known) and the 'Spirit of God' hovered over the waters (Gen.1.2). So clearly something was happening even before creation began. The midrash Bereshit Rabba (1.4) interprets this pre-existence as follows:

> 'In the beginning God created.' Six things preceded the creation of the world; some of them were actually created, while the creation of others was already contemplated. The Torah and the Throne of Glory were created. The Torah, for it is written 'The Lord made me at the beginning of his way, prior to his works of old' (Prov. 8.22).

In Genesis, there was some sort of existence on to whose bones the midrash gave flesh. But according to Gen. 1.2 there is more. Alongside what was before the world was created is another entity, 'the spirit of God'. Here is the crux of the issue: God is not alone. The Hebrew grammatical form – the construct – can be ambiguous. Is the Spirit of God an independent entity working 'with' God, or is it part 'of' God? We are back into John language, and can see clearly that for John, the 'Word' is the 'Spirit'. But even here, we are not departing from Jewish thought. Many texts describe God as having a partner in creating the world, for example Bereshit Rabba 1.1:

> 'Then I was by Him as a nursling (*amon*); and I was daily His delight' (Prov 8.30) . . . '*amon*' is a workman (*uman*). The Torah declares: 'I was the working tool of the Holy One, Blessed be He.' In human practice, when a mortal king builds a

> palace, he builds it not with his own skill, but with the skill of an architect. The architect, moreover, does not build it out of his head, but employs plans and diagrams to know how to arrange the chambers and the wicket doors. Thus God consulted the Torah and created the world, while the Torah declares 'In the beginning, God created' (1.1), 'beginning' referring to the Torah, as in the verse, 'The Lord made me as the beginning of his way' (Prov. 8.22).

Torah becomes the blueprint by which the world is created. But this still is not exactly what John is talking about. According to this midrash, God created Torah first and then used her to make the world. John's Logos (the Greek for word) appears to have existed alongside God or as God always. The two midrashim we have seen actually reinterpret the original Proverbs text to get rid of an alarming dualism that appears there. If we look at the text itself, we see precisely John's view of creation – only instead of the Word the person who speaks is Wisdom.

> The Lord created me at the beginning of his work,
> the first of his acts of old.
> Ages ago, I was set up,
> at the first, before the beginning of the earth.
> When there were no depths I was brought forth,
> when there were no springs abounding with water.
> Before the mountains had been shaped,
> before the hills, I was brought forth;
> before he had made the earth with its fields,
> or the first of the dust of the world.
> When he established the heavens, I was there,
> when he drew a circle on the face of the deep,
> when he assigned to the sea its limit
> so that the waters might not
> transgress his command,
> when he marked out the foundations of the earth,
> then I was beside him, like a nursling;
> and I was daily his delight,
> rejoicing in his inhabited world
> and delighting the sons of men (Prov. 8.22–31).

This passage of Proverbs has within it a summary of creation, with Wisdom's comment on the process as it went along. John's Word has the precise same function. Just as John's Word is there 'In the beginning', so Wisdom is the beginning of God's work. Just as John's Word is then transported through the stages of creation – of light (John 1.4), of the creation of the world (1.9), to the creation of humanity (1.14) – so Wisdom was there when the waters were cicumscribed, when the earth was formed, in the delight of humankind.

This text of Proverbs is not an isolated one. Wisdom is also mentioned as playing an active part in creation in the book of Job 28.20–28, and some of the apocryphal books take the idea further, as will be seen below. There is a strong argument to say that Judaism was not always as strictly monotheistic as we like to think, and that wisdom had a divine, or semi-divine, status. For the author of John's Prologue, there was no need to look beyond the Judaism of his own time to express his ideas.

And God said

But there is still a difference. The Word remains eternal, while Wisdom is clearly 'brought forth' (Prov. 8.22). The Hebrew word used in this context denotes the action 'to writhe' and is used often as writhing in childbirth, as in Isa. 26.17. It means that Wisdom is God's literal 'first-begotten child'. Ironically, if you consider the other Gospels, there is no sense of 'begetting' in John. Unless you go back to Genesis, and the third verse of the creation narrative. God, having 'hovered' for eternity over chaos, finally goes into production, and . . . speaks. The very first act of creation is the creation of words, and it is through those words that the world comes into being. Thus it is that the Word is also 'brought forth'. God's speech was no idle phrase; in it the whole world lay in essence. To produce those words could be seen as equivalent in pain and in effort to the giving of birth. So the Word – Logos – becomes co-partner with God and the equivalent of Wisdom – in Hebrew *Chochmah* – in its relationship to God and its obligation to the world. John's Gospel was by no means the first to use the concept of the Word; the Jewish world at the time was full of it. The

Targumim, Aramaic translations of the Bible, constantly interpolate the Word – in Aramaic *memra* – into the texts where it is not found in the original. A Greek idea that had entered the realm of Jewish thought was uneasy with the notion of an immanent God. God who speaks directly to people, who has a personal relationship with individuals, did not seem right to much of the Jewish world of that time. Therefore, wherever the biblical text mentioned that God 'spoke', the Targumists added a mediator: 'the word came to' people instead. The Word soon gathered a life of its own. Wherever there was Wisdom, it was the Word that spoke. Wherever there was creation – it was through the Word. Wherever there were miracles, God's Word had effected them. Wisdom and Word (*Chochmah* and *Memra*), both feminine nouns, easily merged into one and the same female companion of God. In the Greek world it was different. Here the Word is found as a masculine noun, and Logos could not so easily join with the feminine wisdom of Sophia, so the two remain separate. We have little other than the works of Philo, but there are enough of them! In fact Philo uses Wisdom as well as the Word, but it is those masculine descriptions of Logos that the Gospel of John seems to utilize.

Philo had that same difficulty with an immanent God that seems to have beset much of the world of the time. He saw God as eternally other and totally separate. Humanity, created in God's image contained a divine element, yet how could this be linked to God? Answer: the Divine Mediator, the Logos, the 'Seal stamped on creation',

> The Logos is the God of us imperfect men. But the Primal God is the God of the wise and perfect,

and, most telling of all in the context of the Gospel of St John,

> for like a flock: earth and water, air and fire and all plants and animals in them . . . are led according to right and law by God, the shepherd and king who has set over them his true Logos and first begotten son as the vice-regent of a great king.[3]

In the light of these texts it seems hardly necessary for the author of John's Prologue to look to Greece for notions of a pre-existent word as son of God, when they are already part of Judaism.

Let there be light

> In him was life, and the life was the light of men. The light shines in the darkness and the darkness has not overcome it (John 1.4–5).

Here, we are on to more familiar Jewish territory – but not for long! In the book of Proverbs we are told that Wisdom is:

> A tree of Life to those who grasp her.
> And whoever holds on to her is happy (Prov. 3.18).

While light is described later in terms of teaching:

> For the commandment is a lamp and
> Torah a light (Prov. 6.23).

The light shining in the darkness comes straight from Isaiah:

> The people who walked in darkness have seen a great light, those that dwelt in a land of deep darkness, on them has light shined (Isa. 9.2).

Daniel 2.22 may also have something to do with it:

> He reveals deep and hidden things,
> knows what is in the darkness,
> and light dwells with Him.

Above all, this passage continues the theme of creation.

> And God said, 'Let there be light', and there was light (Gen. 1.3).

In John's rendition, God's first act of creation becomes associated with the Logos. But the wording is careful: '. . . the life was the light of men . . .' The Word cannot be the light, as that would make him a product of creation. In the same manner, Wisdom is associated with light, without actually being called 'The Light'. In the Wisdom of Solomon, *Chochmah* 'enlightens' the world and, as in John, this light is not overcome by darkness.

Being compared with light, she is found to be before it;
For as the light of day succeedeth night,
But against wisdom evil doth not prevail;
But she reacheth from one end of the world to the other with full strength
And ordereth all things well (Wisdom of Solomon 7.9–30).[4]

John's Word follows the path well trodden by the Hebrew Wisdom.

The world

> The true light that enlightens every man was coming into the world. He was in the world, and the world was made through him, yet the world knew him not (1.9–10).

The Genesis creation continues with the creation of the world, and this John now picks up. He is not interested in the details of the world's formation, as it is the relationship of the Logos to the world that is important to him. Nevertheless days three, four and five are encompassed in these two verses: the creation of the heavens, the earth and the sun, moon and stars.

There is no circumlocution here – in John's passage the Logos is described most definitely as light. And not simply as light, but as the true light. This apparent contradiction can be explained as we are now three days away from primal light. The comparison is with the luminaries.

Isaiah again appears to be the source.

> Arise, shine, your light has come,
> and the glory of the Lord has shone upon you.
> For behold, darkness shall cover the earth,
> and thick darkness the peoples.
> But the Lord will arise upon you,
> and his glory be seen upon you.
> And nations shall come to your light,
> and kings to the glory of your rising (Isa. 60.1–3).

This vision ends with these words.

> The sun shall be no more
> your light by day
> nor for brightness shall the moon
> give light to you by night.
> But the Lord will be your everlasting light,
> Your God will be your glory (6.19).

It is a passage that is messianic in every sense of the word: the end of days and a picture of complete perfection, where God alone and supreme gives light to the world.

Is John's Logos, then, associated with God who will rule alone at the end of time? Well, it could be. The Logos, after all, 'is God' as well as 'with God'. The rejection of the Word echoes the deafness of Israel to the cry of the prophets, when time and time again God threatens to reject the people. But then again, we have passages about Wisdom that also fit this picture, and in view of the close association of Logos and *Chochmah* so far, it seems likely that the connection between these two concepts continues. Here is *Chochmah* roaming the earth to find a home, and finding it among the people Israel.

> Alone I encompassed the circuit of heaven,
> And in the depths of the abyss I walked.
> Over the waves of the sea, and over all the earth,
> And over every people and nation I held sway.
> With all these I sought a resting-place,
> And (said): In whose inheritance shall I lodge?
> Then the Creator of all things gave me commandment,
> And He said: Let thy dwelling place be in Jacob,
> And in Israel take up thine inheritance (Ben Sirach 24.3–8).

Let us make man in our image

> And the Word became flesh and dwelt among us, full of grace and truth; we have beheld his glory, glory as of the only Son from the Father (1.14).

Here we have the most problematic passage. The word becomes flesh and claims sonship of the divine. According to many commentators, it is at this point that John departs from Jewish expectation. A pre-existent word may be one thing, but a word made flesh is quite another. The idea could be based on the assumption of Greek mythology of gods disporting themselves with young girls and producing legendary offspring. Such a view is found in the Gospels, which describe the miraculous birth of Jesus, but there is no hint of this in John. Instead, we see a philosophical metamorphosis which has traits in common with those in Jewish mystical literature of *Adam Kadmon* – the primeval human perfect being of which earthly humans are a pale reflection.

In Philo, the Logos is also

> ... incorporeal man which is no other than the divine image ... for the father of all caused him to spring forth as his eldest son.

If Logos is brought forth at the beginnings of creation, in an action I described earlier as akin to childbirth, then of course Logos is the first-begotten son.

But Philo's Logos remains spirit. The fleshly attributes are those that really trouble. How can God become man? While again, it is tempting to look at Greek mythology for the origins, one must remember that in the context of Greek philosophy the idea of flesh and spirit as being connected at all was problematic. Platonic thought, which has dogged Christianity for centuries, made God so impossibly spiritual that there had to be emanation upon emanation upon emanation before there could be any contact at all between flesh and spirit.

In contrast, biblical Judaism saw no distinction between matter and spirit. All animals are created as *nefesh chaya* – living souls: the most creaturely of creatures has something of the spiritual contained within it. Humanity goes one closer to God's spirit by receiving *nishmat chayim* – living spirit (Gen. 2.7), but at the same time, the bodily essence of the human; dust of the earth is also emphasized.

In his 'Word made flesh', the author of John's Prologue appears to be going back to biblical basics. This is his explanation of the image of God. If in Genesis humanity is created in God's image, then God must equally be in the image of humanity. Neither Philo nor wisdom literature entertain such an idea – they are too Greek in their inspiration. But this, John's most Christian statement of all, might also be his most Jewish!

Judaism has moved on a long way since the first century, and so has Christianity. But in the Prologue to John's Gospel we may have an example of how the two faiths once met in a common language and common ideas. In today's climate of dialogue and tolerance, we can look back at those common roots and study together those sympathetic texts on both sides of the Testament divide.

Notes

1. Many of the ideas in this article derive from classes and conversations with the late J. A. T. Robinson, Cambridge 1976.
2. The translation is that of the Revised Standard Version, second edition 1971. The verses describing John the Baptist have been omitted, as they are not relevant for the purposes of this article.
3. Quoted from Judith Hunt, *The Prologue to John's Gospel*, Lancaster 1969 (unpublished).
4. Translation from R. H. Charles, *The Apocrypha and Pseudepigrapha of the Old Testament*, Oxford University Press 1913.

Christian Influences on the Reading of the Prophets

Michael Hilton

It is now common for religious thinkers to recognize that Jesus was a Jew and that the origins of Christianity are rooted in Judaism. Just as important is the way in which the church has borrowed from the synagogue over the centuries – not only the Bible, but the use of the psalms in worship, the development of the eucharist from Passover and Sabbath rituals, and in many other ways. The remarkable rediscovery of Hebrew by Christian Reformation scholars in Germany, Holland and England required rabbinic input and help. In modern times, the Passover Seder, with the help of Jews, has found its way into many churches.

Less well known, but equally important, is the influence of Christianity on Judaism.[1] In the ancient world such influences were always attempts to combat Christian doctrine: arguments were intense in a world with active competition between the two faiths for allegiance and membership. In medieval and modern times the situation has been more complex, but Jewish-Christian dialogue continued to focus on the discussion of scriptural texts. For the Hebrew Bible is the common book of Jews and Christians, a scripture debated and argued over for 2000 years. Throughout the centuries, Jewish responses to Christian claims have influenced Jewish interpretations of Scripture. This article examines one small aspect of these debates, the effect of which lives on in synagogues today.

On Saturday morning in the synagogue, the contrast between the reading from the Torah and the reading from the prophets is immediately apparent. The Torah is read from a manuscript scroll, which is wrapped in a finely decorated mantle and adorned with silver. It is processed round the synagogue with great ceremony. Worshippers consider it a high honour to be called up to the reading to say the blessings before and after a section is read. In most synagogues, the scroll is read by a professional rabbi or cantor, or some person the community wishes to honour – a barmitzvah or batmitzvah, a bride or groom, and at the festival of Simchat Torah chatanim chosen by the congregation to honour two of their members. (In Orthodox synagogues, all honours are offered only to men.)

By contrast, the reading from the prophets (known as the haftarah) seems almost an afterthought. It is read from a book instead of a scroll, and the only ceremony is the chanting of one blessing before and one or more afterwards. Although it is an honour to be asked to read the haftarah, in Orthodox synagogues the reader is called up to the Torah beforehand, as if to emphasize that the haftarah is a mere adjunct. The very word haftarah means conclusion, dismissal. Traditionally, the whole of the Torah is read in the yearly cycle (a few passages more than once), but only a tiny fraction of the prophetic books is read, and the readings are very much shorter than the prescribed sections of the Torah. The Babylonian Talmud (Megillah 23a) mentions at least 21 verses, while Talmud Soferim 14.1 prescribes 22 verses, one for each of seven men called to the reading of the Torah, plus one for the cantor of the synagogue.

The wording of blessings said before and after the reading of the haftarah also emphasizes that reading the prophets is second in importance to the Torah:

> Before: who has chosen the Torah, and Moses your servant and prophets of truth and righteousness.
>
> And after: For the Torah, and for the Service and for the prophets . . .

In Christian practice, by contrast, it is the first reading, from the Old Testament, which is of lesser importance. It may be followed by one or more readings from the New Testament. In the Catholic tradition, the reading from the Gospel is always read by the priest (or his deputy) in person, thus highlighting its importance over the other readings. It is the New Testament, not the Hebrew Bible, which is the kernel of the Christian faith. Church liturgies are very diverse, but most centre on preaching the gospel.

When was the reading from the prophets introduced into Jewish tradition? When I was at Leo Baeck College I was taught the traditional explanation that at the time of the Maccabees, when Antiochus IV Epiphanes outlawed the reading of the Torah (I Macc. 1.56), the Jews turned to the prophetic books instead. Much to my surprise, I recently discovered that there is no ancient evidence for this theory at all. Elbogen[2] attributes it to Elijah Levita (1469–1549). The reading of the prophets is mentioned in the Mishnah, but the earliest historical evidence for it can be found in Luke's Gospel, Chapter 4, where it is recorded that Jesus read Isaiah 61. 1–2 in the synagogue at Nazareth.[3]

The Christian Scriptures are now recognized as a valuable source for the history of some Jewish practices and customs, but must not be read uncritically. Luke was certainly a Gentile: in all probability he never visited Palestine, and his knowledge of Jewish practice came from the Diaspora. There is little evidence for the existence of synagogues in Palestine in the first century.[4] It may be that the haftarah (and indeed the synagogue itself) had its origins in the Diaspora, for the purpose of educating Greek-speaking Jews.

When Luke wrote his Gospel and Acts (where a haftarah is also mentioned), Christian groups were clearly established. They seized on many prophetic texts to show that Jesus had come 'to fulfil the Scripture'. The rabbis would have good reason to wish to present a different argument. Ever since the rise of Christianity, the prophetic books have provided ample material for debate between Jews and Christians. It is possible that the very origin of the reading of the haftarah comes from such debates. The Aramaic term for the haftarah is *ashlamta*, and it has been suggested that this indicates the reading is a 'fulfilment' of the Torah of Moses.[5] Another theory is that the word haftarah corresponds to the Latin *missa*, Mass, which also means 'dismissal'.[6] This Latin term was used by Catholics to designate the eucharist, when the communicants shared in the bread and wine. Just as the synagogue service ended with the words of the prophets, so the church concluded with 'the word made flesh'. Which of the two terms was used first remains a mystery.

So we do not know for certain how the haftarah began; nor do we know when the readings began to form a regular cycle. Although the Mishnah, the Tosefta and the Talmud mention a few specific haftarot for special sabbaths and festivals, the earliest full lists of readings which we have come from the Cairo Genizah. The custom was to read the Torah over a three-year cycle in Palestine, but in one year in Babylon.[7] As one haftarah was linked to each section of the Torah, this gives us over 154 readings in the Palestinian tradition, 54 in the Babylonian. What influenced the choice of readings? We have only the barest of information. The Talmud tells us (Megillah 29b) only that the reading was chosen to resemble or be linked to the Torah reading.

But often the connection is tenuous. The researcher needs to examine the lists of readings quite closely to see if other reasons are involved. Lajos (Ludwig) Venetianer (1867–1922) was a Hungarian rabbi who was a long-forgotten pioneer in studies of Christian influences on Judaism. Like many Leo Baeck College lecturers today, he combined work in the congregational rabbinate with seminary lecturing and writing: for twenty-five years he served as a professor at the Landesrabbinerschule in Budapest and the principal rabbi of the nearby town of Ujpest. His article 'Ursprung und Bedeutung der Propheten-Lektionen' was published in *Zeitschrift der Deutschen Morgenländischen Gesellschaft* in 1909, and runs to nearly 70 pages. Venetianer suggested that a major factor in the selection of the haftarot was the desire of Jewish apologists to counter Christian claims during the first three centuries of Christianity. The article contained a detailed comparison of church and synagogue lectionaries. Unfortunately, Venetianer was not rigorous enough in the dating of his evidence. In particular, he based his article on the Catholic lectionary of his own day, without thinking that church readings might well have been subject to change over the centuries. The mistakes he made have meant that his article lies neglected and unread.

In 1959 Eric Werner rediscovered and re-examined the evidence put forward by Venetianer in his book *The Sacred Bridge: The Interdependence of Liturgy and Music in Synagogue and Church during the First Millennium*. Werner had access to a wide range of early church lectionaries. Werner found that although many of Venetianer's conjectures were wild, others could be corroborated. In particular Venetianer had accurately pointed to the links between passages connected with various prophetic readings in the church which are also found in the midrash known as Pesikta Rabbati, a collection of sermons now thought to have been complied around the ninth century. Some passages in this midrash are clearly attacks on Christianity. For example, in Piska 23.1 the nations of the world are criticized for neglect of the Sabbath, and Jeremiah 10.8 is interpreted to mean, 'The wooden emblem (i.e. the cross) by which they are instructed is no more than vapour'.

Venetianer discovered that in its discussions of several haftarah passages, Pesikta Rabbati brings quotations from the psalms which are read in churches on the same date as the same readings from the prophets. Though his examples are trivial enough, there are several which seem convincing, and the possibility of Christian influence is thus established. Christian practice must have influenced either the choice of the haftarah itself, or its exposition by the preachers quoted in the midrash.

An examination of the haftarot read today shows that the Jewish-Christian debate may sometimes have influenced the choice of reading in two opposite ways. Sometimes, a particular text may have been chosen to allow a preacher to 'correct' interpretations given by the church. But sometimes, it seems likely that texts known to be widely used by the church were deliberately avoided. It may be that these two different reactions to Christianity come from different times and/or places, where different attitudes may have prevailed. Some examples follow.

Many passages from Deutero-Isaiah are read in synagogues today in the seven weeks leading from Tisha B'Av up to Rosh

Hashanah. This short series is especially important, for it forms the oldest fixed week-to-week group of prophetic readings still in use.[8] However, the two verses read by Jesus in Nazareth are unaccountably omitted. Haftarah Ki Tavo ends at the end of Isaiah 60, and Nitzavim begins the following week at Isaiah 61.10. This suggests the possibility that the first part of Isaiah 61 was omitted from the synagogue readings because of its association with Jesus. The omission is particularly surprising because it is a text with practical halachic implications: this was one of the texts used to derive the duty of *pidyon shivuyyim* – the ransoming of captives. After the Jewish revolts against Rome in early Christian times, many would have been sold as slaves had not the Jewish communities redeemed them. Another known omission is Isaiah 52.13–53. 12 – the 'suffering servant' passage. This omission is the more startling because the following passage, Isaiah 54, is read twice (*Ki Tetze* and *Noach*).

However, other texts associated with Christian interpretations were not omitted by the synagogue. The rabbis seem to have taken particular trouble to include Isaiah 9. 5–6 ('unto us a son is born') by adding it on to the end of haftarah Yitro: we continue to include these verses even though the preceding chapter is now omitted.[9] This is read on the same Sabbath as the Exodus version of the Ten Commandments and the account of the giving of Torah at Sinai. Another controversial text is Ezekiel 37, the valley of the dry bones, read on the Sabbath during the week of Passover. This is found in many early Christian lectionaries for Holy Saturday, the day most likely to correspond. This text, dealing as it does with resurrection, may be thought more appropriate to a festival of resurrection than to one of liberation. It may well be that the Christian choice of the reading preceded the Jewish – the synagogue wished to demonstrate that Ezekiel could be interpreted in a way appropriate to rabbinic Judaism, demonstrating God's future redemption of a suffering people. The explanation that Ezekiel 37 is read on Passover because the resurrection of the dead will take place during Nisan is found no earlier than the ninth century.[10]

Haftarah Parah, which is read approximately three weeks

before the Passover festival, is taken from the previous chapter of Ezekiel (36. 16–38) and deals with the theme of repentance:

> A new heart also will I give you, and a new spirit will I put within you; and I will take away the stony heart out of your flesh, and I will give you a heart of flesh.[11]

This haftarah is quoted in the Day of Atonement liturgy: the connection with the coming Passover festival is tenuous. The time of year when the passage is read marks the Christian penitential season, not the Jewish. The church transferred many readings from the autumn season in the Jewish calendar to the period of Lent and of Easter.[12] This may have influenced the rabbis to transfer this passage to the spring season.

The name *shabbat haggadol* ('the great sabbath') is used for the sabbath before the festival of Passover. There are several theories about the origin of its name: one is that it displays the influence of the Greek church, which called Holy Saturday the Great Sabbath (*Sabbaton megalon*). One church lectionary preserves Malachi 3 as the reading: the same text is used in the synagogue on this special sabbath.[13] This reading is also concerned with the theme of repentance.

Another text from Malachi (1.1–2.7) is read as haftarah Toledot, the prophetic reading which accompanies the stories of the birth and upbringing of the twins Esau and Jacob. The rabbis frequently viewed Esau as a symbol of the enemies of the Jews, including Christians. Part of this passage (Mal. 1.10–12) was frequently cited by Christians of the first centuries to support their claim of the superiority of their cult to the Jewish religion.[14] Perhaps its use as a haftarah represents an attempt to reclaim the text for the Jewish community.

The third blessing recited after the reading of the haftarah includes a specific prayer for the coming of the Messiah. Texts linked with messianism have formed a crucial part of the Jewish-Christian debate: indeed, it is likely that messianic ideas have been kept alive in both faiths by the Jewish-Christian debate. In effect, the reader here asks for a true fulfilment of the messianic hope of the prophets, not the false dawn the rabbis saw in

Christianity. Some have seen also a debate with Christianity in the words which follow, where God is asked to ensure that no stranger will sit on the throne of David. Another theory is that the wording reflects a debate between Jews of Babylon and Palestine: Babylonian Jews were proud of the Davidic ancestry of the *resh galuta* ('Head of the Exile'), the officially recognized head of their community. In his very full account of the haftarah blessings in his book *The Sabbath Service*, B. S. Jacobson ponders why the reading of the prophets is adorned with so many more blessings than the reading of the Torah itself.

> One answer readily comes to mind, if we accept the premise that the Haftarah was originally instituted as a demonstrative refutation of those sectaries who denied the sanctity of the Prophetic Books (279).

This theory was first proposed by R. Judah Leib Maimon (Fishman) (1875–1962), who considered the haftarah to be originally a polemic against the Samaritans who rejected the Davidic monarchy and hope for its restoration.

But if there was danger in the Samaritans' rejection of the Prophets, how much more so in the Christians, who accepted the sanctity of the prophetic books but used them to justify their own claims to the truth. There is ample evidence that the meaning of prophetic passages was debated vigorously between Jews and Christians from the second century onwards. The haftarah therefore gave a text for the week on which the Jewish preacher could base his remarks. The blessings afterwards reminded the people of a distinctively Jewish hope – the return to Zion and the restoration of the Kingdom of David.

These remarks on Christian influences on the haftarah are no more than a few brief introductory remarks on a subject which deserves much fuller consideration, and a full comparison of early lectionaries. There is, I am sure, much more waiting to be discovered by a diligent researcher into this topic. A fuller understanding of the reasons for the choice of our prophetic readings would be of help to those who wish to introduce new ones. The Reform Synagogues of Great Britain has returned to the idea of a three-year cycle for the reading of the Torah, and has taken the opportunity to experiment with new *haftarot*. An attempt is made to link thematically each reading from the prophets with the corresponding section of the Torah.[15] It seems to me that it would be equally in accordance with Jewish tradition to consider what scope the choice of each reading gives to a preacher. And it may be that in an ecumenical age we should consider how the choice of prophetic reading could contribute to our modern dialogue with Christians, to which Leo Baeck College has made such an important contribution.

Notes

1. For Christian influences on Judaism, see Michael Hilton, *The Christian Effect on Jewish Life*, SCM Press 1994.
2. Ismar Elbogen, *Jewish Liturgy. A Comprehensive History*, JPSA Philadelphia and Jerusalem 1993, 143.
3. See my full discussion in Michael Hilton and Gordian Marshall, *The Gospels and Rabbinic Judaism. A Study Guide*, SCM Press 1988, 43–51.
4. Hilton, *Christian Effect* (n.1), 213–14.
5. Charles Perrot, 'The Reading of the Bible in the Ancient Synagogue', in *Mikra. Text, Translation, Reading and Interpretation of the Hebrew Bible in Ancient Judaism and Early Christianity*, ed. M. J. Mulder, Compendia Rerum Iudaicarum ad Novum Testamentum, Section 2, Vol. 1, Assen/Maastricht and Philadelphia 1988, 153.
6. See Elbogen, *Jewish Liturgy* (n.2), 143, and Eric Werner, *The Sacred Bridge*, London and New York 1959, 95.
7. The earliest known reference to the contrasting Palestinian and Babylonian customs is in the Babylonian Talmud Megillah 29b.
8. The midrash known as Pesikta de Rav Kahana (complied in fifth-century Palestine) is based on this group of readings: see Perrot, 'Reading of the Bible' (n.5), 147, and Raymond Scheindlin's remarks in Elbogen, *Jewish Liturgy* (n.2), 145 and 425.
9. The controversial verses are mentioned by Maimonides in his list of readings.
10. Rav Hai Gaon (see Werner, *Sacred Bridge* [n.6]), 100 n. 109.
11. Ezek. 36. 26.
12. Werner, *Sacred Bridge* (n.6), 75.
13. Ibid., 86–8.
14. See Charles Bobertz, in Harold W. Attridge and Gohei Hata (eds.),

Eusebius, Christianity and Judaism, Studia Post-Biblica 42, E. J. Brill, Leiden 1992, 200.

15. *Calendar of Torah and Haftarah Readings 5755–5757*, Reform Synagogues of Great Britain, London 1994. The calendar is edited by Rabbi Dr Jonathan Romain.

Spinoza – A Jewish Heretic for Our Time?

Reuven Silverman

Progressive Judaism has long been associated with Spinoza's thought, especially with his critique of the doctrine of the divine revelation of Scripture. How strongly may that association be upheld, and how far may Spinoza's ideas in general be accommodated within a Progressive Jewish framework?

In his *Response to Modernity*, Michael Meyer describes how Reform Judaism had its genesis amongst nineteenth-century German Jewish thinkers who sought to harmonize their expression of Judaism with contemporary modes of thought to make it intellectually respectable.[1] Among their formative influences was Spinoza. Baruch Spinoza (1632–1677) was the most trenchant critic of religion in general and of Judaism in particular, replacing the personal transcendent Creator with the God that is another name for Nature. For this he was, and is still by some, regarded as an atheist in disguise. His critique of Judaism, as Meyer notes, was for the most part unacceptable even to the most radical Reformers. Nevertheless, Spinoza's pioneering historical approach to Bible was most influential. The fact that its influence did not extend as far as his philosophy suggests that Spinozism is beyond the boundaries of Progressive Judaism. Why should that be so?

Spinoza's 'heresies'

Spinoza was excommunicated (in the Jewish sense of being ostracized) in 1656 by the rabbis of Amsterdam, for heterodox ideas which were not spelled out by his accusers. At the age of twenty-three he had not yet developed his philosophy. From contemporary documents it would appear that he then claimed that everything physical is as divine as everything spiritual and that this is supported by the Bible. He rejected all notions of the supernatural, such as angels. He held that, in Hebraic thinking, the soul is synonymous with life.[2]

Spinoza's mature philosophy, arising out of these ideas, is a kind of pantheism. The constraints of space here permit only the most simplified summary. He begins his main work, the *Ethics*,[3] with a definition of God as the self-caused Being, the Substance of the universe, independent of everything for its existence. God is that from which everything derives its being, since everything is a 'mode' of the one Substance. God is not merely the sum-total of all that exists, for that would be a finite entity, but is also the process by which everything exists, which is infinite. God has an infinity of attributes of which we know only two, 'thought' and 'extension' (roughly equivalent to mind and matter).

For many modern religious Jews, this approach to God seems too impersonal. Martin (1878–1965) Buber, a theological mentor for both Jews and Christians, whilst strongly influenced by Spinoza's naturalism, taught that a third attribute of 'personality' must be added for God to be addressable.[4] Franz Rosenzweig (1886–1929) and Leo Baeck (1873–1956), also erstwhile Spinoza devotees, preserved the traditional relationship between God, man and world. In Spinoza too, man relates to God, not as an individual, rather as the One in which everything is contained. Hence Spinoza still speaks for those who cannot understand a one-to-one relationship with God, but can appreciate a one-to-All relationship.

Human beings, like all natural phenomena in Spinoza's thinking, are modes of God. We are distinguished by our intellectual powers, the capacity to have 'true' or 'adequate' ideas, that is, ideas which correspond with their objects. The highest level of thought, or 'intuition', is cognition of the interconnectedness of all things. It is the knowledge of God. Below that is 'reason', which includes the understanding of mathematics, logic and causality. The latter helps man to master his passions. The lowest level is 'imagination', which covers basic sense-perception, opinion, and false or confused ideas. Unfortunately, for the religiously committed, this would seem to undervalue the creative power of imagination. Spinoza did not set out to abolish religion; his intention was to purge religion of 'superstition' to make for a freer, dogma-less society.

Spinoza developed a philosophy which he believed to be better designed than religion to achieve personal and social salvation. It was an entirely deterministic system where God, man and everything else in the universe function in accordance with fixed laws. There could be no exceptions to natural law, no miracles, no ultimate purposes. Freedom could not mean the choice to alter anything, since everything can be explained by physical and psychological causes. In modern terms this translates into the determinism of genetics and environment, or 'nature' and 'nurture', but it seems to conflict with the freedom of choice which must be assumed if there is to be moral responsibility. Spinoza, nevertheless, does have a concept of freedom, defined as acting out of a full consciousness of one's nature, and using one's reason to master passions, that is, emotional responses to external compulsion. It is a paradoxical freedom in which we are empowered to realize our true potential.[5] Only God could be free in the sense of totally independent, since by Spinoza's definition God is not a separate entity, but rather the One that embraces all.

From the absolute universality of Spinoza's God it follows that the knowledge of God cannot be restricted to any particular revelation. The ultimate goal of knowledge is to understand our interconnectedness with all things. It is at once a scientific and a philosophical task. It is both a knowledge and love of God. This is presented as the goal of human existence, bringing happiness or 'blessedness'. What stood in the way of the religious goals which Spinoza reformulates philosophically were superstitions and prejudices threatening the welfare and peace of society. At their root was the error of thinking that any person or group might be in the possession of a special revelation or providential favour.[6]

The Hebrew prophets, the subject with which he begins his *Theological-Political Treatise*,[7] were not endowed with any superhuman intellectual qualities; they displayed no special insights into the nature of God and the world. Their sole great contribution was their message of justice and righteousness. They were not superior to the prophets of other peoples. They excelled in the use of their powers of imagination, which they displayed through their visions. As in all things, Spinoza relies entirely on the *prima facie* evidence of the Bible, and tries to understand it on its own terms. He accepts that Moses was, as the Bible tells us, the greatest of all prophets, but he was essentially a lawgiver, and the law of Israel was entirely limited to its times. It was centred upon a theocracy, the priesthood and Temple, adapted to the agricultural conditions of a small strip of territory. It could not be an 'eternal law', since this term could only be applied to the laws of nature.

The idea of a special purpose for the Jewish people, the concept of the vocation or election of Israel, is dismissed by Spinoza as imaginary, prejudiced and harmful to human relations. If ancient Israel had any special quality at all, it was in its social legislation, which was a temporal phenomenon. It is interesting that Spinoza, despite this extremely narrow view of the Jewish *raison d'être*, does in fact endorse a predominant Jewish affirmation that Judaism is essentially for Jews and is related to the land of Israel. He ventures to predict that the Jewish people may one day re-establish their own state. His is not a missionizing faith. The scope of Judaism emerges from this as very much limited in time and space. The universal element in Judaism, especially its ethical wisdom, is nonetheless valued by Spinoza. He praises the universal ethics of the prophets and of Jewish wisdom literature.

In accordance with his philosophy, Spinoza regards the whole Bible as a natural phenomenon, a product of human history. It must be studied as any other human product. Every text must be interpreted against the background of its times. For this purpose its likely date and authorship has to be determined. Its language, literary structure and style have to be analysed. Following these and other scientific criteria, Spinoza set about establishing his own analysis of Scripture. His *Theological-Political Treatise* was thus to become a chief cornerstone of the modern discipline of critical Bible study for all non-fundamentalist Jews and Christians.

A severe limitation on the value of Spinoza for modern Jews is his dismissal of rabbinical interpretations of the Torah. He finds that they read too much into the text. The same is true of all attempts to allegorize or to find philosophical wisdom in the Scriptures. In this respect Maimonides comes in for bitter criticism from Spinoza. To be sure, he is even-handed in applying this criticism to theologians of all faiths. It is understandable, although perhaps not condonable, that his principle target is Judaism because, after all, this was his background from which he suffered restrictions on his freedom of thought. Had he been living in later times, he might have been able to remain within the Jewish fold.

'Progressive revelation'

Spinoza's Bible criticism effectively divested Torah of its classical cloak of rabbinical authority, which had traditionally been traced back to Moses at Sinai. He also refuted the attempts of medieval Jewish philosophers to harmonize the Scriptures with reason. The concept of a gradual unfolding of divine truth independent of Scripture has been traced back to Spinoza. This is what is commonly called 'progressive revelation'.

Michael Meyer shows how Spinoza's idea of a progression from the biblical vision of God's revelation to Moses on Sinai carved in stone to the revelation to modern individuals through their hearts and minds was taken up by Reform Jewish theologians. It was espoused most fervently by the eighteenth-century Enlightenment Christian thinker Gotthold Ephraim Lessing (1729–81),[8] who saw it as an endorsement of the Christian claim that the Gospels had superseded the Old Testament. The Jewish Reformers countered this with a strong assertion that Judaism had progressed beyond the Bible and that divine revelation continued to occur through the minds of Jews ever since. In this way Reform Judaism adapted the arguments of Spinoza and Lessing in its own favour.

The concept of progressive revelation has been criticized as arrogantly implying that modern Jews have advanced to a stage superior to that of their ancestors.[9] Lessing certainly saw ancient

Israel as a childhood stage and subsequent history as leading towards maturity in the adult church. Judaism is an eternal childhood. This idea stemmed from Spinoza's assertion that:

> Religion was imparted to the early Hebrews as a law written down, because they were at that time in the condition of children, but afterwards Moses (Deut. 30.6) and Jeremiah (31.33) predicted a time when the Lord should write His law in their hearts.[10]

For Spinoza, the divine law in our hearts was the revelation of reason, or 'intuition'. Many Reform Jews have their own version of this idea. They would not concur with Spinoza's interpretation of God's law in our hearts which makes most of the Bible redundant. Reform Judaism is based upon Torah and rabbinic interpretation, which Spinoza rejected. His main argument in the above quotation was directed against the worship of the letter of the Bible. He did, it is true, limit the validity of Jewish law to the period of the first and second Jewish commonwealths. This view was taken up by some early Reformers, principally Samuel Holdheim (1806–1860). He was in fact the only founding father of Reform who accepted Spinoza's critique of Jewish law.[11]

How far was Lessing's view actually held by Spinoza? This question is crucial for determining the extent to which Reform Jewish thinking was dependent upon Spinoza. First of all, Spinoza did not advocate any version of Christianity. It is true that he asserted that the message of the apostles was more universal than that of the prophets. He also contrasted God's 'face-to-face' revelation to Moses with what he regarded as the more intimate 'mind-to-mind' revelation of Jesus, not dependent on visions. In this, however, Jesus only represented what any man was capable of through pure thought. Spinoza himself did not hold a doctrine of Progressive Revelation, if what we mean by that term is a process by which sets of ideas supersede each other in time on an evolving scale. Spinoza did not hold the idea that God issues progressively superior versions of the truth throughout history. To be sure, he frequently asserts that the ancient Hebrews, as their miracle accounts show, were limited by their inadequate understanding of the causes of natural phenomena.

They were thus hampered in achieving his goal of knowledge and love of God through scientific understanding of all things natural: 'the more we know of individual things, the more we know of God'. On the other hand, the capacity to find the revelation of God within was always present in the thinking of the prophets. It is a revelation of practical ethical teaching, however, not of metaphysical theory. It is, moreover, eternal truth which, by definition, cannot be superseded. Philosophical ideas cannot be found in Scripture. They are of a different order from religious ideas and hence cannot be part of a progression emerging from them. Moreover, Scripture is the 'word of God' for him in so far as it is a natural, human phenomenon. Man is part of nature, hence part of God.

The human mind, for Spinoza, is a mode of 'thought' which is an attribute of God. It is in this respect that Spinoza holds that the soul (another term for mind) is immortal. Our minds bear the 'true handwriting of God, sealed with His own seal, namely the idea of Himself, the image of His own divinity, as it were'.[12] The only admissible idea of God for Spinoza is his own. If one is unable to subscribe to it, the word of God is still accessible to us, since it also consists in 'charity and sincerity of heart'. Such virtues would qualify as the 'word of God', since they are tenable by the light of reason and tend towards the preservation of human life. Spinoza holds, however, that this is not his own opinion alone. It is borne out by the Bible itself. The Prophets and the Apostles proclaim the same message that God's word is internal. Their religious teaching was nonetheless something quite separate from philosophy. Spinoza does not attack it. His criticisms are primarily reserved for the ecclesiastical authority of his day, whether rabbinical, pontifical or Calvinist, which claims exclusive rights to interpret Scripture with the ultimate aim of establishing theocratic rule. For Spinoza, it was only through its universal elements that Judaism, like any religion, could make for a peaceful society.

Spinoza's value today

Whilst Spinoza's philosophy *in toto* cannot be said to have had any significant effect on Progressive Judaism, only on some individuals, the indirect influence of his critique of revelation has been considerable. His scientific Bible study helped to pioneer the whole modern discipline. Principally this means the rejection of the 'documentary doctrine' of revelation, the verbatim dictation of a divine text to man. In place of that is the historical study of Bible as literature. This is not cold analysis alone, but rather analysis accompanied by the search for ethical teachings for the enhancement of life and the peace of society. Scripture is not the sole source of truth and meaning, which may be discovered anywhere. Spinoza's rejection of ceremonial and of historical and mythical narratives as ways to discover God, is, however, the main factor that continues to alienate him from all expressions of Judaism except the purely secular.

Spinoza's conception of knowing God is a philosophical ideal, not a religious programme. Where he gives recognition to religious teachings he does not say that such teachings have progressed towards greater perfection throughout history from biblical times. Spinoza's project was to reformulate vague religious concepts in a more precisely stated form and to re-evaluate the essential teachings of sacred books. Instead of the haughty sounding notion of progressive revelation, such continuous re-evaluation and reformulation would also seem to be the true task of Progressive Judaism. If there is any progression, it is towards completion of a task set by tradition, perfection of our understanding of what is already there and putting it into practice. Here, there may be a sense in which we can draw on Spinoza. 'Perfection', in the special way he used the term, was another word for 'reality'. The two terms are equivalent, since nature cannot be other than it is. Individuals become more perfect, the more they realize their potential, the more they achieve that which tends towards their self-preservation with an active consciousness of their nature, and not passively in response to external compulsion. This is true freedom, the only freedom that can exist in Spinoza's deterministic theory. The idea translates well into Progressive Jewish theology as an endeavour to preserve Jewish values through discovery of what corresponds best to current realities.

Notes

1. M. Meyer, *Response to Modernism*, Oxford University Press, New York 1988, 62–5.
2. A. Wolf, *The Oldest Biography of Spinoza*, New York 1927.
3. E. Curley, *The Collected Works of Spinoza* I, Princeton University Press 1985.
4. M. Buber, on Spinoza, Sabbetai Zvi and the Baal Shem Tov, in *The Origin and Meaning of Hassidism*, Horizon Books, New York 1966.
5. I argue this in Chapter 4 of my *Baruch Spinoza – Outcast Jew, Universal Sage*, Science Reviews 1995.
6. Emil Fackenheim, *To Mend the World*, New York 1982, criticizes Spinoza's universalism as supportive of the philosophical climate which eventually produced the Holocaust. See the Epilogue to my *Baruch Spinoza* (n.4), where I discuss this with regard to inter-faith relations.
7. B. Spinoza, *Tractatus Theologico-Politicus*, E. J. Brill, Leiden 1989.
8. G. E. Lessing, 'The Education of the Human Race', in H. Chadwick (ed. and trans.), *Lessing's Theological Writings*, A. & C. Black 1983.
9. See M. Ish-Horowicz, *Halachah – Orthodoxy and Reform*, RSGB 1994.
10. *Tractatus Theologico-Politicus* (n.7), ch. 12, p.205.
11. Solomon Formstecher (1808–1889), who propounded an idea of progressive revelation, rejected Spinoza. So did Abraham Geiger (1810–1874), despite his admiration for Spinoza's liberalism and his Spinozistic belief that 'revelation was the point of contact between human reason and the deep underlying ground of all things'.
12. *Tractatus Theologico-Politicus* (n.7), 208–9.

1956 And All That

Michael Leigh

Eleven years after the Second World War, Britain had practically returned to normal, though in the Anglo-Jewish community the effects of the Holocaust were still evident. Jewish refugees from the Continent and 'displaced persons', as they were called, were still trying to resettle their lives. Amongst them were rabbis and intellectuals whom Harold Reinhart, the Senior Minister of the West London Synagogue, helped in a variety of practical ways, including securing professional positions for them. In the Council Room of his synagogue a group met regularly on Mondays, including Leo Baeck, to hear lectures in the tradition of Berlin of old. Amongst this group were many graduates of the former Liberal seminary there, the Hochschule, and the Breslau Theological Seminary. They were to have an influence on the subsequent foundation of the Leo Baeck College.

Reform in Britain in the 1950s was just over a century old, but lacked the size and intellectual depth of its European counterpart. It had a vague centralist theological position, and in 1903 one of Reinhart's predecessors, Rev. Morris Joseph, had written a volume on Judaism, *Judaism as Creed and Life*, based squarely on Rabbinism, criticized by early Reform, in which he 'sought a middle way between an unbending orthodoxy . . . and the radicalism which lightly cuts itself adrift from Jewish history and tradition'. However, by now the continental rabbis had injected something of a new lease of life into Reform. A Reform Assembly of Ministers, a religious Court and sixteen Reform congregations were now in place, all encouraged by Harold Reinhart. Rabbi Ignaz Maybaum from Berlin, now a London rabbi, had started to publish works of Jewish theology influenced by the Holocaust and the creation of the State of Israel. By 1956 there was a small but growing movement which presented itself as holding the middle ground in Anglo-Jewry.

It was now obvious that there was a challenge which British Reform would have to face squarely. From where would new spiritual leaders and teachers come, especially if it was set to grow? Hitherto rabbis had been supplied from some who had left the United Synagogue, a few from America and, as we have seen, an influx from the Continent. The supply was uncertain and hit-and-miss, especially as two promising rabbinical candidates had gone to America for training and had not come back! Furthermore, two graduates had been training for the Reform rabbinate (Lionel Blue and myself) at the Hebrew Department of University College, London, and had been having some Talmud lessons under the auspices of the Society for Jewish Study. There was pressure to provide rabbinical training for them. Memories of the Hochschule and the Breslau Seminary, tragically destroyed, were in the minds of some of their graduates who were now working in Britain. It was not just institutions that had been destroyed, but an embodiment of Jewish piety and open scholarship in the European mould associated in the case of the Berlin Hochschule with such names as Ismar Elbogen, Franz Rosenzweig, Hermann Cohen and, of course, Leo Baeck. Many felt that it was almost a duty not to let the tradition which the Hochschule represented die. Here was an opportunity to recreate in England, in different circumstances, another college, a centre for Jewish study rising from the ashes of the Holocaust, yet another symbol of the undying nature of Jewish existence.

The establishment of any new educational institution usually needs someone with a sense of vision and the drive that must go with it. Rabbi Dr Werner van der Zyl of the North Western Reform Synagogue in London provided this. He had arrived in England shortly before the war and became an established rabbi after a period of teaching and welfare work with Jewish refugees during the war. He was himself a graduate of the Hochschule and a great admirer of his former teacher, Leo Baeck, who now attended his congregation. Isaac Meyer Wise had been the driving force behind the establishment of the American Hebrew Union

College in Cincinnati in 1875, and Solomon Schechter re-established the Conservative Jewish Theological Seminary in New York in 1901. Van der Zyl planned and worked hard for the foundation of the College, and all credit must go to him. He was supported by scholar rabbis and also Leonard G. Montefiore, a benefactor and enthusiast for the scheme. Harold Reinhart had hoped, naively, that one institution, Jews College, would be sufficient to train all Anglo-Jewish rabbis, whatever their denomination. Some, like Albert Polack, wanted the new college to be at Oxford or Cambridge.

And so on 30 September 1956, at a ceremony at the West London Synagogue, the Jewish Theological College – a grand title – was opened after a long period of academic and financial preparation. Professor Leon Roth, in an opening speech, pointed to the failure of the Alexandrian Jewish community in the years before the Common Era, because it had no school to reproduce itself.

Lessons were started immediately and were given in the large Old Council Room of the West London Synagogue (incidentally the Jewish Theological Seminary had started in 1887 in the synagogue of Shearit Israel in New York). In this massive room there were two students with five lecturers. The quality of the courses was extremely high and the syllabus was based on that of the Berlin Hochschule. The staff included Dr Aryeh Dorfler, who taught Talmud and liturgy, with the former course figuring prominently. Dr Erwin Rosenthal from Cambridge prepared in great detail specialized lectures within seventeenth-century Jewish history. Dr Joseph Heller, recently retired from University College, London, lectured brilliantly on Jewish philosophy. Because of the small number of students, I recollect that the work was very intense. However, no instruction was given in 'practical rabbinics' like counselling, and participation by the growing number of students in pastoral work was discouraged on the grounds that all the time was required for study. The College was a Reform institution in 1956, and the Liberal movement joined the project later in 1964. Rabbi Leo Baeck died in November 1956, a month after the College's foundation, and its name was changed, in his honour, to Leo Baeck College.

In the whole context of the growth of British Reform some years later, the reviewer of a volume of essays in the *Jewish Chronicle* (*Reform Judaism*, edited by Dow Marmur, 1973) referred to what he called 'A Second Chance for Reform'. The first had been in the nineteenth century, when Reform made little headway and soon became 'a refuge for the fashionable and assimilated', a half-truth. Now in the post-Second World War years another opportunity was presented, but this time the outlook was more propitious. 'Its spiritual leaders,' he wrote, were 'more positively Jewish and driven by a missionary zeal, and take considerable pains to remain firmly rooted in traditional Judaism with . . . Halachah (Jewish religious law) a recurrent theme.' The Reform Synagogues of Great Britain were now firmly in place and a Reform rabbinical college had been established, a positive step in the right direction. The founding of the college had been a significant step towards this 'second chance'.

The founders of the College in 1956 still lived in the world of the nineteenth-century Science of Judaism, and spoke affirmatively of objective historical study and a learning institution catering for no particular denomination. This position assumed that you could coldly stand 'outside', as it were, and that rabbis could become potential research workers in Jewish scholarship. Although the syllabus was theoretically based on this principle, in practice the emphasis changed and loosened over the years with the growing multiplicity of movements in the Jewish world and the input of lecturers from across the whole religious spectrum, from neo-Orthodox to Liberal. Furthermore, according to the current (1996) Principal of the College, Rabbi Dr Jonathan Magonet, the Holocaust had dramatically changed the situation. For many the certainties of faith were shaken in the post-war world, and there were unthought-of challenges in the areas of halachah and Jewish survival. For others, as happened previously in Jewish history, catastrophe reinforced a return to religious isolationism and fundamentalism. Magonet observes that the philosophy of the College became concerned with training rabbis towards a caring ministry for Jewish people, starting with where people actually are and coming to the sources from a more human and subjective perspective. This led to a greater emphasis on counselling training, which encouraged 'going to people before the book', as he put it, with all the theological challenges which this position presented.

The College has become a sort of academic focal point for the Reform and Liberal movements and has ordained to date 120 rabbis, including several women since 1975. These have gone mainly to pulpits in the UK but some also to the European continent, including France, Germany, Holland and Switzerland, many being students from those lands who came to London to study and then returned to the Continent qualified. Others have gone further afield, to the USA, South Africa, Australia and New Zealand. The five-year course for rabbinic ordination includes a study year in Israel, and some graduates have later chosen to settle in Israel after years in the active ministry. Of late students have been coming from Eastern Europe, especially from the former Soviet Union. The potential for the College to make a spiritual contribution in this challenging area of post-Cold War Europe is immense.

Beyond rabbinic training, the College has tried to reach a wider public. Graduates have played a role in the re-editing of Prayer Books which indirectly, through reaching a wider public, have provided insights into rabbinic and contemporary Jewish thought by means of the 'study sections' contained in them. The College provides Bachelor and Masters degree courses in Jewish subjects which give greater academic possibilities to laypeople. Furthermore, it has also been in the forefront with programmes in the fields of psychotherapy, feminism, and dialogue with Christians and Muslims.

But British Jewry has changed over the forty years since 1956. Though it is smaller, now estimated at 300,000, in many ways Jewish organization has tightened and in some areas intensified. There are far more educational and social agencies devoted to increasing a sense of Jewish identification and indeed self-preservation. Although in 1956 world Jewry was still reeling only a decade after the Holocaust, remnants present of a more relaxed Anglo-Jewish tradition were still in place. Over the years assimilation has proceeded apace. The implications of the State of Israel have become more clearly apparent. Religious institutions and movements have become more professionalized and efficient, defining their aims more clearly. And all this has been proceeding under the influence of recession and financial constraint. The Leo Baeck College has been part of this process and has made good, increasing greatly in sheer size of 'output' and multiplying its activities and possibilities.

There were no clear theological goals in 1956 beyond providing theoretically 'unlabelled' rabbis and teachers. But there was an implicit assumption that the new college would provide rabbis for Reform synagogues and possibly the non-Orthodox world in general. The approach was both religious and, as we have seen, non-fundamentalistic, though styles in teaching depended on the individual lecturers, which in turn depended on availability. These considerations obtained for many years to come. An air of 'cobbling together' hung over the College for many years, with lecturers coming and going and the syllabus undergoing constant review. What is certain is that Dr van der Zyl and the founders of 1956 could never have dreamed that forty years on, the potential which they had launched would have developed to the multi-faceted institution the College has become. Almost exactly a century after the founding of Jews' College (1855), another Anglo-Jewish seminary had opened, a challenge to the Orthodox Establishment's monopoly. A new contribution had been made to the small collection of the community's institutions devoted to Jewish learning. Above all, the ambition of the Holocaust to eradicate not only the Jewish people but the Jewish spirit could not be allowed to succeed. Rabbis and teachers would be needed to help to recreate the still stunned Jewish world, and the foundation of the College was truly, in the words uttered at the opening ceremony, 'an act of faith'.

PREPARING FOR THE FUTURE

The challenges that lie ahead

This last section prepares us for the future. Dow Marmur urges Jewry to seek a higher goal than mere survival, and formulates a theological critique by which those who have managed to outlive Hitler can ensure that Judaism outlives the threat of assimilation, too. Jonathan Romain considers the fate of British Jewry in particular, and whether it will become a distant memory or remain a vibrant reality. He looks at practical ways of tackling key issues, including that of mixed-faith marriage, and how to include and enthuse the large number of Jews on the periphery of communal life. Barbara Borts presents a task that is vital for all Jews to address: 'repairing the world', and making determined efforts to improve the condition of life around us. Moreover, she points out that this is not just a worthwhile aim but an inescapable duty. For some Jews, the main centre of attention is what is happening in Israel. This certainly applies to Michael Boyden, who has lived there for many years and tells of the particular problems that Reform Judaism faces there, but is equally forthright about the positive contribution that it can make to the life of the country. Jeffrey Newman takes up one of the most controversial aspects of recent Israeli history, the relationship between Israelis and Palestinians, and charts the remarkable progress achieved by a Jewish-Palestinian group here in Britain and its attempt to bring a religious calm to troubled political waters. A problem that is common to all people and transcends their political or religious differences is the way in which we treat the earth itself. This is Hillel Avidan's theme, and he gives a Jewish perspective to an urgent universal problem.

The Future of the Jews

Dow Marmur

Emil Fackenheim's oft-quoted assertion that it is our duty not to give Hitler a posthumous victory – and, therefore, we must survive as Jews – had a profound impact on many of us who came into active Jewish life in the 1960s. As his statement was first published around the time of the Six Day War in 1967, it gave added impetus to the charged atmosphere that prevailed then in the Jewish world. The formula brought encouragement to those determined to help protect and defend Jews in the face of renewed adversity and danger. If Israeli soldiers would declare their allegiance to the State of Israel by pledging that Masada shall not fall again, many Jewish activists in the Diaspora gave legitimacy to their work by pledging that Auschwitz shall not happen again.

Though Fackenheim's statement was intended to be religious, it was its acceptance of secular Judaism as a legitimate expression of the collective Jewish struggle for survival that caught the attention of the Jewish public at large. Though he may not have intended it, he had become one of the theologians of Jewish civil religion, which defined its primary purpose in terms of reactive survival, rather than proactive purpose. Those who wanted to be Jews without necessarily affirming Judaism found their teacher in Emil Fackenheim.

But what was very powerful in the 1960s has become largely irrelevant in the 1990s. Even those who continue to stress the importance of Jewish survival have come to realize that more is needed to safeguard the future of Judaism than merely to prove Hitler wrong. Though Fackenheim's message was essential for the generation of survivors, it is inadequate for their children. The new generation needs to know *why* it should survive before deciding *how* it should survive.[1]

The limitations of Jewish survivalist ideology, as manifest in Jewish civil religion, have been explored by Jonathan Woocher. In identifying those contemporary Jewish thinkers who helped shape the horizontal, rather than vertical – people-centred, rather than God-centred – theology, Woocher treated Fackenheim with sympathy and understanding, even when he was critical of him:

> Yet, some of its very strengths also render Fackenheim's thought somewhat problematic as public theology. Fackenheim's vision is dominated on the one hand by the Holocaust and state of Israel, and on the other by a sense of radical challenge emanating from the secularist philosophies of the modern era. It is not clear, however, whether these are in fact the starting points from which all American Jews today (and certainly all civil Jews) approach the task of defining the nature of their Jewish commitment. Insightful as it is, Fackenheim's thought is not really aimed at those Jews who live in a more prosaic world than he describes, who begin not from anguish and questioning, but from relative contentment. This does not mean that Fackenheim errs in putting forward his vision of the critical choices which the contemporary Jew must face. It means only that a civil Jewish theology must seek additional ways to focus and to elaborate the religious implications of civil Jewish faith.[2]

The implications of Woocher's analysis are behind the fresh initiatives that have come to dominate the Jewish world, particularly in the realm of education, in the closing decade of the twentieth century. As Rabbi Jonathan Sacks put it: 'The 1990s have brought the discovery that survivalism has not proved strong enough to ensure Jewish survival. A generation raised on knowledge of the Holocaust and Israel is now choosing to disaffiliate from the Jewish people at the rate of one young Jew in two.'[3]

The new call in the Jewish world is, therefore, not for *survival* but for *continuity*; not for a largely 'secular' response to Hitler, but for a more conventionally 'religious' response to the call from

Sinai. Not just, 'Don't give Hitler a posthumous victory!', but the *veshinantam levanecha* of the Shema, 'You shall teach [Torah] diligently to your children.' Fackenheim had spoken of a new commandment to be heard from between the chimneys of Auschwitz. Contemporary exponents of Judaism, of whatever denomination, plead for a return to the original 10 – or, more often, as many as possible of the 613 – commandments as heard at Sinai. They fear that the call for survival has only an impact in the present; the future requires a formula for Jewish continuity, which must be based on the affirmative content of Judaism.

Most of those who speak for Judaism today assert that traditional Jewish values, based on God and Torah, will, by definition, safeguard the existence of Israel, the people and the state. Preoccupation with survival, while neglecting God and Torah, is bound to fail, because survival depends on purpose, and only God and Torah can provide it for Judaism.

That is why secular Jews remain more concerned with Jewish survival than religious Jews; defending Israel and fighting antisemitism have become secular substitutes for Jewish religious life. But it is a futile enterprise. For, as Rabbi Sacks states, those who so loudly clamour for Jewish survival are least likely to succeed, because it is God and Torah that ensure it by providing Jewish content-continuity.

A case must therefore be made against those who minimize the importance of the Diaspora, at times even negate its legitimacy, in favour of what has been loosely described as 'the centrality of Israel'. However, though this critique makes sense – for there is no reason why any of us should live our Judaism vicariously through the Israelis, or through the Jews in the former Soviet Union by seeking to settle them in Israel – the juxtaposition itself points to a more ominous dichotomy. David Vital defines it. Whereas many regard the move toward greater affirmation of Diaspora existence as positive, he sees dangers in this 'bifurcation of Jewry'. Vital reminds us that participation in Jewish life in the Diaspora is voluntary. We can opt out at any time and, because of the decrease in antisemitism, we often do – and succeed. Thus, when Diaspora existence ceases to be precarious, it becomes ephemeral, left to our personal discretion and whim. Whether or not our sporadic excursions into Jewish life are 'religious' seems irrelevant.

Jewish existence in Israel, on the other hand, is controlled by state power. Israel affirms the Jewish nation; the Diaspora has only nebulous, and precarious, communities of vaguely concerned and interested individuals. Thus only Israel, however 'secular', can provide consistent Jewish continuity. If the Diaspora wants to have a share in it, it must seek partnership with Israel, organizing its activities and priorities in conjunction with, and with the support of, the Jewish state.

Whereas for us in the Diaspora Judaism is a matter of individual choice, for them in Israel it is a matter of collective decision. Whereas Diaspora Jews 'are subject to a sovereign power which is not and cannot be in any significant sense Jewish', Jews in Israel 'are governed by Jews, by their own people or kind'.[4] Jewish existence in the Diaspora is, therefore, not only more precarious than in Israel, but it has also become more problematic because of Israel. The attempt to divide between the secular and the religious masks a much deeper rift.

If Vital is right, as long as we stressed survival, we could affirm Israel without reservation and satisfy our needs for Jewish identity through philanthropy on its behalf, because – as Fackenheim himself and most other so-called Holocaust theologians asserted – the Jewish state is vital for Jewish survival. But once we come to speak of continuity, we need our financial resources for education and institution-building at home. This means giving less to Israel, especially now when money in the Diaspora has become scarce and Israeli economic prosperity obvious. Moreover, decrease in antisemitism here and the problematical politics associated with occupation and disengagement there make us believe that we are less emotionally and intellectually dependent on Israel.

This points to a growing division between the people of Israel – the Jewish nation in the sovereign state – and the faith of Israel, adhered to by individuals who come together in voluntary communities and often quarrel amongst themselves as to the nature of that faith. The division is dangerous, for if we are concerned for our future, it must be the future of *Jewry* no less than the future of *Judaism*, the future of Israel no less than the future of the Diaspora. To distinguish between them is to damage them both, perhaps beyond repair: Jewry without Judaism becomes like all other peoples; Judaism without Jews is reduced to a relic. Neither Jewish nationalism on its own nor Jewish antiquarianism, whether religious or academic, deserve our passion and our commitment. To plan for the future of Judaism is to assert the indivisible nature of the faith and the people of Israel.

The covenant between God and Israel, which constitutes the foundation of Judaism, celebrates the unity between faith and people. But it also has a third element: the land. The covenant assures the people of Israel that if it lives by its commitment to the God of Israel – its faith – it will be brought to the land of Israel, the Promised Land. Neither the faith of Israel nor the people of Israel can exist without the land of Israel. The dichotomy between Israel and Diaspora is false, because the land has no meaning without the people, and neither makes sense without faith in the God of Abraham, Isaac and Jacob to whom the land had been promised by God.

Secular Judaism, in Israel and in the Diaspora, is as meaningless as is the abstraction 'the Jewish religion'. The future of Judaism rests on the integration of faith, people and land, and thus the abolition of the distinction between 'religious' and 'secular' Judaism, as well as the dismantling of Vital's dichotomy between Israeli and Diaspora Jews.

Some tend to refute the stress on land as ahistorical. After all, Jews have lived for some 2000 years outside the land and managed to survive, often much better than if they had stayed at home. Exile may not have been as much a punishment as it was an opportunity. For while other peoples, ostensibly sovereign and securely landed, came and went, the Jewish people, insecure and seemingly homeless, lives on. Even when there was such a thing as Jewish sovereignty, it was often more in name than in substance. And even then, many Jews lived outside the land of Israel. Why should not Jews continue in the same way, especially in countries where they prosper? An articulate exponent of this view is George

Steiner. The only Jewish homeland he is prepared to recognize is the text.[5]

I have argued against this stance. Following Martin Buber and others, I have tried to present Judaism as a triangle the corners of which are faith, people and land. Every attempt to choose one of the corners, and identifying it as 'the essence of' Judaism at the expense of the others, constitutes a distortion of Judaism of which many contemporary Jewish movements are guilty. Applying Thomas Kuhn's theory,[6] I have suggested that a paradigm shift has taken place in Jewish life: after some 2000 years of being removed from our land, with only a token remnant present there, the Jewish people has come home again. Zionism has been vindicated. At a time when the faith of Israel was threatened by the Enlightenment and by modernity, and the people of Israel by antisemitism, culminating in the Holocaust, both had been renewed by the Jews' return to the land of Israel.

Whereas in earlier epochs the faith was strong enough and the people cohesive enough to allow for collective Jewish existence outside the land, that is no longer possible today. The only way for a viable self-contained Diaspora in our time is the creation of voluntary ghettos; it is unlikely that more than a small number of Jews will ever want them. On the other hand, it is evident that the sovereign Jewish state, established in the land of our ancestors, is the main reason for the revival of the Jewish faith and the renewal of the Jewish people in our time and as such the best guarantor of our future.

Exponents of Orthodox Judaism will not agree, for they believe that halachah, Jewish law, is still operative in Jewish life, wherever Jews may be. I do not hold such a view, because I do not see Jewish law at work other than on a voluntary basis – which brings us back to David Vital's charge. The State of Israel is most certainly not ruled by halachah, yet it compels Jews to follow Jewish precepts and, at the same time, inspires their sisters and brothers in the Diaspora to greater Jewish commitment. And Jews in the Diaspora who wish to submit to halachah, do so voluntarily and, very often, highly selectively.

This does not mean that I wish to minimize the importance of

Jewish observance, or ignore its growing impact in the service of continuity. But I am suggesting that those who observe, do so usually as a result of free individual choice in search of content for themselves, not out of compliance with the law. That is why I prefer the term mitzvah, commandment, to halachah, law. Jewish continuity will not be conditioned by law, even if it is informed and directed by observance.

Nor does it mean that access to the land has, by definition, secured the future of our people or our faith. The use of power by Jews – in one sense, the epitome of the new paradigm – paradoxically also endangers the Jewishness of Israel by rendering it like all other states. Hence the warning by Irving Greenberg that 'exercise of power must be accompanied by strong models and constant evocation of the memory of historic Jewish suffering and powerlessness'. Greenberg reminds us that 'it is so easy to forget slavery's lessons once one is given power, but such forgetfulness leads to the unfeeling infliction of pain on others'.[7]

Though neither the secular intellectuals nor the halachic minority can safeguard the future of Judaism in the way the Israeli collective might, both groups can help promote the corrective as outlined by Irving Greenberg. But they can only do so if they, first, work for an Israel that exercises power with the memory of powerlessness. The fact that many Diaspora Jews are currently part of the extremist problem, rather than the corrective solution, should be a further reason for exponents of liberal Judaism to affirm ways that point beyond temporary survivalism and inadequate civil religion.

The Holocaust is the bitter illustration of the old paradigm: the despair of exile and powerlessness. Israel is the vision of the new which, as so often in paradigm shifts, ends up as a restatement of the very old – in our case, the biblical paradigm. It is not unreasonable, in this scheme of things, to look at the future of the Jews in terms of a new biblical era, with all its dangers of abuse of power and worship – and all its opportunities for making the voice of God heard in the world.

This perspective differs fundamentally from the predictions of social scientists. They look at demographic figures and *foretell dire consequences*. But there are also reasons to *forthtell good things to come*, almost in prophetic fashion, by pointing to the possibility of growing links between Israel and Diaspora based on mutual recognition and respect. And there is evidence in the Diaspora that suggests a revival of commitment to Judaism based on the recognition of the faith, the people and the land of Israel.

Fackenheim's original statement was not only about survivalism. Though it contained four distinct points, his contemporaries seem to have heard only the first. Reading it now, we must also hear the other three and recognize its affirmation of the organic bond between Jews and Judaism, consistent with the new paradigm that blends particularism with universalism and makes for the authentic old/new Judaism of today and tomorrow:

> If the 614th commandment is binding upon the authentic Jew, then we are, first, commanded to survive as Jews, lest the Jewish people perish. We are commanded, second, to remember in our very guts and bones the martyrs of the Holocaust, lest their memory perish. We are forbidden, thirdly, to deny or despair of God, however much we may have to contend with Him or with belief in Him, lest Judaism perish. We are forbidden, finally, to despair of the world which is to become the kingdom of God, lest we make it a meaningless place in which God is dead or irrelevant and everything is permitted.[8]

If the call for *survival* concentrated on not giving Hitler a posthumous victory by staying alive and remembering the Holocaust, the call for *continuity through content* tells us also to affirm God and the world. Our best chance to achieve it is through orientation toward the *place* we call The Land of Israel, whatever *space* we may occupy in the world.

Notes

1. This is the main theme of my *Beyond Survival*, Darton, Longman and Todd 1982.
2. Jonathan S. Woocher, *Sacred Survival: The Civil Religion of American Jews*, Indiana University Press 1986, 188f.
3. *The Jerusalem Report*, 10 March, 1994, 30ff. Rabbi Sacks develops

the theme in his *Will We Have Jewish Grandchildren?*, Vallentine Mitchell 1994.

4. David Vital, *The Future of the Jews*, Harvard University Press 1990, 115.
5. See George Steiner, 'Our Homeland, The Text', in *Salmagundi*, Winter-Spring 1985, 4ff. See also my 'The Struggle Between Text and Land in Contemporary Jewry: Reflections on George Steiner's "Our Homeland, The Text"', *History of European Ideas* 20/4–6, 807–13. For a comprehensive treatment of the relationship between faith, people and land, see my *The Star of Return*, Greenwood 1991.
6. Thomas S. Kuhn, *The Structure of Scientific Revolutions*, University of Chicago Press 1970. See also Hans Küng, *Judaism*, SCM Press 1992.
7. Irving Greenberg, *The Third Great Cycle of Jewish History*, The National Jewish Resource Center (now CLAL) 1981, 25.
8. Emil L. Fackenheim, 'Jewish Values in the Post-Holocaust Future', in *Judaism* XVI/3, Summer 1967, 272f.

British Jewry, The Eleventh Tribe, Lost or Saved?

Jonathan Romain

Is history about to repeat itself with a re-enactment of a major fissure within the Jewish community two and a half thousand years after the first traumatic one?

Let me explain. After the death of Solomon, the twelve tribes of Israel split into two kingdoms, with ten tribes forming the Northern Kingdom and the remaining two being known as the Southern Kingdom. Eventually both were defeated by different foreign powers and taken into exile, albeit with a crucial difference. Despite being seventy years in Babylon, the Jews of the Southern Kingdom maintained their identity, and returned to the Land of Israel. They ensured that Jewish life carried on and reached subsequent generations. There is a direct line between them and the Jews of today. The Northern tribes never returned from exile in Assyria, but were assimilated into its empire and disappeared from history. Their only legacy is a host of fantastic legends about the Ten Lost Tribes and supposed sightings of them in mythical lands.

Two startling thoughts arise. First, that Jewish history ever since 723 BCE has been functioning at only two-twelfths of its original size. How much more dazzling might it have been at full strength? Second, how secure is that remaining two-twelfths? The margin for absorbing losses and still surviving is dangerously narrow; what if ten-twelfths of today's Jews disappear? Would the loss form another legend, or would it be the final chapter in the book of Judaism?

The question is neither academic nor fanciful, particularly with regard to British Jewry, for assimilation is widespread in the latter half of the twentieth century. The more pessimistic commentators are even doubting its ability to survive and have begun writing its obituary.[1] Perhaps talk of British Jewry's demise might have been prevalent much earlier but for successive waves of immigration that boosted its numbers. Most important was that of the Jews of Eastern Europe in the 1880s, while the influx of Jews from Germany and Central Europe in the 1930s also provided a significant injection of ethnic adrenalin. However, their descendants also fell prey to the aura exuded by British society at large, whose condition of acceptance was the tacit declaration: 'You are welcome – but please don't be too different. Be Jewish – but look British, act British and think British.' It was a message of genuine tolerance, but carried a price tag that encouraged Jews to be invisible Jews, and hence less and less Jewish. The result was that, starved of further reinforcements from abroad, British Jewry began to decline in number and commitment.

The losses were due to a range of interlocking factors. One is the high rate of Jews marrying non-Jews. A recent survey has shown that 44% of Jewish men under forty are marrying non-Jewish partners, with a lesser but growing number of Jewish women having non-Jewish husbands.[2] Marrying out does not always mean opting out – but it can do. There are many Jews who either give up their Jewish ties on setting up home with a non-Jewish partner, or who try to maintain some vestige of Jewish life but find that their efforts become increasingly minimal and eventually evaporate altogether. They are lost to Judaism, and so are their children.

A second factor in British Jewry's decline is the number of Jews who are in Jewish-Jewish marriages yet give up Jewish connections through inertia. Even for those who do keep the annual fast at Yom Kippur and have bread-free family gatherings at Passover, the rest of the year is entirely secular. They may be vaguely interested in Judaism's past and find its history fascinating, but have no burning ambition to be part of its future. They, too, are lost to Judaism, whether in their lifetime or in that of their children who inherit little and keep nothing.

A third factor in the decline is that many of those who feel intensely fired by their Jewish identity emigrate to Israel, whose vibrancy and sheer Jewishness offers the self-expression they seek. The number of such emigrants has been around 1000 a year for the last three decades. Taken together, they form a sizable group, but there is a much more important aspect: they are among the most Jewishly active and committed of the community's sons and daughters. Israel's undoubted gain is British Jewry's certain loss, depleting it of leadership and creativity. There has been a conspiracy of silence about this loss, for in the post-1967 enthusiasm for all things Zionist, it is considered disloyal to do anything but applaud the flow of talent from Britain to Israel. Yet however joyous it may be in one respect, such emigration has, and is continuing to have, a serious negative impact on British Jewry and deserves to be acknowledged.

A fourth factor is that even among those committed Jews who do remain in Britain and who do marry fellow-Jews, many of them have exceedingly low birth-rates. With the exception of the ultra-Orthodox, the average Jewish family size tends to be 1.6 children. This means that British Jewry is not only failing to grow but is unable to reproduce itself. A low birth-rate is in itself a common symptom of assimilation, although Jews have taken it even lower than in other groups. The end-result of all four factors is that the perhaps generously estimated Jewish population of 500,000 after the war decreased to 450,000 in the 1960s, to 400,000 in the 1970s, to 350,000 in the 1980s, and has sunk to 300,000 in the 1990s. The message is clear: British Jewry is decreasing, and rapidly. Despite occasional success stories and local rejuvenations here and there, the overall figures are inexorably downwards. Will the Ten Lost Tribes now become Eleven?

Enough of the problems, what of the solutions? If the assumption that solutions are possible seems a cavalier leap of faith, it is worth noting that doomsayers have often been wrong. Indeed it is a peculiarly Jewish act of self-flagellation for virtually each generation to award itself the title of the last generation. It is possible that British Jewry can be spared being labelled as 'a once thriving Jewish community now extinct' in the history books of the next millennium.

The solution, if it is to be successful, has to recognize the factors against which it is competing. This means a two-fold strategy: first, encouraging those Jews still within the community to remain Jewish, and to do so in a positive way that will inspire their children too; secondly, persuading those Jews who have left the community to return and re-adopt their religious roots. This dual approach assumes neither that affiliated Jews can be taken for granted, nor that unaffiliated Jews are irrevocably lost.

Reaching out to unaffiliated Jews who are not part of the community has been epitomized in recent years by 'the Maidenhead Experience', although what follows will apply to some other congregations too. Maidenhead is a Reform synagogue that has engaged in an energetic outreach campaign over the last decade with stunning results. From a congregational point of view it has increased the size of the community more than seven-fold and grown from 80 families to over 600. What is more, the newcomers have not been mere statistical additions to the membership list, but a very high percentage of them have become involved in synagogue life and taken positions of responsibility in it. From an individual point of view 'the Maidenhead Experience' has touched the lives of many Jews who felt estranged from the Jewish community and who have been brought back into it. Virtually all of them would say that it has enriched their lives, and some would add that it has changed the very course of their lives.

They had left the Jewish community for a variety of causes: some had unpleasant experiences elsewhere; some had been made to feel unwanted for economic or social reasons; some had drifted away accidentally; some had not realized there was a synagogue locally or made the effort to enquire; some knew but felt too unsure of themselves to come along ('I don't know when to stand up or sit down in services'); some did not think that being Jewish meant that they needed to belong to a synagogue (although they forgot that the synagogue might need them, while they also under-estimated their own needs too); some were fearful of what commitments might be involved; some were fearful of high costs; some felt that people of their status (mixed-marriage, single parents or divorcees) were not welcome; some had an aversion to rabbis based on their days at Religion School or insensitive encounters at funerals; some reckoned that their doubts about the existence of God meant they were not eligible to join.

In all cases the strategy was not to wait for them to approach the synagogue, but for the synagogue to approach them. This entailed discovering all unaffiliated Jews in the area and then contacting them with a letter, followed up a few days later with a phone call. Unless the person was totally opposed to any contact with the community, a home visit was arranged. This was enormously time-consuming but absolutely crucial for dismantling their preconceptions and establishing a positive relationship. The suggestion 'Can I pop round for a few minutes to say hello?' invariably turned into a stay of an hour and a half. The conversation was both about them and about the synagogue and what it could offer them. For many people it was 'the first time a rabbi has ever visited my house' and showed the friendly and caring side of Judaism, helping overcome many of the objections that had led to their alienation.[3]

Those with theological doubts were disabused of the notion that everyone else was a firm believer, and told that being Jewish means seeking God, often being puzzled but considering the search worthwhile. Those with financial problems were accommodated and made to feel that they could contribute to the community just as well in other ways. Those with concerns about their private lives were reassured that the synagogue was a place for real people and real situations, not supposedly model families untouched by any conflict or set-back. Those in mixed-faith marriages were informed that marrying a non-Jewish partner did not make them any less Jewish, while their partner and children were equally welcome to attend if they wished to do so.

The result was that in 50% of all cases, the people eventually joined the synagogue and became involved to some degree, with many attending the adult education classes in particular so as to improve their Jewish knowledge. The process was predicated on the belief that one of the tasks of the synagogue is to reach out to the unaffiliated. It is also based on recognizing people's right to be as they are and that there are many different ways of being Jewish. Of course, a 50% success rate also means a 50% failure rate, but it showed that a substantial part of those outside communal life could be brought back if synagogues were to take the initiative in contacting them.

Most of the unaffiliated joined the synagogue in their front living rooms. Whether they remained members depended on what they met when they came to the synagogue. This is the second part of the strategy and applies both to new members who have come back into the fold, and to existing ones whose loyalty still needs to be earned.

The three different Hebrew terms for the word 'synagogue' may offer a clue for ways of re-invigorating an institution that needs to be much more dynamic and proactive. *Bet Tefillah* – house of worship – suggests the need not only for prayer but also for spirituality. Services must not just take one through the prescribed liturgy but push out ladders to heaven – be it through angelic choirs, or enthusiastic communal singing, or elevating instrumental music, or quiet time for meditation, or new prayers that speak to people meaningfully, or inspirational sermons, or creative services or anything that touches the soul and makes people emerge feeling enhanced in some way.

Bet Midrash – house of education – reminds that those who do not understand Judaism will not feel at home in it or wish to maintain their association with it. The recent explosion in courses for adults at Jewish centres in London needs to be replicated on a synagogue level (and throughout the country) so as to turn interest in general Jewish knowledge into participation in communal life. In the case of children, however much religion school teachers urge parents to practise more at home, they must accept that in many cases the burden of education will lie with them alone. Whilst transmitting Jewish knowledge will be one goal, even more important is inculcating an enthusiasm, a sense of enjoyment, and pride in being Jewish, which will have a much more long-term impact on their development. Equally vital are educational activities for those in the thirteen to eighteen age group – after their *bar/batmitzvah* and before they leave home for college or a flat nearer work – a time when they are most searching for an ethical framework and personal identity. Until now Judaism has often been absent at this critical period, and has left a vacuum that other philosophies – religious or secular – have quickly filled. Instead, a stimulating programme for the teenage generation has to be provided which can allow access to Jewish teaching and the range of guidelines it has to offer. At the same time, those over eighteen should not be abandoned, but provision made for them and the search for Jewish knowledge and identity that can last a lifetime.

Bet Knesset – house of meeting – emphasizes that a synagogue should also be a social and cultural centre, with activities that provide something for everyone. They should encompass both events for the community as a whole and those for specific groups – such as students, singles, young marrieds or the retired. Activities should be as extensive as possible, so that whatever Jews enjoy doing, they can do through the synagogue – be it bridge club, cricket team, knitting circle, drama group or photographic society. Where appropriate, these should have a Jewish element to them, so that one is exploring one's Jewish heritage at the same time (such as mounting plays or photographic exhibitions on Jewish themes). In addition there should be occasional projects dealing with special issues that affect the lives of members, such as divorce, intermarriage, bereavement, alcoholism or care for elderly relatives. Dominating all these diverse elements is the notion that nothing that Jews do should be alien from the synagogue, so that it is not peripheral to the lives of its members but central to it.

A fourth dimension should be added to the three traditional models of the synagogue: that it should also be a *Bet Tzedek* – house of righteousness – concerned with putting Jewish ethical teachings into practice and turning piety into action. The synagogue should be a co-ordinating centre and stimulus for social action, communal care, charity work, fund-raising, or visitation committees, and with a brief to assist individuals in need within the congregation, those in the wider Jewish community, society at large, and matters of broader horizons, such as human tragedies abroad or ecological concerns. With this extra dimension not only will synagogues be a channel for the clarion call of the biblical prophets to 'let justice roll down like water and righteousness like an everlasting stream' (Amos 5.24), but they will allow the deep sense of social justice that exists among many Jews to be given expression in a Jewish context.

The issue of mixed-faith marriage deserves particular attention, partly because, as was indicated earlier, it affects so many Jews today, and partly because of the intemperate language and emotional response that is so often used about it. Descriptions such as 'giving victory to Hitler' and 'a cancer destroying Judaism from the inside' express the view that Jews who marry out are either deliberately rejecting their Jewish heritage, or are beguiled by the physical attractions of non-Jews into adopting their ways. Hence the reaction of many Orthodox authorities who reject those who have married out. However, a different view is possible which is not only more realistic but is also more constructive: that in the vast majority of cases Jews who marry out do so unintentionally, without dogma and without malice aforethought. They would have been content to marry a Jewish partner, perhaps would have preferred to do so, but in an open pluralist society they had mixed with non-Jews in college or at work, and had fallen in love with someone with whom they found much in common but who happened to be of a different faith.

The haphazard, almost accidental way in which most Jews marry out of the faith may be a cause for alarm, but is also a source for hope. It highlights the Jewish identity that *remains* a characteristic of many outmarried Jews. They want to attend synagogue services and practice home observances as much as do most other 'middle of the road' Jews. They also wish to pass on their Jewishness to their children, have them circumcised, give them a *bar/batmitzvah*, and often express a desire that their children will marry within the faith, precisely because they themselves value it, even if they have broken one of its taboos.[4]

Given this situation, it is clear that although outmarriage can lead to abandoning Judaism, it need not necessarily do so. Much depends on the person concerned and, just as crucially, on the response of the community. Do we regard outmarried Jews as still fully Jewish? Do we welcome them into the community? Do we treat their non-Jewish partners with courtesy and respect? Do we allow the children (whether technically Jewish or not) to attend Religion School and receive a Jewish education? In short, do we make every effort to include them? I would urge that the answer in each case should be a resolute 'yes'. The effect of such a policy over the last decade, particularly at Maidenhead but also at some other communities, has been that outmarried Jews have not only become involved in synagogue life but have contributed to it. Moroever, in a substantial number of cases it has brought their non-Jewish partner and children into Jewish life. It has highlighted the fact that a high percentage of the non-Jewish partners do not have any religious affiliation of their own and, if given a warm welcome, come to feel at home in the Jewish community and either convert or become philo-Jewish. Others wish to remain without any religious attachment, but are happy to support their partner's Jewish involvement, and let the children be exposed to his or her Jewish roots.

It is a success rate that contrasts strongly with the results of the policy of rejection – which has not deterred Jews from marrying out, and has only succeeded in guaranteeing that they do not play any part in the Jewish community. This should not detract from the fact that marrying within the faith may well be much better at keeping Jews Jewish, but it does mean that a new policy has to be formulated with regard to those Jews in mixed-faith marriages. This is reinforced by evidence that the numbers look likely to increase – in America the figure is over 50% – and affect a significant proportion of the community.[5]

Beneath all these strategies lies the need to respond creatively to the challenge that emancipation and acceptance has brought to British Jewry. We know from history that if only two out of twelve survive, that is enough to keep going for over 2,500 years. The effort we make in the next few decades will help determine whether British Jewry's name will be associated with the ten tribes that disappeared or the two that flourished.

Notes

1. This essay was written immediately before the publication of two books (Norman Cantor, *The Sacred Chain*, HarperCollins 1995; Bernard Wasserstein, *Vanishing Diaspora*, Hamish Hamilton 1996) which argue that Diaspora Jewry is facing extinction.

Unlike this article, however, neither holds out any hope that it can be avoided.

2. Stephen Miller, Marlena Schmool and Antony Lerman, *Social and Political Attitudes of British Jews*, Institute for Jewish Policy Research, London 1996.
3. The exact method of locating and approaching unaffiliated Jews is set out in detail in Jonathan A. Romain, *How To Grow*, RSGB 1995 (2nd edition).
4. For further analysis of intermarriage in general, see Jonathan A. Romain, *Till Faith Us Do Part*, HarperCollins 1996.
5. Egon Mayer, *1990 Jewish Population Survey*, Council of Jewish Federations, New York 1991.

Repairing the World – A Task for Jews?

Barbara Borts

Introduction

In the beginning, so the Kabbalists [Jewish mystics] taught, God was all – God's presence so filled the world that Divinity was synonymous with the world. In order for the process of creation, differentiation, to proceed, God needed to contract Godliness from the world, which was termed *tzimtzum*, to allow space for life. Without God's *tzimtzum*, contraction, there could be no creation, no independent life. God's *tzimtzum* was a divine declaration of independence which allowed the world to be established in all its diversity: land and sea, trees and shrubs, animals and humans, good and evil. 'See, today I offer you life and good, and death and evil . . . I have set before you life and death, blessing and curse' (Deut.30.15,19).

God so withdrew from the world of creation that none of the divine light was visible in this world, and God, the *Ein Sof*, the Totally Other, was absent until God breathed sparks of light back into the world. This divine light was contained in *kaylim*, vessels.

Somehow these vessels shattered, and sparks of divine light were released into the world. These lost traces of divine light and the shards of their holy containers float about awaiting repair and recontainment by human beings. This is *Tikkun Olam*: repairing the world through a commandment observed; a deed of loving kindness proffered; a blessing offered with devotion – all these are potentially restorative acts which capture a spark of light and enclose it once again. Were we by some miracle, somehow, to succeed in accomplishing this *tikkun*, this repair of all shattered vessels, reuniting them with their sparks of light, we could bring about the days of messiah.

A simple version of a complex concept, this explanation of Lurianic Kabbalah's version of the creation. *Tikkun Olam*, the repair of the *kaylim* and the gathering of the lost sparks of divine light. This idea, *Tikkun Olam*, has other, more ancient meanings. But it was really the mystics who bequeathed to us this theological paradigm for a new Jewish agenda: *Tikkun Olam* as a commandment for Jews to repair the world, mend the shattered pieces, heal the broken creation. *Tikkun Olam* has, for many, been transformed from an esoteric mystical concept to an inspiring model of a Judaism with a religious/spiritual social action imperative.

We derive from here not only a task, but also our responsibility: God has contracted out of the world to create space for our lives. Those of us who find a modern moral imperative in this reconstructed understanding of an old concept believe that into the void of God's *tzimtzum* came a world and a humanity charged with being first this world's overseer and then its moral/ ethical guardian. 'There is no quality and there is no power in people that was created to no purpose. But to what end can the denial of God have been created? It, too, can be uplifted through deeds of charity. For if someone comes to you and asks your help, you shall not turn them off with pious words, saying "Have faith, and take your troubles to God!" You shall act as though there were no God, as though there were only one person in all the world who could help this person, only yourself.'[1]

It is upon this basis, this space in the world given to human beings, the world in need of repair, the divinity in need of recontainment and the teachings about how to live one's life, that one asks the question, '*Tikkun Olam*: A Task For Jews?'

I

In autumn 1986 a new magazine was published. It was called *Tikkun*, and it has become an important forum for Progressive Jewish essays and creative writing. The opening passages of the first editorial statement state:[2]

> TIKKUN: To Mend, Repair and Transform the World.
>
> The notion that the world could and should be different than it is has deep roots within Judaism. But . . . it is an idea that seems strangely out of fashion – and those who still dare to hope often view themselves as isolated, if not irrelevant. In the context of Western societies too often intoxicated with their own material and technological success, in which the ethos of personal fulfilment has the status of 'common sense', those who talk of fundamental transformation seem to be dreaming . . .
>
> It is this refusal to accept the world as given, articulated in the Prophetic call for transformation, that has fuelled the radical underpinnings of Jewish life . . . The universalistic dream of a transformation and healing of the world, the belief that peace and justice are not meant for heaven but are this-worldly necessities that must be fought for, *is* the particularistic cultural and religious tradition of the Jews.

The necessity for such a magazine grew out of concern about the rightward and parochial drift of the American Jewish establishment and the increasing and heretofore almost unprecedented conservative stance of the mainstream Jewish community.

The term *Tikkun Olam* as a Jewish concept for social action was first used in 1979/1980, partly as a protest against what has been called the result of the empowerment of the Jewish community. There is a hoary sociological truism that one changes one's affiliations – religious, political, social and even recreational – as one becomes empowered by money or status. The Jewish world has undergone a double empowerment. In England, the United States and elsewhere, Jews have made it. Clearly there are pockets of Jewish poverty, particularly amongst the elderly, and there are still real working-class Jews. Nonetheless, our incomes and careers, our level of education and our pre-eminence in many important endeavours, has established us as a well-off, well-educated, articulate and powerful force in British and North American life. And the establishment of the State of Israel, with its new strong Jew and its warrior image, but beleaguered by enemies all around, gave the Jew a radical new identity in the post-Holocaust world. It also gave Jews a rationale for new political alliances with those who would promise good things for the State.

This combination of money and status and the symbolic importance of a Masada-vision of Israel, led to a shift in Jewish voting patterns, Jewish charitable donations, Jewish involvements, and Jewish social action platforms. It has also generated a shift in some quarters from old platforms of Judaism and social action into an arena qualitatively different – into *Tikkun Olam* – from universal moral calling to divine imperative.

II

In the 1960s, particularly in the United States, Reform Judaism was synonymous with social action. There was little emphasis on ritual, and Jews were roused by the words of the prophets. And this was not just those who attended synagogue:

> One element of the Jewish tradition, it is often argued, remains alive, even if in secularized form, and still guides Jewish behaviour. This is the Jewish concern for social justice . . . In short, Jews play a significant role, far greater than their numbers suggest, in all the tendencies that come under the heading of liberalism, progress, and reform. Do we not have here a secularized version of the passion for social justice expressed by the Hebrew prophets? Many Jews – and non-Jews – believe so, but the matter is not so simple.[3]

However, there is a history of official Jewish concern for causes, as an intrinsic part of early Reform Judaism. The Reform movement was the first to have a distinct social action policy. This was partly a result of an attempt both to minimize the importance of the ritual tradition and to remake Judaism into a religion, not a people, to bring Jewish teaching and practice into line with both contemporary philosophy and a Christianity perceived as the standard bearer of generic, universal religion unfettered by tribalism and distinctiveness. The early reform placed the prophets in the centre of Judaism and the belief in a personal Messiah metamorphosed into a messianic age for all, with progressive Jews as its vanguard. A quotation from the influential Pittsburgh Platform of 1885 illustrates this:[4]

> In full accordance with the spirit of Mosaic legislation which strives to regulate the relation between rich and poor, we deem it our duty to participate in the great task of modern times, to solve on the basis of justice and righteousness the problems presented by the contrasts and evils of the present organization of society.

Although later Reform platforms modified much of the platform, the emphasis on social action remained. The sociologist Nathan Glazer points out that much of the impetus for this type of work came from the rabbis, who were often in opposition to their communities, increasingly a middle-class mass, as Glazer terms them. In a sermon supporting the establishment of a union, which Rabbi Stephen Wise gave to his congregation of wealthy businessmen, he wrote: 'I know there are penalties, many and grave, which are likely to attach themselves to this address. It is clear to me that there are scores of manufacturers . . . within the ranks of this congregation, who may for a time in any event take serious exception to my thought. Some of them will doubtless determine to refuse to lend their help to the building of the Synagogue Home that has long been planned. I am ready to bear every burden and to pay every penalty. The one thing I am not prepared to do is to conceal my inmost convictions . . .'

The middle classes and the well-to-do were (and remained) known for their philanthropy, and, although it was by no means universal, a general Jewish sense prevailed that justice and righteousness were Jewish values to be pursued, sometimes for their own sake, as a religious ideal, as the rabbis would have it, and sometimes because they were seen as part of a political and social process which would lead to the amelioration of Jewish life. And this was also the case with the Jewish Communists and socialists of both Europe and America, as noted above in the passage from Glazer.

III

With the end of the 1960s, a new Jewish movement began to appear. Rabbi Gerry Serotta was one of the first to use the concept of *Tikkun Olam* as a new banner under which to rally Jews and social issues. The term first appeared in a paper circulated to a number of people before the inaugural conference of an organization called New Jewish Agenda. In the opening Statement of Purpose, NJA wrote:

Statement of Purpose

> We are Jews from a variety of backgrounds and affiliations committed to progressive human values and the building of a shared vision of Jewish life.
>
> Our history and tradition inspire us. Jewish experience and teachings can address the social, economic, and political issues of our time. Many of us find our inspiration in our people's historical resistance to oppression and from the Jewish presence at the forefront of movements for social change. Many of us base our convictions on the Jewish religious concept of *tikkun olam* (the just ordering of human society and the world) and the prophetic tradition of social justice.
>
> We are dedicated to insuring the survival and flourishing of the Jewish people. Jews must have the rights to which all people are entitled. But survival is only a precondition of Jewish life, not its purpose. Our agenda must be determined by our ethics, not our enemies . . .
>
> . . . New Jewish Agenda's national platform upholds progressive Jewish values and affirms that the goals of peace and justice are attainable.[5]

Dedicated to their vision, New Jewish Agenda sought to stress a continuity between Jewish tradition and observance *and* people's political and social concerns, *and* to bring together Jewish and universal concerns under one umbrella of involvement and analysis.

IV

This brief historical background was necessary in order to begin to establish an answer to the question: is *Tikkun Olam* a task for Jews? The world is still in a state of brokenness, and there are many Jews, in pockets across the world, who work for *Tikkun Olam* (and, as has been indicated, in social endeavours unrelated to their Judaism). These are also difficult times. As the radicals of the 1960s married and entered into professions, they often did change. And the activists of the 1980s were assailed by Thatcherism. So much was damaged during those years and so much surplus powerlessness (as Michael Lerner, the editor of the magazine *Tikkun* calls it) set in, like a disease, sapping the optimism and energy of the committed. In the face of a major social revolution to the right, one launched so completely and with so much general acquiescence, what will survive from the progressive world?

For many Jews, the answer to our opening question is obviously, yes. *Tikkun Olam* is a distinct Jewish response to working on the problems of the world. It has a lot in common with radical theologies of the Christian tradition, some of which were built upon Jewish sources, but it remains a uniquely Jewish mission.

Many Jews ask, 'Why a Jewish vehicle for expressing concerns about the world?' There are many reasons. We have particular religious and textual insights missing from the other traditions, which fit into a general Jewish picture of things. Furthermore, we have a recent and painful historical perspective to add to the debate. Our tradition has a rich legacy, and our history is full of experiences which need to be added in all of their particularity to the richness and diversity of the work of repairing the world. That is not to say that non-Jews do not and should not do the work, nor that we do it better – only that our voice, grounded in our tradition and in our and our ancestors' lives, offers an important perspective to others.

These are perhaps some of the extrinsic reasons for *Tikkun Olam* as a Jewish task. There are some intrinsic ones as well.

The Reform movements were not wrong in what they propounded – they were just rather shallow. Social Action is the prophets and their message taken to the world, as expounded by the great Reform rabbis. *Tikkun Olam* is the command to create a whole and just world. One is a noble endeavour, inspired by selected Jewish teachings. The other is an obligation, informed by the whole of Jewish tradition, Jewish texts, Jewish historical experiences, all layers of Jewish civilization. *Tikkun Olam* seeks to be continuous with the Jewish heritage, and to reconstruct this Kabbalistic idea to become a religious category of command and a holy task. *Tikkun Olam* seeks to be part of all Jewish life and to be nurtured by all of Jewish life, to recapture the essence of the time when there was no distinction between so-called real life and religious existence. As one lives and works and studies and prays, one also does *Tikkun Olam*.

This wholistic, integrated approach is probably in a strange way quite akin to the early Kabbalistic view. The Kabbalists also strove to bring repair to a world which was once all God. Such is the view which would inform *Tikkun Olam* as a task for Jews – to bring to bear on the world a wholeness, a togetherness, which it lacks.

We have a fundamental problem to overcome if we are to move into the forefront of work for social change, our newly-found empowerment. Rabbi Levi Olan writes:

> A tragic destiny served to keep the Jewish people lean and alert. It has been bad for the nerves but good for the soul. But there are constant imminent dangers; as of today urbanization, over-sophistication, almost complete absorption into a bourgeoisie, loss of self-respect, loss of belief and loss of the tragic-heroic sense of destiny.[6]

We Jews are now a middle-class people, but is the God to whom we pray a middle-class God? Or is the fact that we were once slaves and were delivered, and then enjoined to love our neighbour and take heed of the rules of fair treatment of others, not a sign to us that this God asks more of us than our seeing to our own comfort? We may not need economic liberation because we are not poor peasants in South America. But we need other kinds of liberation from that which we have brought upon ourselves by our way of life and our skewed values, and we have to realize that our neighbour must now include that poor Brazilian peasant, whose destiny is our destiny, and whose liberation is linked to our liberations.

Radical Christianity portrays God as suffering the pain of the world through the body of Christ. One does not, however, need an incarnation to portray God as a sufferer, nor in fact does one need an incarnation as a proclamation of human solidarity. The fact that Genesis proclaims that we are created 'in the divine image' and that God has breathed 'the spirit of life' into us shows that we are all children of God and partake of God's essence – the point in Judaism is not how to make the Divine human so the Divine participates in our suffering, but how to encounter the Divine in each human so as to create the bonds of kinship which will cause us to work to eradicate suffering.

The rabbi and scholar Henry Slonimski has done extensive work in Midrashic theology, and writes convincingly of the other God, who does not appear in our liturgies, but who is implicit nonetheless:

> God's own special suffering as the Rabbis conceive it: his weeping, his helplessness, his need of comfort . . . is the mythological form of expressing the philosophical thought of God's limited power in the world as it stands.[7]

God needs us. We hear it as a statement of hope – the beginnings of our own theologies of liberation:

> The assertion of God in a godless world is the supreme act of religion. It is a continuing of the act of creation on the highest plane. It adds slowly to . . . the translation of God as ideal and vision into the God of empirical embodiment and power. Man, in whom God's creative effort had achieved a provisional pinnacle, so to speak God's own self-consciousness of his aims, becomes from now on God's confronting partner, and the two together a reinforcing polarity of give and take . . . But in a very real sense, the fate of God and of the future rests on the heroism of man, on what he elects to do, for he is the manifesting God and the focus of decision.[8]

But this is not the Jewish, nor the Christian way. The Christian theologian Hans Jonas writes:

> Bound up with the concepts of a suffering and a becoming God is that of a *caring* God – a God not remote and detached and self-contained, but involved with that He cares for . . . This caring God is not a sorcerer who in the act of caring also provides the fulfilment of His concern: He has left something for other agents to do and thereby made His case dependent upon them. He is therefore also an endangered God, a God who risks something.[9]

Judaism has always emphasized *this* life, and hope as a central aspect. We are in effect prisoners of hope, of a sort of pessimistic optimism. A God who requires woman and man to become partners in creating the world cannot be anything but a force toward perfection. The qualities which God has, of grace, loving-kindness, compassion, are only actualized in inter-human encounters. God and God's epithets are weak until realized by humans. And that, as Buber has pointed out, is a message of *ehyeh asher ehyeh* (Exod. 3.14), not 'I am what I am', but rather 'I will be what I will be', a God of becoming, a God of possibility.

A hope for the future, but not boundless optimism, is what separates *Tikkun Olam* from its liberal predecessors, a hope and a future not based on miraculous promises but on a realistic understanding of humanity and of a God who always expects a greater effort towards the bringing of the messianic era, who waits on us to do what is necessary to hasten the day.

One man was able to draw all of these together and gave to all Jews involved in social change who take their Judaism seriously a way and a model. That man was Abraham Joshua Heschel. He derives a call to Jewish political theology and practice from prayer:

> Prayer is either exceedingly urgent, exceedingly relevant or inane and useless . . . Prayer should be an act of catharsis, of purgation of emotions, as well as a process of self-clarification, of examining priorities, of elucidating responsibility. Prayer not verified by conduct is an act of desecration and blasphemy . . . Prayer is meaningless unless it is subversive, unless

> it seeks to overthrow and to ruin the pyramids of callousness, hatred, opportunism, falsehoods. The liturgical movement must become a revolutionary movement, seeking to overthrow the forces that continue to destroy the promise, the hope, the vision.
>
> The hour calls for a revision of fundamental religious concerns. The wall of separation between the sacred and the secular has become a wall of separation between the conscience and God . . . Prayer is private, a service of the heart; but let concern and compassion, born out of prayer, dominate public life.[10]

It is a task for Jews, with our image of God, with our historical suffering, with our understanding of life on the boundary, to develop and deepen the idea of *Tikkun Olam*, to answer yes to the world and to the God who awaits our response.

Notes

1. *Forms of Prayer for Jewish Worship*, Volume I (Daily and Sabbath), RSGB 1980, 396.
2. *Tikkun Magazine* 1/1.
3. Nathan Glazer, *American Judaism*, University of Chicago Press, 16–18.
4. Walter Jacob (ed.), *The Pittsburgh Platform in Retrospect*, Rodel Shalom Press, Pennsylvania, 108–9.
5. New Jewish Agenda National Platform, adopted 28 November 1982.
6. Levi A. Olan, 'Reform Judaism in a Post-Modern World', *Journal of Reform Judaism*, Winter 1981, 1–14.
7. Heny Slonimski, 'The Philosophy Implicit in the Midrash', *Hebrew Union College Annual* 27, 1956, 258.
8. Ibid.
9. Hans Jonas, 'The Concept of God After Auschwitz', in Albert Friedlander (ed.), *Out of the Whirlwind*, Union of Hebrew Congregations, New York 1968, 470.
10. Abraham Joshua Heschel, 'On Prayer', in *Understanding Jewish Prayer*, KTAV Publishing House, New York 1972, 74.

The Challenge for Reform Judaism in a Jewish State

Michael Boyden

Theodor Herzl, the founder of modern political Zionism, wrote his classic work *The Jewish State* during the summer of 1895 while working as a newspaper correspondent in Paris. At the time, he could hardly have imagined that, just 100 years later, the State of Israel would have taken centre stage in the history of the Jewish people. As the Israeli novelist, Amos Oz, has contended, Diaspora Jews have become the audience and critics of a drama in which Israelis are the actors.

Whether one accepts the analogy or not, the fact remains that over 50% of Jewish babies entering the world today are being born in an Israel whose Jewish population – just 600,000 in 1948 – is predicted within a generation to overtake that of the 6 million strong Jewish community of the United States.

A Reform Judaism that believes that it has a central role to play in the Jewish world of the twenty-first century will need to come to terms with the State of Israel and make a significant impact upon her society. Alternatively, it will be defined and condemned by some as having been a Diaspora experience that failed the test of Jewish nationhood.

However, Reform Judaism is important to Israel not only to prevent the marginalization of what is a major religious movement in the Diaspora, but also to save the Jewish State from the ravages of an ultra-Orthodoxy that threatens both her democratic character and the nature of Judaism itself.

Theodor Herzl was aware of the dangers of religious power when he wrote:

> Shall we end by having a theocracy? No, indeed. Faith unites us, knowledge gives us freedom. We shall therefore prevent any theocratic tendencies from coming to the fore on the part of our priesthood. We shall keep our priests within the confines of their temples in the same way as we shall keep our professional army within the confines of their barracks. Army and priesthood shall receive honours high as their valuable functions deserve. But they shall not interfere in the administration of the State which confers distinction upon them, else they shall conjure up difficulties without and within.
>
> Every man will be as free and undisturbed in his faith or his disbelief as he is in his nationality . . . We have learned toleration in Europe.[1]

Herzl's fears have, alas, proved to be well-founded, and the spirit of toleration to which he refers has yet to be embraced.

The history of the State of Israel has been chequered by the ongoing pressures of religious parties extracting concessions from one or other of the two major political groupings as their *quid pro quo* for bolstering up the government of the day. Holding the balance of power, their influence and impact have been out of all proportion to their numbers. When governments threaten to fall, when elections are pending and when new political parties are formed, their secular leaders make what has become almost a ritual pilgrimage to the home of Rabbi Ovadiah Yossef, spiritual leader of Shas, one of Israel's ultra-Orthodox parties. Although it holds less than ten per cent of the seats in the Knesset, proportional representation has enabled this relatively small grouping to become one of the king-pins in the process of coalition building.

Such manoeuvrings and machinations have resulted in an Israel in which religious power has tarnished the values of liberalism and democracy. The law stipulates that marriages and divorces between Jewish citizens can only be conducted by Orthodox rabbis. Those whose Jewish status is uncertain, or who fall into one of the categories of what Orthodox Jewish law considers forbidden unions, have no alternative but to marry abroad. The Chief Rabbinate maintains computer files of over 3,000 of Israel's citizens who are described as 'disqualified for marriage'.

Even more serious is the problem of the offspring of mixed marriages – an issue that has become particularly acute as a result of the massive wave of immigration from the former USSR over the past few years. It is estimated that over 100,000 of Israel's citizens are unable to marry in their own country. In consequence, a growing number of them are marrying abroad. Such weddings account for some ten per cent of the marriages registered in 1994 by the Ministry of the Interior. Indeed, this problem has now reached such crisis proportions that the former Minister of Religious Affairs suggested that funds be established to enable those who cannot marry in Israel to do so elsewhere.

Similar difficulties have arisen over burial. Municipal cemeteries, operated by Orthodox burial societies, are closed to Gentiles. Soviet immigrants, seeking to bury their non-Jewish dead, have been forced to turn to kibbutzim or Christian cemeteries. Israel's government is only just beginning to take the first steps in making provision for such families.

Unfortunately, the approach to these problems has been slow and piecemeal in a society in which any attempt to change the *status quo* and thereby break the monopoly of the Orthodox rabbinate can have serious consequences for the stability of the government of the day.

The effects of Orthodox political power are evident in many fields of public life. Billboard advertising must by law be 'modest', bread cannot be sold in Jewish neighbourhoods during Passover, the national bus company and Israel's airline El Al do not operate on the Sabbath, the import of pork is forbidden and massive sums of national and local government funds are channelled to Orthodox synagogues, seminaries and other institutions. All this and more is the price that is paid by successive governments for the support of the religious parties.

It is, then, hardly surprising that many Israelis have turned away in repulsion from established religion. What has particularly incensed them is that Orthodox seminary students and religious women are entitled to exemption from military service. In a country in which the army is an important unifying factor and where the price of military service exacts a constant toll on Israeli society as a whole, the ultra-Orthodox are exempted.

The fact that Prime Minister Rabin's assassin, Yigal Amir, is himself an ultra-Orthodox Jew, who alleges that he was inspired to carry out the attack by his rabbinical mentors and teachers, has only served to heighten the resentment felt by many for anything to do with Orthodox Judaism.

Judaism in Israel is in crisis, and Orthodoxy is ill-equipped to cope with a Jewish society that is breaking down. Even sadder is the fact that fifty years of Orthodox monopoly and religious coercion have alienated so many Israelis from their Jewish heritage.

It is within this context that the task of Reform Judaism must be assessed. Our role in Israel is a difficult one. Orthodoxy has done everything in its power to delegitimize us and to suggest that there is only one expression of Judaism. Many Israelis choose to collude with this view and opt for secularism as an expression of their disgust for the religious establishment rather than seriously seeking an alternative.

Meanwhile, the religious parties use their political power to obstruct us. Reform Jews are barred from local Religious Councils even when elected. Local and national government funds are rarely given to Reform institutions and programmes. Public land is generally only allocated for the building of Reform synagogues after appeals to Israel's Supreme Court.

However, things are changing. Following years of struggle to achieve a level of credibility in Israeli society and discard its image of being an American import, the Israel Movement for Progressive Judaism is beginning to make an impact, and secular Israelis are turning to us in their attempt to connect with their Jewish roots. After a recent marriage conducted at Kibbutz Gal'on by the present writer, the bridegroom wrote, 'On Kibbutz they can't stop expressing their amazement . . . They had finally attended a wedding at which they felt the symbols and values were related to their way of life.'

A handful of Reform rabbis in Israel are now being swamped with approaches by secular Israelis wanting them to officiate at their marriages. The decision by such couples is not an easy one.

Not only are they breaking away from the norm, but they also have to meet the expense of a civil marriage outside Israel to ensure that the Ministry of the Interior will register them as married. It should be emphasized that the overwhelming majority of such couples could easily have married under the auspices of the Orthodox rabbinate, but chose rather to express their dissent by seeking a Jewish alternative.

The same is true of the large number of Israeli parents who turn to the congregations of our Movement to celebrate the *barmitzvahs* of their children. The demand has become so great that our congregation in Tel Aviv, Beit Daniel, has been forced to institute such ceremonies on Sabbath afternoons, since there are insufficient Sabbath mornings to cater for the number of applicants.

A similar dramatic upturn has taken place in the field of education. Reform day schools in Haifa and Jerusalem are filled to capacity in a country in which quality education combined with a non-coercive approach to Judaism has proved to be an attractive option.

The rabbinic court of the Israel Council of Progressive Rabbis is inundated with requests by non-Jews wishing to convert to Judaism. The vast majority of applications come from the non-Jewish spouses of Israeli citizens. Many are the partners of Soviet Jews who have recently immigrated to Israel. Included within their numbers are those who have Jewish fathers but Gentile mothers. In the former USSR they were considered Jews. Upon arriving in Israel under the Law of Return, which grants those with Jewish ancestory an automatic right to citizenship, they discover to their amazement and distress that the Jewish State does not recognize them as such.

It is to the discredit of the Orthodox rabbinate that it has generally failed to meet the challenge of the recent Soviet immigration and has not found a way to convert the non-Jewish members of their families. While respecting Orthodoxy's right to condition conversion upon the observance of Jewish Law as understood by them, it is harder to justify the Ministry of the Interior's refusal to recognize those converted in Israel by Reform and Conservative rabbinic courts. At the time of writing, we are fighting for the recognition of Reform conversions by Israel's civil authorities. Should the Supreme Court find in our favour, such a decision would inevitably lead to attempts by the Orthodox political parties to introduce legislation to overturn the consequences of such a ruling.

There is much for Reform Judaism to do in Israel. If Zionism has been the political response of Jewry to the Emancipation, then Reform Judaism is its religious counterpart. As liberals and pluralists, our approach to Judaism is eminently suited to make a significant contribution to a Jewish democracy. Our task is to build a just society in which the values of prophetic monotheism, which are so central to the message of Reform, will turn Israel into a country that is an expression of our highest ideals.

Given these aspirations, which could offer so much to the character of a Jewish State espousing the values of democracy, it is hardly surprising that we find ourselves engaged in a bitter *Kulturkampf* against the intransigence of a medieval, monopolistic Orthodox establishment obsessed with ritual and seemingly unconcerned with the struggle for justice. The credo of Orthodoxy and the principles of a Western, liberal democracy are, it would seem, inevitably irreconcilable, and it is a tragedy both for Israel and for Judaism that these Siamese twins have not been separated.

To those outside Israel, these words may appear unduly harsh. However, those who live in the Jewish State and are constantly faced with the consequences of a Judaism that enjoys political power are only too aware of the need, as the former Knesset member Avraham Burg – himself an Orthodox Jew – has put it, to separate religion from politics.

Israel, then, is ripe for change at a time when the dissonance between the demands of Orthodoxy and the realities of everyday life in a Jewish State are being increasingly felt. There is little doubt that the recent Soviet immigration has served to heighten an awareness of the problem. Furthermore, the encouraging progress of the peace process is causing some secular Israelis, such as the writer A. B. Yehoshua, to re-examine their relationship to Judaism in recognition of the fact that a post-Zionist Israel without a common enemy will need to strengthen her sense of unity and national identity by reaffirming her religious roots.

However, just when Reform Judaism might have been well placed to offer an appropriate response to Israel's needs, our very Movement in Israel is under threat. Diaspora Jews, who have been our main source of financial support over the years, are becoming increasingly inward-looking as they consider their own future in societies in which the forces of indifference and assimilation threaten their own survival. At the very time when we are most in need of the assistance of our fellow Reform Jews from abroad, the supply line is beginning to dry up. In consequence, our capacity to offer a serious religious alternative in the Jewish State is likely to be dependent upon our ability to find independent sources of funding within Israel as the only viable way to expand our Movement and reach out to society at large.

The price of our failure would have serious consequences for Israel as a whole. Over 50% of schoolchildren in Jerusalem who enrolled for the first time in 1994 come from Orthodox and ultra-Orthodox families. Indeed, it has been suggested that Ehud Olmert may be the last non-Orthodox mayor of Israel's capital. At the other end of the spectrum, secular Israelis, in their espousal of Western consumer values, are increasingly losing touch with their Jewish heritage. El Al and Turkish Airlines laid on extra flights last Passover to the Turkish tourist resort of Antalya for those Israelis for whom the traditional prayer of 'Next year in Jerusalem' has been exchanged for 'Next year in Antalya'.

Reform Judaism must show these Israelis a way back to their religious heritage and thereby demonstrate that there is an alternative to the polarized choice between Orthodoxy and secularism.

Fortunately, the mood in Israel is changing in our favour. The peace process, started with the signing of the Camp David accords between Menachem Begin and Anwar Sadat, has been followed by treaties with Yassir Arafat and King Hussein of Jordan. At the time of writing, there is still talk of the possibility of an accommodation with Syria. If this dynamic is maintained, then, for the first time since Israel became an independent state in 1948, the issues of defence and peace will disappear from her political agenda. Such a development will have a major impact on present party-political alliances and on the balance of power between right and left that has resulted in a stalemate in Israeli politics ever since the right-wing Likud party led by Menachem Begin first came to power in 1977. Up until now, the inevitable centrality of security as the only real political issue at election time has resulted in major social concerns such as the plight of the poor, the housing and employment of new immigrants and the role and power of established religion being pushed into the background. Whenever Reform leaders have tried to raise the issue of religious pluralism with Israeli politicians, the response, even by those who sympathize with our position, has always inevitably been, 'Don't expect us to help you now. The peace process is so important that we cannot afford to risk antagonizing the religious parties at a time when their support is a precondition for our remaining in power and pursuing this goal.' All this is now likely to change.

For the first time, economic and social concerns, which constitute the key political issues in 'normal' democracies, are beginning to come to the fore in Israel. Natan (Anatoly) Sharansky, a prisoner of conscience for so many years in the former Soviet Union, recently formed a political party primarily supported by Soviet immigrants disgruntled by the high cost of housing in Israel and lack of suitable employment. Their sucess in the recent elections in which they won seven seats in Israel's Knesset, resulting in their being allocated two ministerial portfolios in Likkud's coalition government, has shown how the peace issue does not have to dominate Israeli politics.

Indeed, the recent change in Israel's electoral system, resulting in the separation of the vote for Prime Minister from that for a particular party list, caused many voters to abandon Labour and Likkud in the 1996 elections in favour of smaller sectarian interest groups, while expressing their views on the peace process and security issues through their choice of Prime Minister. In such a setting, a civil rights movement could attract considerable support as a reaction against the growing power of the religious parties.

All of this bodes well for the future of Reform Judaism in Israel. Once the monopoly of Orthodoxy has been broken and other streams in Judaism are granted the same status, influence and public funding as at present enjoyed by the religious establishment alone, there seems little doubt that our Movement will assume a major role in Israeli society in the same way as it has done in Jewish communities in other parts of the world.

Those who have witnessed the progress of Reform Judaism in Israel over the last decade, in spite of limited funding and a lack of rabbinic leadership, know only too well that the potential is there. Once we are able to compete on an equal footing, large segments of Israeli society will turn to Reform as the expression of Judaism best suited to meet the needs of those seeking a way to relate to their Jewish heritage in a non-coercive and tolerant framework.

As a result, Israel will become a country that not only embodies the aspirations of Theodor Herzl and has achieved, please God, a lasting peace with her Arab neighbours, but will also be a society that has learned to combine the values of democracy with the spirit and traditions of Judaism. Such a synthesis will not only enrich the Jewish State but will also refresh and give new meaning and purpose to our religious heritage. Then, and only then, will 'Zion be redeemed with justice and they that have returned to her with righteousness' (Isa. 1.27).

Notes

1. Theodor Herzl, *The Jewish State*, H. Pordes 1967, 71.

Jews and Arabs: Can We Make Our Enemies Our Friends?

Jeffrey Newman

I have a vivid memory of sitting in a room of Arabs and Jews and being totally unable to distinguish who was who! The room belonged to Saida Nusseibeh, the woman who more than anyone else in Britain has laboured to bring together the two peoples. Her guests were mainly British, including Diaspora Jews, and some Israelis and a similar mix of Palestinians, many of whom had been born and brought up in the West.

I was astonished. There were the same semitic faces, and since the evening was for discussion and non-confrontational, what people said heightened my sense of confusion. Surely that man speaking of the Jewish pain and suffering in the Holocaust must be Jewish – but just now he seemed to have an intimate understanding of Palestinian politics. Maybe he's an Israeli journalist – but, on the other hand . . .

I realized that I could introduce many of the Arabs – many but not all of whom were Palestinians – to my community, and they would be indistinguishable from my own members. Equally, their attitudes ranged from hard-line and intransigent to deeply empathic.

The occasion of the meeting was a visit by Gershon Baskin, the Israeli Chairman and founder of the Israel-Palestine Centre for Research and Information (IPCRI). I had met Gershon a couple of years previously when I had been arranging a twinning between my community (Finchley Reform Synagogue) and Kol HaNeshama, Rabbi Levi Weiman-Kelman's lively community in Jerusalem. Gershon had been the first Chairman of Kol

Haneshama – originally an American who during his service as an Intern for Peace had spent two years working in an Arab village, learning the language.

But the story really begins even longer ago, while I was at the Leo Baeck College, in 1967, during the months of April and May. To all of us, to almost every Jew at that time, it was evident that Nasser was planning the destruction of Israel. We could not believe what we read, saw and heard as the Egyptian-Syrian Pact (the United Arab Republic it was called) was formalized and the Arab countries, united only by their hatred, prepared openly for war. Nasser's request for the withdrawal of the small United Nations' Sinai force and U Thant's agreement to this made the war inevitable.

At that time, I was learning Bible with Dr Ellen Littman, who had been born in Germany but who had emigrated to Palestine (as it then was) before the war. She had been an old friend of Rabbi van der Zyl's, and he had persuaded her to come from Israel to teach when he started the college. For me, she epitomized one central group of Israelis – those who had already suffered enough. She was a sweet, fussy old lady with a deep love for and understanding of the Bible, and she had lived in Jerusalem through the horrifying siege of 1948. And now she, or thousands exactly like her, who had lost their families in the Holocaust, or had themselves been in camps, were once again about to relive all the terrors of those years.

Here we were, Jewish rabbinical students, future leaders of the community. There was no way that we could just sit back and watch what was going on. So, what did we do? We called a meeting!

Leo Baeck College became a hive of activity. Some of the students went to the Israeli embassy and 'enlisted'. Awraham Soetendorp and I brought together all the Jewish Youth organizations, Zionist and non-Zionist, religious and wildly atheistic, from B'nei Akiva to Habonim/Dror, and with the encouragement of Chief Rabbi Jakobovits even Orthodox students from Jews' College were included. Blankets and masses of first-aid equipment and other supplies were collected in West London Synagogue, where the Leo Baeck College then was based, and at two other centres in London; we organized poster and radio and television appearances, as we tried to wake the world to the feared annihilation of Israel.

In six days it was all over. It was a miracle – though different people of course have very different understandings of that word. But, what was to be done now? Unexpectedly, the real victims of the war were the Palestinians, thousands of whom had lost their homes.

During the lead-up to the war, Avraham and I had become quite friendly with the Israeli Consul-General, Raanan Sivan, with whom we had had a number of meetings. Now we went to him to help arrange the distribution of all the medical supplies to those who needed them: the Palestinians. He was quite in favour and agreed to telegraph Jerusalem. The answer came back: on reflection, this would not be a wise move – it might appear that Israel had something to be guilty about.

At that moment, I realized that I was most certainly not a politician. Gradually, the blanket mountains, the food and supplies were dispersed and with them any hope that I had of being involved with the real reconciliation work that was necessary between Jew and Arab.

And so the situation remained for twenty years, as I watched the politicians, as it seemed to me, squander all possibilities for constructive conflict resolution and the beginning of any true peace. Only the occasional courage of a hero like Anwar Sadat broke through the monotonous cycle of violence and accusations.

The intifada changed everything. Palestinians, particularly those in Gaza and the West Bank, discovered to their astonishment that they had power and, through that, hope. They were not merely reliant on others outside the country.

At this time, IPCRI was born. Gershon Baskin, too, realized that his work in Jerusalem – providing Arab and Israeli teachers with materials about each other's culture and heritage – was not enough. He identified six principal areas of conflict: security, refugees and returnees, borders, economic development, water and Jerusalem. In each of these, it was necessary to find options which could lead to a mutually satisfactory solution for both Israelis and Arabs/Palestinians. A breakdown over any of the six was sufficient to rekindle violence. He began to set up task forces, and working parties and round-table discussions – and he needed help and money.

When we met on his first trip to England, I too felt hope. For the first time in twenty years I could make a contribution. It was an overwhelming and terrifying feeling – May 1991, long before the handshake between Rabin and Arafat, when the Likud government was still in power. I knew that any such work would quite possibly be unpopular in the Jewish world and in my community and I wondered whether I would have the strength to do it. In any case, I was in no way a fund-raiser.

But the odd thing was to discover that doors were open: literally. I found myself sitting in the Foreign Office, and the House of Lords, in Arab homes, and Barings Bank (before the collapse). People wanted to help.

With virtually no resources, we organized three major conferences: the very first meeting between the Israeli and PLO military took place in a hotel in London under our auspices; with the Development Planning Unit of London University we arranged an international seminar on the needs of Jerusalem; and we brought Palestinian and Israeli businessmen, economists, bankers and officials together to look at the barriers to investment which exist in the West Bank and Gaza.

Over and over again, it becomes obvious that personal relationships are the foundations for change. Understanding and trust only emerge out of shared experience, particularly of working, eating, laughing, arguing and sometimes praying together. For five years, we have held together a Steering Group made up of Jews and Palestinians; some of the Palestinians have been, for me, easy to work with and have shared values and aspirations, and some of the Jews have been almost impossible. The 'labels' have been less important than the people who bear them. Saida Nusseibeh, for example, has remained an inspiration for all of the work. A tireless woman whose family has lived in Jerusalem for a thousand years, she is the finest of ambassadors, a woman of kindness and deep humanity who scorns politics and is concerned only about people, all people, and especially children. All who meet her, trust her.

Most of all, I have appreciated the time that I have been able to spend with my Co-Chair Ahmad Khaldi, an outstanding and humane man, a 'Diaspora' Palestinian as I am a Diaspora Jew. We have shared recognitions of the mirroring which has taken place in our respective communities, in terms of suffering and humiliation, of organization and dispersion, of politics and problems, and of fluctuating hope. We have raised questions about our children, their identification with what is important to us, our hopes and thoughts for their future.

Simplistic hope and being 'nice' are not enough, however. Pious words about turning enemies into friends may sound good, but how can such a revolution actually be achieved? How, for example, do we hold a check on our feelings while identifying and progressing 'the task'. Is it better, perhaps, to 'let go of' anger and express it and let the other side know, or will this lead to escalation and blow all hope?

There are in fact some very clear and central procedures, which begin with clarification of aims. We have been looking for mutually acceptable solutions – we have not needed or wanted to 'become friends'; in fact we have deliberately continued to regard and treat one another as enemies, or potential enemies. As Jonathan Magonet pointed out in his St Paul's Lecture on Dialogue,[1] in work like this members of each side also have to reckon themselves as ambassadors for their respective communities and work out how they will communicate any progress to the more sceptical on their own 'side'.

It has been necessary throughout to act and speak with the greatest caution, whilst ensuring that we take into account each other's worst suspicions and hostilities, as if they were based on reality. 'Judge no person until you stand in their place.'[2] The truth is less important here than what is perceived.

However, each side has needs, and progress is possible only when these are articulated and understood by the other. At this point it can become a logical and imaginative enterprise to discover whether those needs are contradictory (as they so often appear to be at the outset), or whether they can all be accommodated.

What is needed, however, is more than goodwill, or intuition.

As in all human intercourse, there are ways of talking, being and acting which are facilitative, and others which are blocking. One other excellent opportunity which the Leo Baeck College afforded me was the chance to work as a rabbinic student not at a congregation but at the West Central Club and Settlement at a time when a new pattern of 'non-directive' youth work was evolving.

The first weekend I went on with Alec Oxford, the scheduled leader, was a revelation. The club was in an Association of Jewish Youth (AJY) 'hotel' in Folkestone, and after the Friday night meal and a service, we assembled for the first session, and expectantly waited for Alec Oxford to begin. After a few very brief opening remarks, like 'this session is for you', he waited. So did we. In the pause (what were we supposed to do?) someone brought up the question of smoking. It was a Liberal club – was it or was it not all right to smoke in the 'hotel' on Shabbat? Various arguments and counter-arguments were introduced, with, all the time, other angry interventions that this was not what the session was supposed to be about. At a certain time the session just ended.

I felt as deeply challenged as in any of my studies at the College. In a bizarre way, my life was changed, though I only realized just how important that session was many years later. A group of people had been given the chance to talk about what was important to them. Buber speaks about it, in a discussion on trust and dialogue: 'If instruction is aimed at the "what", it is not educational. If it aims at the "how", it is educational.'[3]

The purpose of our discussion was not to make a group decision on smoking, nor to think about aspects of tradition and other peoples' sensitivities, nor even how we make decisions. Much more, it was learning about how we talk to one another, how some dominate and others keep silence, and the value of each and every person. It gave us opportunities to listen and understand, each in our own way and according to our own needs.

From that point, until now, the way we are as people, and the ways we change, have been of as much importance to me as the particular decisions that we come to, or who we are (our labels), or our history, traditions and customs. I saw the people-based values that I enjoyed in youth work as a direct expression of the teaching that we are all, whether Jew or not, made in the image of God,[4] or, as the Quakers put it, that there is that of God in every person.

The 'how' of which Buber speaks is the fundamental question about change. How do we bring it about? How can reconciliation and peace be obtained? There are more skills, experience and understanding available in our world now than ever before. Hope is no longer in vain: progress, with obstacles and setbacks, is possible. The Israeli-Palestinian work with which I became engaged was possible for me only because subsequent to my youth work experience for many years I undertook a Jungian analysis with Fred Plaut and then followed this by training with Eugene Heimler. But how to make your enemy your friend is almost as profound a change as one is likely to want to make, and Neuro-Linguistic Programming (NLP) is one of the most recent and significant tools for bringing it about.

Robert Dilts, one of the originators of NLP, has shown, for example, how human action and communication can take place at a number of different 'logical levels': environment, behaviour, capabilities, beliefs and identity. Mismatch takes place when one person or 'side' is working at one level, and the other responds from a completely different level.

Andrew Acland paints a graphic picture from a 1993 conference of the Centre for International Understanding, where he was one of the facilitation team.[5]

> Participants, including several ambassadors, came from all over the Middle East to discuss the then deadlock in the peace process. During the conference it became apparent to me that one source of the current deadlocks stemmed from the tendency of the Israeli and Palestinian representatives to address the issues at different logical levels.
>
> For example, when the subject of local elections was raised, the Palestinians spoke about the issues in terms of their relevance to the Palestinian sense of identity and nationhood, and the values implicit for them in the holding of such elections. The Israelis responded at the levels of capability (how the results could be secured fairly), behaviour (how

voters might be intimidated) and environment (the roles of such elections within the wider political context).

So, for example, writes Acland:

The local elections' relevance to Palestinian nationhood would be countered by an Israeli point about safeguarding ballot boxes. An Israeli point about local economic management would be met with a Palestinian point about the need for local autonomy as a vital part of building a stable political identity. The apparent failure to respond directly to the points at issue led to accusations of bad faith by both sides.

The work of a facilitator in such an encounter is to gain a rapport with both sides by carefully attending to every aspect of language and behaviour and analysing precisely what is taking place. It then becomes possible to bring about change, providing one has the tools to do so.

There is now an art and science of conflict resolution and mediation which can make a major contribution to the search for solutions. With these tools we can increase goodwill and accelerate the process without losing precision. (The same techniques are available in our synagogue and marital work if we wish.) Judaism provides us with values often expressed in pithy aphorisms, and it has a legal tradition for solving disputes. Israel Salanter and the Musar movement devised ways to encourage and teach ethical behaviour, but we now have new ways. Neveh Shalom (the Arab-Israeli settlement outside Jerusalem) and its School for Peace, for example, has learnt from those involved with the Irish conflict and from trainers from Bradford University and the United States. When anger and envy, fear and the sense of injustice take over, even the United Nations is not enough to avoid widespread bloodshed and slaughter. So we have to foster any hopeful signs and development in the Middle East Peace Process in the face of those who would wish to subvert it.

Thinking about this area of work, however, I have wondered how I really became involved with it, and there may well be another, deeper and more important answer than my anecdotal tales. I come from an Anglo-Jewish family, my parents and two of my grandparents being born in this country. We were therefore far less touched by the war, and I wonder if this might have allowed me a sense of security denied to many others. If this were so, it provides another reason why it is so hard to break through cycles of violence.

In any case, this work seems the most important in which I have ever been involved. I only wish it were possible to do more.

Notes

1. Jonathan Magonet, 'Risk Taking in Religious Dialogue', 1992.
2. Pirke Avot 2.5.
3. A. Shapiro, 'Meetings with Buber', *Midstream* 24/9, November 1978.
4. Gen. 1.26–27.
5. Andrew Acland, 'Conflict Resolution: Micro Decision-Making and NLP', *ITS Journal* 7, June 1995.

Collective Survival: Judaism and the Environment

Hillel Avidan

As the twentieth century draws to a close, some look back with pride on tremendous technological achievement, while others look back in sadness at horrific destruction of life – human, animal and plant. The coincidence of scientific success and moral failure enabled war, genocide and environmental degradation on a scale which could hardly have been imagined, even by a Nostradamus.

During the 1980s it finally dawned upon millions of well-educated Westerners that technology was a mixed blessing and that a finite planet could not sustain the indefinite plundering of its resources. 'Sustainable growth' became a fashionable phrase and was hastily adopted by economists as a palliative. Applications of this phrase varied widely in accordance with the intellect and integrity of those applying it. In the late 1990s there is increasing doubt over the ecological validity of any degree of economic growth.

Does this mean that the millions who languish in Third World poverty can never enjoy the material plenty which most Westerners take for granted? Must the 'underdeveloped' world remain so?

Such questions presuppose constant development in Third World countries when, in truth, most of today's poor societies were less poor in the past. Their current 'underdevelopment' is the consequence of exploitation by those more technologically advanced. The Iberian navigators of the fifteenth and sixteenth centuries paved the way for European annexation of vast areas in the Americas, in Africa and in Asia. Mercantile imperialism implemented the transference of considerable mineral, animal and vegetable wealth to Europe in exchange for much that was likely to degrade the native peoples of the conquered territories. Indigenous cultures and religions were treated with arrogant disdain and European norms were imposed, often at the point of a sword. The tragic fate of Amerindians is but one example of how those who lived in harmony with their natural surroundings were brutally supplanted by those who regarded nature as an enemy.

Even the benefits of European science have sometimes proved harmful. Twentieth-century medicine reduced the incidence of death at precisely that time when populations in Africa and Asia were beginning to outgrow available land and food resources, thus further increasing pressure on the environment and consigning millions to malnutrition. Infant mortality is hardly something to be desired yet was, in the past, a natural curb on population increase.

European intrusion into Asia, Africa and the Americas has resulted in the impoverishment of hundreds of indigenous groups which once enjoyed freedom from want.

If Third World poverty has been caused by European ethnocentrism, then the moral onus is upon Europeans (and their descendants living outside Europe) to reduce the striking economic inequalities of our time, without further ravaging the environment. While increased economic growth in global terms is highly dangerous, it may well behove richer nations to accept a measure of economic decline at home so that poorer nations may raise their living standards to a level where adequate food and shelter are available to all.

What would motivate wealthier nations to share their wealth with those less fortunate, or to accept economic decline so that others might enjoy a degree of economic growth and the natural world be safeguarded? Only self-interest, it would seem, yet one should not ignore nor underestimate altruism as a factor for change. The great world religious still boast many millions of adherents who are taught the value of foregoing satisfactions now so that the future may bestow its blessings. Religious leaders may justifiably demand austerity of their followers so that what there is may be shared by more.

In an age of widespread environmental pollution and chronic resource depletion it is only prudent to consider ways in which we might protect what is fragile and conserve what is valuable. Yet for the religious Jew, 'caring for creation' is more than a matter of prudence. It is a response to God's commandments.

Each morning the devout Jew praises God 'who daily renews the work of creation'. Creation is viewed by Judaism as an ongoing process, and the Jew should view himself as a junior partner in that process. Aware of his status as God's steward, the religious Jew should strive to recognize the boundary between responsible utilization and irresponsible exploitation.

When it comes to care for the environment, Jews may rightfully claim the status of pioneers, for in the Hebrew Bible it is written, 'God took man and placed him in a garden, to work it and to conserve it' (Gen. 2.15). The earth's riches may be sensibly utilized to enhance human existence, but they should never be squandered. Modern consumer societies are notoriously wasteful and place enormous strains upon delicate environmental balances, so restraint is essential in the battle to conserve what we can.

Many are so damaged by a lifetime of exposure to relentless commercial advertising that they just cannot consider a simpler life-style than the one they currently enjoy. Yet if prosperous and relatively prosperous people do not volunteer to live more simply, in the end they will be forced to through resource depletion. In a finite world, infinite appetites and aspirations are sorely misplaced.

The first half of Genesis 1.26 states that human beings are created in God's image, and the second half that they may exercise control over their natural surroundings. Taken as a whole, the verse teaches us that in our control of the environment we must behave as God would behave, because we are created in the divine image. As God displays justice and compassion in His dealings with the world, so must we. Too often in the past, the second half of this verse has been quoted in support of human spoliation of nature. In considering our God-given mastery over nature, we must sensitize and educate ourselves so that we distinguish clearly between 'use' and 'abuse' of nature.

Self-interest alone would dictate more caring attitudes and behaviour towards the world about us, but Judaism seeks to lift Jews above the level of mere self-interest by demanding that they 'image' God in their relations with other creatures, with plants, soil, air and water, all of which are inextricably interconnected and interdependent.

'The earth is the Lord's and the fullness thereof: the world and all who dwell within it' (Ps. 24.1). In these words we are reminded of who is in charge of the universe. Our role is one of stewardship. Acceptance of God as ruler and humanity as subject leads to responsible conservation of the earth and its resources.[1]

The theocentric view of the psalmist is reinforced by the regulations concerning the fiftieth year of Jubilee, when all leased land reverted to its original owners who were themselves understood to hold the land in trust for God. 'And the land shall not be sold in perpetuity (i.e. the freehold shall not be sold) for the land is mine . . .' (Lev. 25.23).

Urban dwellers are apt to forget that the most valuable of international resources is not oil but arable land. We are hopefully flexible enough to adjust to a life without the ease afforded us by machinery, but we cannot live without food, and certainly in the foreseeable future, if not beyond, most food will continue to be grown on the land.

Many once-fertile areas of the world have been rendered arid through deforestation or soil exhaustion, and it was in order to prevent the latter that the Israelite farmer let his land lie fallow in every seventh year (Lev. 25. 2–7). If modern farmers would consider God as the rightful landlord and themselves as His stewards, answerable to Him for the way they use His land, then the adequate nutrition of future generations would be more assured. Whereas in some places land is not fully utilized and could quite safely produce more and better crops, in other places the relentless demand for increasingly higher levels of food production has led to the eventual collapse of the soil. The greed of some producers for ever rising profits contrasts dramatically with the diligent yet restrained methods employed by the farmer in biblical times or even more recently. 'Organic farming' was the norm when I was a child in the 1930s and 1940s.

Whenever men and women work in harmony with the rhythms of nature, displaying both deep affection and profound respect for the land and its life-supporting capacities, the results are beneficial to all concerned. Nature is not an enemy to be conquered or circumvented, but a potential ally with which we must come to terms.

Jewish environmental legislation rests in the main upon a prohibition against destroying fruit-bearing trees in time of war (Deut. 20.19). From this prohibition were drawn many others which in sum total served to prevent wanton destruction of anything useful to humanity. The judging of what is useful cannot exclude considerations of effect upon the environment because assaults against nature are also assaults against ourselves.

Judaism assigns the fifteenth of the Hebrew month of Shevat as a day to plant and celebrate trees. For the past hundred years afforestation has been an important feature of redeeming the ancient Jewish homeland, and hills that were denuded of trees by Romans, Arabs, Crusaders and Turks have been restored to the verdant glory that was theirs in biblical times. As a consequence, the water table has risen, soil erosion has ceased, and bird life has multiplied in the Holy Land.

In contrast to Jewish regard for trees is the cruel and steady destruction of tropical rain forest with disastrous consequences for the human, animal and plant life within and the atmosphere above. In much of Europe the loss of broad-leaved hardwoods has adversely affected flora and fauna, together with the waterways which depend for life upon an indigenous habitat.

Water is such a precious commodity, yet so thoughtlessly spoiled and squandered. Toxic wastes from factory and farm have so seriously polluted many of Europe's rivers and lakes that they are virtually beyond redemption. In Africa and the Americas, the construction of vast dams has brought ecological catastrophe to many an ancient river valley. Israel may justifiably take pride in its afforestation programs, but now regrets the drainage, fifty years ago, of the Huleh Valley wetlands.

One of the greatest threats to planetary well-being is uncontrolled expansion of the human population, which has already upset the stability of many Third World countries, exacerbating land and food shortages, and even inspiring civil war. Jewish teachers have traditionally cited Genesis 1.28 ('. . . be fertile and increase and fill the earth . . .') as an argument against birth control, but now that the earth has been 'filled', it could be argued that the commandment 'to increase' has ceased to apply. While wishing to avoid coercion and poignantly aware of declining Jewish numbers, Progressive Jewish teachers do encourage voluntary family limitation. A smaller population will obviously use less of the earth's finite resources to satisfy its basic needs. However, it must be borne in mind that one North American can use as much of the earth's resources as a hundred South-East Asians, suggesting that family limitation is as necessary in prosperous countries as it is in poorer countries.

Assaults against the environment often begin with abuse of animals. In its concern for animal welfare Judaism has always displayed a rare sensitivity.

In Proverbs 12.10 we can read, 'A righteous man has regard for the life of his animal'; that is, he shows consideration for its needs and feelings. Exodus 20.10 teaches that work animals must rest on the Sabbath, and the need for such consideration is repeated in Exodus 23.12 and Deuteronomy 5.14.

In Leviticus 22.27 it is stated that a young domestic animal may not be separated from its mother till at least seven days old, and in Leviticus 22.28 it is prohibited to kill an animal together with its young, mainly in order to prevent the one witnessing the death of the other. Commenting on these two verses, the twelfth-century philosopher Maimonides wrote: 'The pain of animals under such circumstances is very great. There is no difference in this case between the pain of humans and the pain of other living beings, since the love and tenderness of the mother for her young is not produced by reasoning but by feeling, and this faculty exists not only in humans but in most living things' (*Guide of the Perplexed* 3.48).

In Jewish post-biblical literature much is written about the need to spare animals from pain or stress. The Talmud forbids gladiatorial shows and hunting (Avodah Zarah 18b), so that bull-fighting, dog-fighting, cock-fighting and fox or big game hunting are quite abhorrent to the observant Jew. So too is the trapping of animals for such luxury items as fur coats, the mowing down of elephant herds for ivory, or the merciless hunting of whales for the production of pet foods. A high percentage of the exotic creatures imported for sale as pets in Britain die of starvation before their crates or cages are opened. The observant Jew ought to avoid the purchase of imported animals, birds or reptiles.

Much has been written and spoken against the Jewish method of slaughter, but this method (known in Hebrew as *shechitah*) is actually designed to minimize animal suffering. *Shechitah* renders an animal unconscious in a matter of seconds and it is doubtful if pain can be registered in such a short time. If it is, it can only be momentary and is as nothing compared to the life-long suffering endured by so many farm animals in our day. 'Factory farming' is an abomination, and as the Talmud (in a summary of previous teachings on the subject) demands that animals be spared pain at all costs (Baba Metsia 31a–32b), the products of intensive animal husbandry must be considered as unsuitable for Jewish consumption.[2] To deprive God's creatures of sunlight, fresh air and exercise is utterly sadistic, and it is against intensive animal husbandry, rather than against particular methods of slaughter, that the efforts of animal welfare societies ought to be directed. *Shechitah* is at least as humane as any other method of slaughter, but if one has serious doubts about the morality of depriving other creatures of life, then the course to pursue is that of vegetarianism, which has always occupied an honorable position in Jewish tradition and is anticipated as the norm that will prevail in the Messianic Age.

Criticism may be levelled by Judaism against research laboratories where millions of animals have been tortured yearly, supposedly to advance the frontiers of science. At the very least one should distinguish between experiments intended to assist medical development and those conducted for the benefit of commerce.

'*Tzaar baalei chayyim*' (animal suffering) is the rabbinic term employed to embrace all Jewish law and lore concerned with animal welfare. Such concern is global, and includes reference to animals in the wild, on farms, in laboratories, in zoos and circuses, in pet shops and in private homes. The earth has been given by God for the benefit of all creatures, and we humans, as God's stewards, must exercise restraint and recognize the rights of non-humans, be they furred, feathered or scaled.

The abuse of animals desensitizes the abuser and facilitates the abuse of fellow humans and the spoilation of soil, air and water and all that they support. The sensitive person will possess some awareness that the various components of creation are interconnected, and that damage done to one component is liable to cause damage to others. Jewish mystics like Isaac Luria, Shneur Zalman and Abraham Kook have stressed that a divine thread binds all the segments of the universe together – an essential unity reflecting the oneness of God.

Tikkun ha-Olam (repair of the world) is an important feature of the teachings of Isaac Luria, who lived in the Galilean town of Safed during the sixteenth century. For almost two millennia Jews have recited the prayer known as *Alenu*, and in the second paragraph of that prayer are the words '*Letaken olam bemalchut Shaddai*' (to repair the world for the rule of God). 'Repairing the world' is viewed in Judaism as a necessary prelude to the Messianic coming, whether that coming be understood as the advent of an era or the appearance of a special human individual. The ancient Messianic longing is for a world free of strife and suffering, and *Tikkun ha-Olam* is the formula for transforming such longing into reality. We are here to repair the world.

Jews who have prayed the *Alenu* for nearly two millennia have less excuse than others for ignoring environmental crisis. Many Jews have striven to improve society, but too many have not. The Holocaust has emotionally maimed most twentieth-century Jews and is responsible for so many of us looking only inwards – only to the perceived needs of our own people. Yet without a viable planet the Jewish people is as doomed as any other. The survival of our planet does not depend upon Jewish survival, but Jewish survival does depend upon planetary survival. Planetary survival depends upon 'repairing the world' and upon limitation of appetites so that something is left for those too young to make decisions or those as yet unborn.

Human greed and arrogance lie behind most environmental despoliation, and they are fed by the humanist slogan that 'man is the measure of all things'. Acceptance of God as ruler is likely to breed attitudes of humility and reverence in the face of wondrous nature. Judaism reminds us of our place in the scheme of things and of our duty so to act that God's plans for the world will not be thwarted. Jews are few in number and need to work in concert with others who care equally about the future of our planet. Survival is a collective responsibility.

God created humanity to be a co-partner in the wise and compassionate maintenance of the world. How we have failed God! Now that disaster looms, our selfishness is finally giving way to intelligent action, albeit with painful slowness. At the eleventh hour, humanity confronts God's command 'to repair the world', but is it too late? Perhaps not.

'And God saw all which He had made and behold it was very good' (Gen.1.31). The earth *was* very good, and with the assistance of sufficient numbers of responsible humans it could still be saved and even restored to some semblance of its former glory.

Notes

1. For examples of practical steps being advocated and adopted by the Reform Synagogues of Great Britain, see Jonathan Romain, *Faith and Practice*, RSGB 1991, 232.
2. Ibid., 113.

Glossary

The glossary does not include words and phrases used only once that are explained in the main text itself.

Alenu	Prayer concerning the duties of Israel which occurs towards the end of all services.
Ashkenazi	Jews originating from Central and Eastern Europe.
Bar/batmitzvah	Ceremony for boys and girls aged thirteen in which they are called to read from the Torah to mark the beginnings of Jewish adulthood.
Chanukah	Festival of Dedication, celebrating the survival of the Jewish faith despite attempts to destroy it.
Chasidic	Associated with the Chasidim, a Jewish sect founded in Eastern Europe in the late eighteenth century as a revivalist movement, now part of the ultra-Orthodox establishment.
Chatan (plural: *chatanim*)	Bridegroom; also used for the two members of a congregation honoured at the festival of Simchat Torah.
Chayyim	Life.
Chochmah	Wisdom.
Ein Sof	God as 'The One Without End' in contrast to 'the God of Abraham, Isaac and Jacob'.

Genizah	Storeroom for discarded documents and books
Haftarah (plural: haftarot)	Reading from the Prophets during Sabbath and festival services.
Halachah (adjective halachic)	Jewish law and practice.
Kashrut	The dietary laws concerning permitted and forbidden food and rules of preparation.
Kibbutz (plural: kibbutzim)	Communally-owned settlement in Israel.
Kippah (plural *kippot*)	Head-covering worn during prayer.
L'chayyim	To life! The toast customarily said by Jews.
Metzaveh	God-Who-Commands.
Midrash (adjective: Midrashic)	Homiletical commentary on the Bible by the rabbis.
Mikveh	Ritual pool for immersion used by those converting to Judaism, or by women following their menstrual period.
Mishnah	Codification of Jewish law completed around 200 CE.
Pesach	Festival of Passover celebrating the Exodus from Egypt.
Pirke Avot	The Sayings of the Fathers, a treatise of the Mishnah.
Purim	Festival of Lots, celebrating the deliverance of the Jews of Persia from attempts to kill them.
Rebbe	Leader of a Chasidic sect.
Rosh Hashanah	The Jewish New Year and a time of renewal.
Seder	Service surrounding the Passover meal.
Semichah	Ordination ceremony for rabbis.
Sephardi (adjective: Sephardim)	Jews originating from the Spanish Peninsula and the Mediterranean countries.

Shabbat	The Sabbath – a time of rest, lasting from sunset on Friday evening until after dark on Saturday.
Shavuot	Festival of Weeks, celebrating the revelation at Mount Sinai.
Shechitah	Jewish method of killing animals for food.
Shivah	The first seven days of mourning after the death of a close relative.
Shloshim	The first thirty days of mourning after the death of a close relative.
Shoah	The Holocaust, in which six million Jews were murdered.
Simchat Torah	Festival of the Rejoicing of the Law, celebrating a new cycle of public readings in synagogue from the Pentateuch.
Sukkah	The booths erected during Sukkot.
Sukkot	The Festival of Tabernacles, commemorating the wanderings of the Israelites in the wilderness.
Tallit	Prayer shawl worn at morning services.
Talmud	Rabbinic commentary on the Mishnah completed around 500 CE; the main repository of Jewish law.
Tikkun Olam	'Repairing the world' – the concept of the duty of all Jews to better the world and improve its condition.
Tisha B'Av	The Ninth of Av, a fast day commemorating the the destruction of the First and Second Temples in Jerusalem, and other tragedies in Jewish history.
Torah	The five books of Moses; also used to refer to the entirety of Jewish teaching.
Tosefta	A parallel work to the Mishnah.
Tzimtzum	The Jewish mystical concept of God limiting the divine presence to make room for creation.
Yom Kippur	The Day of Atonement, a time of prayer, repentance and fasting.

Contributors

All the contributors are rabbinic graduates of the Leo Baeck College. Their dates of ordination are given in brackets after their names.

Hillel Avidan (1966) is Chairman of the Southern African Association of Progressive Rabbis and Rabbi of Bet David, Johannesburg.

Tony Bayfield (1972) read law at Magdalene College, Cambridge and served the North West Surrey Synagogue for thirteen years before becoming the first Director of the Sternberg Centre for Judaism in North-West London. In January 1994 he was appointed Chief Executive of the Reform Movement in Britain. He has written a number of educational books and co-edited the pioneering *Dialogue with a Difference* (SCM Press 1992). His *Sinai, Law and Responsible Autonomy* was published by RSGB in 1993. He is the founder editor of the quarterly journal *Manna*.

Lionel Blue (1958) was born in the East End of London and educated at Balliol College, Oxford. He has officiated as rabbi, cook, liturgist, author and broadcaster. For twenty-five years he has provided morning spirituality for the BBC's 'God slot'. He has been awarded the OBE, the Jewish Chronicle Book Prize (for *To Heaven with Scribes and Pharisees*, Darton, Longman and Todd 1990) and the Templeton UK Prize.

Barbara Borts (1981) is the former Rabbi of Radlett and Bushey Synagogue. She is the founder of the Social Action Group of the

Reform Synagogues of Great Britain, has worked with the homeless and with psychiatric patients, and written in the field of Judaism and feminism. She is currently the Director of Education and Associate Rabbi of Temple Emanu-El-Beth Sholom, Montreal, Quebec.

Michael Boyden (1972) is a graduate of London University in Hebrew Literature. He served as Rabbi of Cheshire Reform Congregation and became Chairman of the Assembly of Rabbis of the Reform Synagogues of Great Britain before immigrating to Israel with his family in 1985. He is at present a rabbi in Ra'anana, Israel, Chairman of the Israel Council of Progressive Rabbis and Convener of its rabbinic court.

Henry G. Brandt (1966) is Landesrabbiner of Westfalen-Lippe and is Jewish President of the German Co-ordinating Council of the Societies for Christian-Jewish Co-operation in Germany. He holds an honorary doctorate of the University of Marburg and is holder of the great seal of the city of Oldenburg, as well as the Hedwig Burgheim Medal of the city of Giessen. He is a regular broadcaster on radio and contributes to various journals.

Douglas Charing (1970) is a freelance educational consultant who lectures and writes on Judaism and is founder director of the Leeds-based Jewish Education Bureau.

Jeffrey Cohen (1979) currently holds the position of Chief Executive Officer of the Sydney Jewish Museum: The Holocaust and Australian Jewish History, in Sydney, Australia. Prior to that, he served as Director of Pastoral Resources within the Missouri Department of Mental Health as well as consultant to Pathways to Promise: Congregational Response to Mental Illness. He has lectured on three continents on the relationship between faith and mental and physical well-being as well as designing a religious history and spiritual assessment tool which is used in hospitals in North America and beyond.

Howard Cooper (1980) is an analytic psychotherapist in private practice and a lecturer on biblical, psychological and spiritual themes. He is the editor of *Soul Searching: Studies in Judaism and Psychotherapy*, SCM Press 1988, and co-author of *A Sense of Belonging: Dilemmas of British Jewish Identity*, Weidenfeld and Nicolson 1991.

Michael Hilton (1987) obtained his DPhil in Renaissance English Literature and serves Menorah Synagogue, Cheshire Reform Congregation. He has been involved in Jewish-Christian dialogue all his life, and his book *The Christian Effect on Jewish Life*, SCM Press 1994, was written while he was on sabbatical in Kingston, Jamaica.

Michael Leigh (1958) was educated at Lincoln College, Oxford, where he studied Modern History, and University College London, where he studied Hebrew; he was awarded an Honorary DD by Jewish Theological Seminary, New York in 1985. He was Assistant Minister of West London Synagogue from 1958 to 1963, and Senior Minister of Edgware and District Reform Synagogue from 1963 to 1993.

Jonathan Magonet (1971) gained his PhD in Heidelberg and then returned to lecture at the Leo Baeck College in Bible. He has been Principal since 1985. He is the author of *A Rabbi's Bible* (1991), *Bible Lives* (1992) and *A Rabbi Reads the Psalms* (1994), all published by SCM Press, and has co-edited with Rabbi Lionel Blue three volumes of *Forms of Prayer*, the prayer books of the Reform Synagoges of Great Britain, as well as three collections of more popular writings, most recently *Kindred Spirits*. He has taken a leading role in Jewish-Christian and Jewish-Muslim dialogue and is a Vice-President of the World Union for Progressive Judaism.

Dow Marmur (1962) was born in Poland in 1935 and educated in Sweden. He served the South-West Essex Reform Synagogue (1962–69) and the North West Reform Synagogue (1969–83). Since 1983 he has been Senior Rabbi of Holy Blossom Temple in Toronto. While in Britain, for many years he edited *Living*

Judaism, the RSGB journal, as well as two books on Reform Judaism. He is the author of four other books and numerous articles.

Rachel Montagu (1986) was formerly Rabbi of Cardiff New Synagogue and Assistant Rabbi of the North Western Reform Synagogue. She teaches Judaism at Birkbeck College, as well as writing and doing interfaith work.

Julia Neuberger (1977) chairs Camden and Islington Community Health Services NHS Trust. She is a patron of the North London Hospice, a Vice-President of the Royal College of Nursing, and a member of the General Medical Council and Medical Research Council. She is also Chancellor of the University of Ulster.

Jeffrey Newman (1970) read Philosophy and Psychology at Oxford before a short spell in the world of retailing. He undertook a considerable amount of youth work and training, which led subsequently to an interest in counselling and then Jungian analysis. He also trained for several years with Eugene Heimler. He has been chair of Rabbinic-in-Service-Training at the Leo Baeck College, and for some years co-ordinated its Pastoral Care and Community Skills programme. He was founder and co-chair of the UK branch of the Israel-Palestine Centre for Research and Information. He is at present Rabbi at Finchley Reform Synagogue.

Jonathan Romain (1980) is the minister of Maidenhead Synagogue and is also a regular broadcaster on the radio. He gained his PhD in Jewish History from the University of Leicester. His previous publications include *Signs and Wonders* (a Hebrew primer), M. Goulston Educational Foundation 1992; *The Jews of England*, M. Goulston Educational Foundation 1988; *Faith and Practice: A Guide to Reform Judiasm Today*, RSGB 1991; and *Till Faith Us Do Part: Couples who Fall in Love across the Religious Divide*, HarperCollins 1996. With Anne Kershen, he *wrote Tradition and Change: A History of Reform Judaism in Britain 1840–1995*, Vallentine Mitchell 1995.

Sylvia Rothschild (1987) is Rabbi of Bromley and District Reform Synagogue. She is particularly interested in terminal care for the Jewish patient and in creating liturgy and ritual for the dying and bereaved. She also sits on the local Research and Ethics Committee.

Elizabeth Sarah (1989) worked for five years as a congregational rabbi and is now director of the Programmes Division of the Reform Synagogues of Great Britain. She is also a member of the Executive of the Assembly of Rabbis and the Co-ordinating Group of the Half-Empty Bookcase for Progressive Jewish Women's Studies. Her most recent publications include: 'The Biblical Account of the First Woman', in *Women's Voices*, ed. Teresa Elwes, HarperCollins 1994; 'Rabbi Regina Jonas, 1902–1944' and 'Beruria: A Suitable Case for Mistreatment', in *Hear Our Voice*, ed. Sybil Sheridan, SCM Press 1994; and 'Judaism and Lesbianism: A Tale of Life on the Margins of the Text', in *Jewish Explorations of Sexuality*, ed. Jonathan Magonet, Berghahn Books 1995.

Robert F.Shafritz (1987), from Philadelphia, USA, is Rabbi of Wimbledon and District Synagogue and Chairman of Exodus 2000. He previously served as Associate Rabbi at the West London Synagogue. Before entering Leo Baeck College he taught EFL and history, and lectured in teacher training at the universities of Tours and Strasbourg, and in Iran for the American Peace Corps. He died unexpectedly shortly after completing his contribution, and is much mourned by his rabbinic colleagues.

Sybil Sheridan (1981) read Theology and Religious Studies at Cambridge University. She is Rabbi of the Thames Valley Progressive Jewish community based in Reading, and lecturer in Life Cycle and Festivals at the Leo Baeck College, where she also organizes seminars and study days for Christian theology students. Her publications include *Hear Our Voice – Women Rabbis Tell Their Story*, SCM Press 1994, which she edited.

Reuven Silverman (1974) is Rabbi of Manchester Reform Synagogue and honorary lecturer in Hebrew at Manchester University Department of Middle Eastern Studies. He is a member of Leo Baeck College Faculty and a lecturer in rabbinic literature on the part-time MA course in Manchester. He has written *Baruch Spinoza – Outcast Jew, Universal Sage*, Science Reviews 1995, and is a broadcaster on Jewish topics, regularly on BBC Radio 2 and occasionally on Radio 4.

David Soetendorp (1972) was born in Amsterdam. He has been Rabbi of Bournemouth Reform Synagogue since 1972. He is also founder Rabbi of South Hants Reform Congregation. From 1994 to 1996 he was Chairman of the Assembly of Rabbis. His published work includes *Op weg naar het Verleden*, Amsterdam 1990.

Chaim Joseph Wender (1979) studied at Georgetown University in Washington DC and the Hebrew Union College in Cincinnati. While serving as Rabbi of Congregation Children of Israel in Augusta, Georgia, he gained his Doctor of Ministry degree at Columbia Theological Seminary, specializing in Judaism and gerontology. From 1990 to 1995 he served as Rabbi of the Woodford Progressive Synagogue in London. Towards the end of 1995 he was called to the pulpit of Temple Sinai in Delray Beach, Florida.

Rabbinic Graduates of the Leo Baeck College

United Kingdom

A. M. Bayfield (1972)
F. R. Berry (1989)
J. Black (1988)
L. Blue (1958)

M. Carr (1996)
D. Charing (1970)
C. Cohen (1975)
J. Collick (1983)
H. Cooper (1980)

H. Davis (1993)
N. R. M. de Lange (1973)

C. Eimer (1971)
W. Elf (1994)

S. Franses (1971)
D. Freeman (1967)
H. Freeman (1990)

A. Golby (1988)
D. Goldberg (1971)
M. Goldsmith (1996)
A. Goldstein (1970)
D. Goldstein (1968) z"l
H. Goldstein (1967)

G. Hall (1986)
M. R. Heilbron (1973)
M. Hilton (1987)
S. Howard (1987)
D. Hulbert (1989)

H. M. Jacobi (1971)
M. Jacobi (1994)

S. Katz (1975)
S. Kay (1976)
N. Kraft (1988)
S. Kunin (1990)

M. Lawrence (1992)
M. Leigh (1958)

J. Magonet (1971)
A. Mann (1971)
R. Mariner (1976)
M. Michaels (1996)
C. Middleburgh (1986)
R. Montagu (1984)
F. Morgan (1984)
D. Myers-Weinstein (1996)

J. Neuberger (1977)
J. Newman (1970)

D. Rich (1989)
L. Rigal (1985)
S. Rodrigues-Pereira (1981)
J. A. Romain (1980)
E. Rothman (1992)
S. Rothschild (1987)

T. Salamon (1972)
E. Sarah (1989)
R. Shafritz (1987)z"l
S. Sheridan (1981)
M. Shire (1996)
S. Shulman (1989)
R. M. Silverman (1974)
A. D. Smith (1977)
F. Dabba Smith (1994)
D. Soetendorp (1972)

J. Tabick (1975)
L. Tabick (1976)
D. Thau (1983)
P. Tobias (1990)

L. Wax (1994)
J. Wittenberg (1987)
W. Wolff (1984)
A. Wright (1986)

Europe

P. Bebe (1990)
I. ben Yosef (1991)z"l
H. G. Brandt (1966)
G. Farhi (1996)
A. S. Herman (1966)
M. König (1983)
Michel Liebermann (1994)
D. Lilienthal (1971)
M. Marcus (1975)
J. Oppenheimer (1972)
W. Rothschild (1984)
H. Schmelzer (1959)
A. Soetendorp (1967)
E. Stein (1976)
M. ten Brink (1993)
E. van Voolen (1978)
M. Williams (1976)

Israel

T. Ben David (1996)
M. Benjamin (1975)z"l
M. Boyden (1972)
N. Ginsbury (1967)
R. Gradwohl (1966)
S. Howard (1987)

USA

S. Barth (1985)
J. Case (1984)
K. Cohen (1980)
A. Friedmann (1971)
G. C. Goldberg (1975)
S. Greenstein (1973)
R. Leib (1986)
A. Miller (1960)
J. Newman (1981)
J. Panitz (1975)
A. Ungar (1961)
W. Vine (1986)
C. L. Wender (1979)

South America

R. Werner (1979)

Australia and New Zealand

J. Cohen (1979)
A. Kippen (1991)
U. Themal (1968)
H. Vallins (1970)
C. Wallach (1975)

South Africa

A. E. Assabi (1971)
H. Avidan (1966)
I. Richards (1967)
M. Standfield (1968)

Canada

B. Borts (1981)
J. Gale (1980)
D. Komito-Gottlieb (1980)
D. Marmur (1962)
R. Pavey (1967)
P. Sidolfsky (1988)